DISABILITY AND THE GOOD HUMAN LIFE

This collection of original essays, from both established scholars and new-comers, takes up a debate that has recently flared up in philosophy, sociology, and disability studies on whether disability is intrinsically a harm that lowers a person's quality of life. While this is a new question in disability scholarship, it also touches on one of the oldest philosophical questions: What is the good human life? Historically, philosophers have not been interested in the topic of disability, and when they are it is usually only in relation to questions such as euthanasia, abortion, or the moral status of disabled people. Consequently, implicitly or explicitly, disability has been either ignored by moral and political philosophers or simply equated with a bad human life, a life not worth living.

This book takes up the challenge that disability poses to basic questions of political philosophy and bioethics, among others, by focusing on fundamental issues as well as practical implications of the relationship between disability and the good human life.

Jerome E. Bickenbach is the leader of the Disability Policy Unit and a profes-sor in the Department of Health Sciences and Health Policy at the University of Lucerne and Swiss Paraplegic Research, Nottwil, Switzerland.

Franziska Felder is a senior researcher in the Department of Education at the University of Zurich, Switzerland.

Barbara Schmitz is an associate professor in the Department of Philosophy at the University of Basel, Switzerland.

CAMBRIDGE DISABILITY LAW AND POLICY SERIES

Edited by Peter Blanck and Robin Paul Malloy

The Cambridge Disability Law and Policy series examines these topics in interdisciplinary and comparative terms. The books in the series reflect the diversity of definitions, causes, and consequences of discrimination against persons with disabilities while illuminating fundamental themes that unite countries in their pursuit of human rights laws and policies to improve the social and economic status of persons with disabilities. The series contains historical, contemporary, and comparative scholarship crucial to identifying individual, organizational, cultural, attitudinal, and legal themes necessary for the advancement of disability law and policy.

The topics covered in the series also reflect the new moral and political commitment of countries throughout the world to equal opportunity for persons with disabilities in such areas as employment, housing, transportation, rehabilitation, and individual human rights. The series will thus play a significant role in informing policy makers, researchers, and citizens of issues central to disability rights and disability antidiscrimination policies. The series grounds the future of disability law and policy as a vehicle for ensuring that those living with disabilities participate as equal citizens of the world.

Books in the Series

Ruth Colker, *When Is Separate Unequal? A Disability Perspective*, 2009

Larry M. Logue and Peter Blanck, *Race, Ethnicity, and Disability: Veterans and Benefits in Post–Civil War America*, 2010

Lisa Vanhala, *Making Rights a Reality? Disability Rights Activists and Legal Mobilization*, 2010

Alicia Ouellette, *Bioethics and Disability: Toward a Disability-Conscious Bioethics*, 2011

Eilionoir Flynn, *From Rhetoric to Action: Implementing the UN Convention on the Rights of Persons with Disabilities*, 2011

Isabel Karpin and Kristin Savell, *Perfecting Pregnancy: Law, Disability, and the Future of Reproduction*, 2012

Arie Rimmerman, *Social Inclusion of People with Disabilities: National and International Perspectives*, 2012

Andrew Power, Janet E. Lord, and Allison S. deFranco, *Active Citizenship and Disability: Implementing the Personalisation of Support for Persons with Disabilities*, 2012

Lisa Schur, Douglas Kruse, and Peter Blanck, *People with Disabilities: Sidelined or Mainstreamed?*, 2013

Eliza Varney, *Disability and Information Technology: A Comparative Study in Media Regulation*, 2013

Jerome E. Bickenbach, Franziska Felder, and Barbara Schmitz, *Disability and the Good Human Life*, 2014

DISABILITY AND THE GOOD HUMAN LIFE

Edited by

Jerome E. Bickenbach

University of Lucerne, Switzerland

Franziska Felder

University of Zurich, Switzerland

Barbara Schmitz

University of Basel, Switzerland

CAMBRIDGE
UNIVERSITY PRESS

CAMBRIDGE
UNIVERSITY PRESS

32 Avenue of the Americas, New York NY 10013-2473, USA

Cambridge University Press is part of the University of Cambridge.

It furthers the University's mission by disseminating knowledge in the pursuit of education, learning and research at the highest international levels of excellence.

www.cambridge.org
Information on this title: www.cambridge.org/9781107545830

© Cambridge University Press 2014

First published 2014
First paperback edition 2015

A catalogue record for this publication is available from the British Library

Library of Congress Cataloguing in Publication data
Disability and the good human life / [edited by] Jerome Bickenbach, University of Lucerne, Switzerland, Franziska Felder, University of Zurich, Barbara Schmitz, University of Basel.
   pages   cm. – (Cambridge disability law and policy series)
Includes bibliographical references and index.
ISBN 978-1-107-02718-3 (hardback)
1. Sociology of disability.   2. Disabled people – Social conditions.   3. Quality of life.   I. Bickenbach, Jerome Edmund.
HV1568.D5672   2014
305.9′08–dc23   2013023411

ISBN 978-1-107-02718-3 Hardback
ISBN 978-1-107-54583-0 Paperback

Contents

Contents

Acknowledgments

The idea for this book began to take shape in June 2010 at a conference about disability and the good life at the University of Basel. The editors would like to thank the speakers and the participants, some of them also authors in this volume.

Introduction

Rethinking the Good Human Life in Light of Disability

Historically, philosophers have not been greatly interested in disability. Although disability has always been a part of the human experience and therefore a universal feature of humanity, the major figures in the history of philosophy, if they mentioned disability at all, usually spoke of it as the exceptional case or the special issue that, for the purposes of ethical, political, or social theory, could be safely ignored. In the past few decades this has changed dramatically, and ethical and political philosophers in particular have begun to integrate disability issues into their work. Although not the leaders in this trend, bioethicists have perhaps been among the most prominent voices addressing disability.

Much to the chagrin of disability scholars and activists, however, initially this focus was almost entirely negative: having a disability was assumed to be a justification for euthanasia, evidence of disability was grounds for selective abortion, and political theorists looked only at what justice required the state to do by way of compensation for the undeserved misfortunes people with disabilities had to endure. For their part, bioethicists seemed more concerned about justifying the morality of eliminating people with disabilities than with improving their lives (Parens and Asch, 2001). This was ironic because both bioethics and disability scholarship grew out of a rejection of the paternalistic assumptions of the medical community and both expressed themselves ethically in terms of basic human values of autonomy, self-determination, and respect for persons (Asch, 2001).

As the focus of bioethics has shifted in recent years to issues of social justice, philosophers are taking more seriously the importance of accessibility, inclusion, and equality in health care and social policy generally, and the synergy between disability scholarship and bioethics has accordingly been strengthened. Ethical and political philosophers also take great care to integrate disability into their conceptions of equality and systematic political theorizing. This is unquestionably a positive development for both philosophy and disability scholarship. Still, the bulk of this new literature continues to address very specific social and ethical issues, overlooking what philosophers traditionally understood as the fundamental philosophical questions.

This volume seeks to expand and strengthen the links between philosophy and disability scholarship by focusing on what, by any standard, is one of the oldest philosophical issues: What constitutes the good human life? This question is both one of the oldest and one of the most modern of philosophical topics. All classical philosophical traditions have offered approaches, methods, and systematic answers to it. Modern philosophers, at least since the twentieth century, have pursued a variety of methodologies and tactics to address the good life, if not directly then at least obliquely by focusing on moral and political debates that a conception of the good life would inevitably inform. Questions about moral obligations to oneself and the role and proper scope of the obligations of the state to its citizens, and about the proper distribution of subjective happiness and objective resources, invariably shed light on what, as philosopher Derek Parfit put it, "makes life go well" (1984). Philosophical positions in this domain have shaped ethical theory and political ideology, but also, and perhaps more than at any other time in history, have directly affected law, social policy, and our understanding of the content and significance of human rights.

Disability studies scholarship, at least relative to philosophy, is very much in its infancy. But this scholarship is rapidly growing, in part because of its robustly interdisciplinary methodologies that span the natural and social sciences and the humanities (Cureton and Brownlee,

2009; Roulstone, Thomas, and Watson, 2012). Born out of a world-wide political movement and invigorated by the successes of that movement, disability studies has continued to pursue, if not an overtly political, then a politically informed research agenda. The fundamental philosophical question of the good human life has not, at least in that abstract formulation, been the direct focus of disability scholarship; instead, disability scholars have found themselves responding to claims and assumptions that impairments per se undermine the prospects of living a good human life. They have taken up that challenge, but only piecemeal and defensively.

Against those bioethicists who, impressed by new reproductive technologies offering the prospect of "preventing disability" by pre-natal diagnosis and selective abortion (cf. Buchanan et al., 2000), dis-ability scholars have also had to adopt a defensive posture by arguing that disability is a complex and interactive phenomenon and as such the disadvantages of having a disability cannot be traced to the under-lying impairments alone, but to stigma, discrimination, lack of accom-modation, and other social factors (Amundson, 1992; Bickenbach, 1993; Silvers, Wasserman, and Mahowald, 1998; Wasserman, 2001). In particular, they have argued that public health practices of preven-tion, although unobjectionable on their face, also send the clear mes-sage that individuals living with preventable impairments have lives not worth living (Asch, 2001). They insist that the prejudice that often occurs during a life with an impairment is itself a discriminatory stance toward disabled people and their lives.

Political philosophers typically address the impact of disability on the good life from the perspective of the implications of disability on distributive justice generally, and the demands of social and political equality specifically. Confronting the hard fact that the combination of increased longevity and medical improvement more or less guar-antees an ever-increasing prevalence of persons with disabilities and chronic health conditions (WHO, 2001, 2011), the naive view that political theory can ignore disability as a social justice outlier has been

3

recognized as utterly untenable. Political philosophers have debated the consequences of viewing physical and mental impairments as potential decrements in well-being, including the appropriate response by a just society. At this juncture, competing understandings of what disability is direct the discussion: if understood as a purely biological phenomenon only partially within human control, then the situation of persons with disabilities points to some form of charity or social transfers grounded in social solidarity. If understood as entirely or in part a disadvantage created by stigma, discrimination, and lack of accommodation, then a case is made for a human rights–based and antidiscrimination social response. Perhaps the most salient contribution of disability studies to political philosophy has been the insistence that only the latter human rights approach to disability is tenable.

Philosophically, the question of what makes for a good human life arguably presupposes the question of what constitutes a human life of moral value, conceptualized as the grounds of personhood. This in turn raises the question of whether human beings are essentially or merely contingently moral persons, that is, whether some nonhuman animals may qualify as persons, while some human beings with impairments may not qualify. Can some members of *homo sapiens*, in short, have impairments of such kind or severity that they are not persons in the required sense, that is, entities with fundamental moral worth? An engrained philosophical tradition insists that as human moral worth is grounded on rationality – and its preconditions, cognition and consciousness – profound intellectual or cognitive impairments might wholly undermine moral worth, and so the possibility of living the good human life. Against this prejudice, some philosophers have tried to untether moral worth from an overly rational or cerebral conception of humanity to redeem the value of living with severe intellectual impairment. Suggestions of participation in human community, connectedness with others, and membership in the human form of life have been suggested as alternative ways of grounding human worth and the basis for the good human life (Kittay, 2005, 2009; Kittay and Carlson, 2009).

Other than alternative ways of understanding or modeling disability, the fact that there are competing conceptualizations of the good life further muddies the waters. As might be expected, philosophical approaches to human well-being or the good human life has a long and complex pedigree. Derek Parfit's taxonomy of philosophical positions, although itself controversial, is a good place to start (1984): philosophers have either adopted a purely subjective approach to the good life, with accounts grounded in hedonism, preferences, or desire satisfaction, or have looked toward objective accounts, which Parfit called "objective list accounts," in which efforts are made to identify necessary conditions of the good life. Mooted constituent components of the good life range from Aristotle's "eudemonia" – the good that is constituent of the essence of humanity – to John Rawls's more pragmatic "primary social goods" (1971) and Amaryta Sen's capabilities or opportunism for securing what one wishes to do or be (2009). T. M. Scanlon has helpfully labeled these accounts as "experiential theories," "desire theories," and "substantive-good theories" (1998), or more simply, subjective and objective theories of well-being.

Subjectively, the relationship between impairments and well-being is not straightforward, because of either psychological processes of adaptation to impairment or other fundamental shifts in how an individual deals with his or her impairments so that what was originally viewed as a detriment to the good life is subsequently viewed neutrally, or even positively. Thus, if the good life is understood exclusively in terms of what is called *subjective well-being* (SWB), *happiness*, or *positive life satisfaction*, then we should expect that the experience of living with an impairment, even a serious one, will not necessarily reduce or eliminate the goodness of living, at least as it is experienced by that individual. Objectively speaking, however, it seems more intuitive to think of impairments, at least prima facie, as decrements to the good life, although, as the chapters in this collection argue, this inference too is suspect for many reasons: when an impairment such as blindness or lower body paralysis is so thoroughly internalized as to form part of one's identity, it seems insensitive and factually incorrect to continue to insist the impairment is both an objective harm and an essential detriment to that individual's good life.

In the health and social science literature on what makes a life good, which is most often couched in terms of "quality of life," a similar distinction is drawn between objective and subjective quality of life, the former broken down into domains of good things in life, about which there is general consensus. Because of parallel developments from different disciplines, and the general lack of awareness of what is happening outside the researcher's own discipline, significant overlap occurs between the quality of life and well-being discussions, causing considerable confusion in terminology. Until fairly recently, the quality of life work took the lead on developing empirical measurement instruments, which soon became widely used in medicine and rehabilitation as therapeutic outcome measures. Here too the same challenge comes to the fore: What do we make of the considerable evidence that people with severe disabilities, who rank low on objective lists of the good life, report high levels of subjective quality of life? Only fairly recently has the well-being literature followed the trends in quality of life instrumentation and moved from theory to empirical research (Kahneman, Diener, and Schwartz, 1999).

One of the most challenging issues in the growing debate about the effect of impairments on well-being or quality of life is whether it is possible to reconcile two apparently diametrically opposed propositions: first, that the prevention of impairments through public health and safety measures is not merely desirable but a genuine social responsibility; second, that strong self-report evidence demonstrates that people with those impairments live good and valuable lives. The disability community may, in its rush to deny that disability is an utter tragedy that can only ruin one's life, feel compelled to oversteer to say that disability is "just a difference" and the disadvantages a person may experience are entirely the result of social prejudice. More cautious writers point out that impairments are real phenomena, and not infrequently painful and choice limiting, so that even if all social and physical barriers were removed, though the life of a disabled individual would thereby be made easier, disadvantages may nonetheless remain.

Interestingly, a parallel strategic problem has been identified as a political challenge for the disability community at large. Often called the "dilemma of difference" (Minow, 1990), it involves the fact that should people with disabilities and their political advocates concede that impairments, on their own, can have adverse effects on the good life, then they are in effect agreeing with common perceptions that a life with impairments is not worth living. On the other hand, if these advocates insist that impairments have no essential deleterious effect on the good life, if they are, once again, mere "differences," then the advocates seriously jeopardize the case they have to make to the state that positive social response is essential to meet the health and other practical needs impairments create, without which full social inclusion and participation would be impossible.

The central question of this book is, therefore, whether, in any conception of the good human life, disability is an alternative way of living that can be as valuable as any other or whether disability is intrinsically associated with deficiency or defect in the value of life, one that must be tolerated or socially compensated and accommodated. As will become apparent in the chapters included in this volume, this question can be addressed from a variety of perspectives and philosophical methodologies. Despite the diversity of approaches and conclusions, however, all of these chapters share the conviction that disability is a fundamental feature of human existence – neither an outlier to nor an anomaly of the human condition – and that it is well within our grasp to understand the significance of the immense variety of human lives and conditions, and through that understanding to secure the preconditions for achieving the common dignity of all individuals.

THE CHAPTERS

The volume starts with two chapters that focus on the relationship between intellectual impairment or cognitive disability and the good human life. Benjamin L. Curtis and Simo Vehmas discuss the moral significance of severe intellectual impairment and set out to explore how particular mental characteristics are thought to determine an individual's moral status. In particular, they ask why some philosophers argue that people with severe intellectual disabilities have comparable psychological and emotional capacities to animals. They compare two opposing camps on this issue: the "intrinsic property camp," represented by philosopher Jeff McMahan, and the "special relations camp" associated with the work of Eva Feder Kittay. They conclude by motivating and describing their "hybrid view" of the relationship between intellectual capacity and moral status, a view that sets the benchmark of moral worth at consciousness, which, they argue, is an essential precondition for entering into a relationship with the human community. Barbara Schmitz takes up this issue of the moral status of cognitively disabled people, but turns instead to the important Wittgensteinian notion of the "human form of life" as her benchmark. On this view, a truly human life is made up of a multiplicity and plurality of practices, rather than a single, putatively essential human capacity or characteristic. Cognitively disabled individuals, she argues, must not be viewed, by philosophers or anyone else, as "something else," but, in light of what they have and experience in common with everyone else, as full members of the human community with equal intrinsic moral worth.

As noted earlier, the assumption, shared by philosophers and the lay alike, that all serious or severe impairments are always and indeed necessarily harmful to the good human life, dramatically conflicts with a reliable body of evidence that people with disabilities themselves positively rate their well-being. This clash, sometimes called the "disability paradox" (Albrecht and Devlieger, 1999), is addressed by Thomas

Introduction

Schramme in his contribution. He argues there is nothing contradictory about a person with a disability agreeing that having a disability is comparatively worse than not having one, while insisting that, from his or her perspective, it does not adversely affect well-being or the prospects of living a good human life. Because well-being is closely related to one's identity, he argues, it is not unexpected that once a disability has been internalized, its absolute, objective harmfulness will decrease or even disappear. Tom Shakespeare addresses the same perplexity, but in a form more relevant to public policy. He asks how we can reconcile the evidence that many people with disabilities assess their lives positively with the view that prevention of health conditions and impairments is a desirable social aim. He shows that while there are no good reasons for discounting the views of persons with disabilities, it is also naive to deny that impairments limit people's lives and choices, and in a sense are true harms. Because of this, social and public health prevention programs are fully justified, as long as they do not mistakenly reinforce the misperception that disability is a tragedy, that disabled people are useless, or that the prospect of living a good life is forever closed to them.

Halvor Hanisch also addresses this debate, but from a different methodological perspective that takes the discussion in a very different direction. He argues that, ultimately, the question of the impact of disability on the good life depends on what he calls the "recognition of life with a disability" by both the disabled individual and the surrounding community. Integrating the accounts of recognition in the writing of French cultural theorist and psychoanalyst Julia Kristeva and Canadian political philosopher Charles Taylor, Hanisch notes that, in the end, an appreciation of the fact that life with a disability can be a good life crucially depends on resolving the apparent conflict between an acknowledgment of commonality in universal dignity and the recognition of difference, or in other words, the recognition of the goodness in living a fundamentally different kind of human life.

The contribution of David Wasserman and Adrienne Asch takes as given that disabilities need not have a substantially adverse impact on well-being – on any subjective, objective, or hybrid account of that notion – and goes on to explore more deeply the subtle issues that remain and that must be taken into account in the relationship between disability and well-being. They argue it is important to distinguish in this regard between impairments that consist of the loss rather than the absence of a function, between impairments that involve pain, progressive functional decline, and reduced life expectancy and those that do not, and, finally, the different impacts on living caused by the impairments themselves and those that result from social and environmental exclusion. After factoring out the clearly detrimental aspects of disabilities, they try to distill the remaining residue of disadvantage that might account for the intuition that, as a general matter, prevention of impairment is always justified as a social goal.

The relationship between disability and well-being has recently reemerged as a social concern with the advent of the so-called well-being agenda in countries such as the United Kingdom. Jerome E. Bickenbach explores the recent social policy phenomenon of assessing policy in terms of well-being population outcomes, rather than economic or other social indicators. In particular, he scrutinizes the growing disquiet with the agenda voiced by disability advocates who discern in it the potential for identifying the responsibility for unhappiness in the individual, thereby ignoring the impact of external social factors such as discrimination and oppression and legitimatizing a particularly strong version of paternalism. While agreeing that these are potential worries, he warns against overstating the problem by relying on *disability exceptionalism*, namely the view that living with a severe impairment may well be preferable in terms of well-being than living without it.

In many health and allied health disciplines, the standard and widely used tool for assessing how well life is going for a patient is the quality of life questionnaire. Hans Reinders takes up the issue of the validity of quality of life assessment of disabled individuals by considering the story of Sam, a severely handicapped boy who managed not only to survive but, from his own perspective, to lead a high-quality life, despite the fact that his doctors deemed his quality of life very low. Reinders shows us what we can learn from Sam about the difference between presumptively objective and factually subjective quality of life. Arguing that the lack of correlation between the two is probably unresolvable, he suggests we need to transcend the difference between the objective and subjective dimensions entirely. He is led to a more dynamic account of quality of life oriented toward the classical Aristotelian goal of *human flourishing*, according to which human beings flourish to the extent that they are capable of actualizing their own potential.

Anna Stubblefield tackles the quality of life dilemma in the case of persons with profound intellectual impairments by arguing from her experience that, in many cases, the reason for the tendency to judge quality of life as minimal in these individuals has more to do with our failure to find appropriate modes of communication that would allow us more accurate insight into the nature of the lives these individuals are living. In many instances, although perhaps not all, what we take to be a low quality of life is a failure on our part to become fully aware of the mode of experiencing the world that the individual relies on in response to the impairment. In the end, she reminds us that impairment is a fundamental human characteristic and cautions us that to fear disability is to fear our own humanity and that we only devalue ourselves when we devalue the disabled life.

Relying on a very different, phenomenological approach, Havi Carel explores the complex dimensions of chronic illness to reveal the full, subjective completeness of living such lives. She addresses, first, whether and how illness affects one's well-being, and, second, because according to the evidence, illness does not always adversely affect our lives, why do we conceive of it as one of the most terrifying evils that can befall a person? Her multilayered and nuanced analysis makes the case that we are, perhaps surprisingly, far more resilient than we think and can change priorities and values in light of even radically altered circumstances. In this sense, insofar as happiness is an achievement that always requires thought, planning, and work, chronic illness might best be understood as providing us with a context and opportunity for reflection and revaluation that can be, and often is, a preclude to enhance well-being.

In his contribution, Christopher A. Riddle makes the link between the extent to which impairments undermine the good life and the requirements of social justice should we decide that impairments have this effect. Addressing one of the most intransigent problems of social policy implementation, he argues that as a matter of justice it is incumbent on our social, political, and legal institutions to adequately rectify the inequalities that arise from disadvantages associated with disability, but only to do so in a manner that avoids or mitigates the stigmatization that can result when society singles out an individual for compensation. He argues that the requirement that the political theory that justifies such policy as "stigma-sensitive" is grounded in human dignity. Testing the popular capabilities approach of Amartya Sen and Martha Nussbaum, he finds the approach has a potential flaw that opens it to the charge that it cannot sustain a stigma-sensitive attitude toward disabilities.

In the concluding chapter, Franziska Felder further contextualizes the notion of the good human life as it applies to persons with disabilities by taking up one of the central human rights recently enunciated in the United Nations Conventions on the Rights of Persons with Disabilities, namely the right to inclusion. Her aim is to show the relationship between inclusion and the good human life by subjecting the notion of inclusion, long a catchword of the disability movement, to the philosophical scrutiny it requires. She argues there are two spheres of inclusion – inclusion into communities and inclusion in a society – and both involve social intentionality from participants in the inclusive relationship. That is, social inclusion depends on the positive attitudes of others, but also on the freedom to choose the life one wishes to lead. Inclusion thus has a direct impact on the good life as a crucial part of basic human thriving, and an indirect impact as a means for expanding the range of opportunities for achieving the diverse, constituent elements of the good life.

THE AUTHORS

Adrienne Asch is the Edward and Robin Milstein Professor of Bioethics and the director of the Center for Ethics at Yeshiva University as well as a professor of epidemiology and population health and family and social medicine at Albert Einstein College of Medicine, New York. She received her doctorate in social psychology from Columbia University and was a member of the board of the American Society for Bioethics and Humanities and a fellow at the Hastings Center. She has written extensively on disability issues and bioethics. She has edited several books, including, with E. Parens, *Prenatal Testing and Disability Rights*, Georgetown University Press (2002), and many articles and chapters that have been highly influential in shaping the debates between bioethics and disability.

Jerome E. Bickenbach, PhD, LL.B, is the leader of the Disability Policy Unit and a member of the Department of Health Sciences and Health Policy, University of Lucerne and Switzerland Swiss Paraplegic Research (SPF), Nottwil, Switzerland. He is the author of numerous books and articles, including *Physical Disability and Social Policy* (1993), *Disability and Culture: Universalism and Diversity* (2000), *A Seat at the Table: Persons with Disabilities and Policy Making* (2001), *Quality of Life and Human Difference* (2003), and *Ethics, Law and Policy* (2012). He was a content editor of Sage Publication's five-volume *Encyclopaedia of Disability*. He has since been a consultant with the World Health Organization (WHO) working on the revision of the International Classification of Functioning, Disability and Health (ICF).

Havi Carel is senior lecturer in philosophy at the University of Bristol and also teaches at Bristol Medical School. She is currently a British Academy fellow writing a monograph for Oxford University Press provisionally entitled *Phenomenology of Illness*. Her research examines the experience of illness and of receiving health care. She has written on the embodied experience of illness, well-being within illness, and patient-physician communication in the *Lancet, BMJ, Journal of Medicine and Philosophy, Theoretical Medicine and Bioethics, Philosophia*, and in edited collections. She is the author of *Illness*, Acumen (2008), shortlisted for the Wellcome Trust Book Prize, and of *Life and Death in Freud and Heidegger*, Rodopi (2006). She is the coeditor of *Health, Illness and Disease*, Acumen (2012) and of *What Philosophy Is*, Continuum (2004).

Benjamin L. Curtis is a philosopher at the University of Nottingham, UK. His interests are wide and varied, and along with working on issues in disability studies and applied ethics, he works on issues in philosophical logic and metaphysics.

Franziska Felder, PhD, is a senior lecturer at the University of Zurich. She studied special needs education, economics, and cinema studies (2000–5). After that, she was a doctoral student in philosophy and special needs education and attended the graduate program for interdisciplinary research in ethics at the University of Zurich (Switzerland). During this time she was also a visiting student at the University College London (political philosophy). She finished her doctoral degree about the moral rights to inclusion in 2010. Her research interests include justice and disability, especially inclusion, recognition, and the capabilities approach to disability and social justice.

Halvor Hanisch holds a PhD in sociology, as well as an MA in comparative literature. He is now a postdoctoral research fellow at Oslo University Hospital. His research areas include: (1) qualitative work in sociology, emphasizing the relation between disability and different social arenas, such as private spaces, public spaces, and workplaces, as well as the importance of families and other close relations; (2) quantitative research, in particular on the relations between disability, psycho-emotional well-being, and violence; (3) theoretical work on the differentiation of disabling processes, with particular reference to the work of Anthony Giddens; (4) theoretical work on the structural workings of disabling processes, with particular reference to the work of Julia Kristeva; and (5) interpretations of representations of disability.

Hans S. Reinders is a professor of ethics at the Vrije Universiteit, Amsterdam, where he also holds the Bernard Lievegoed chair for ethics and disability. He is president of the European Society for the Study of Theology and Disability (ESSTD), and general editor of the *Journal of Religion, Disability & Health*. His publications include *The Future of the Disabled in Liberal Society*, University of Notre Dame Press (2000) and *Receiving the Gift of Friendship: Profound Disability, Theological Anthropology, and Ethics*, William B. Eerdmans Publishing (2008).

Christopher A. Riddle is an assistant professor of philosophy at Utica College, NY, where he also leads the Institute of Applied Ethics. Previously, he was an assistant professor of philosophy at Concordia University, Montreal. He completed his PhD at Queen's University at Kingston in the Department of Philosophy. His work has been published in journals such as *The Journal of Social Philosophy*, *The American Journal of Bioethics; Medicine, Healthcare, & Philosophy*, and *Disability Studies Quarterly*. He is the author of *Disability and Justice: The Capabilities Approach in Practice*, Rowman & Littlefield (2013).

Barbara Schmitz, PhD, studied at the University of Tübingen, Freiburg und Tromsoe. Her research interests lie in questions of ethics, political philosophy, and philosophy of language. After her PhD on Wittgenstein she worked as an assistant professor in philosophy at the University of Basel, including research visits at Oxford and at the Center for Human Values, Princeton. In 2009, she finished her second dissertation (Habilitation) about "Needs and Justice." Currently she is working on a research project about the concept of disability and its moral and political consequences. She has a cognitively disabled daughter.

Thomas Schramme is a professor of ethics, University of Hamburg (since 2009); before that he served as a senior lecturer at the Department of History, Philosophy and Law in Swansea (UK) and course director of the MA in medical humanities at the University of Swansea. His publications include *Philosophy and Psychiatry*, jointly edited with Johannes Thome, de Gruyter (2004) and "The Significance of the

Concept of Disease for Justice in Health Care," *Theoretical Medicine and Bioethics* (2007).

Tom Shakespeare trained as a sociologist at Cambridge University and has worked at the Universities of Sunderland, Leeds and Newcastle, and at the World Health Organization, Geneva, and is now a professor at the University of East Anglia. He has published widely in disability studies and bioethics, and his books and articles include *Genetic Politics: From Eugenics to Genome*, "The Social Model of Disability: An Outdated Ideology?" *Research in Social Science and Disability* (2002), and *Disability Rights and Wrongs*, Routledge (2006).

Anna Stubblefield is an associate professor of philosophy at Rutgers University-Newark. Her research interests are in disability studies and ethics – particularly communication rights and access, issues relating to intellectual disability, autism, and the intersection of disability and race. She provides communication support to people who use supported typing.

Simo Vehmas is a professor of disability studies at the University of Helsinki (Finland) and the president of the Nordic Network on Disability Research (NNDR). His training is in both special education and philosophy, and he has written many articles and books about the base of disability and bioethics. His publications include *Philosophy and Science: The Axes of Evil in Disability Studies? Journal of Medical Ethics* (2008) and (edited with K. Kristiansen and T. Shakespeare), of *Arguing about Disability – Philosophical Perspectives*, Routledge (2008).

David Wasserman is a professor at Yeshiva University in New York and was previously a research scholar at the Institute for Philosophy and Public Policy, University of Maryland. He has an MA in Psychology and a J.D. from the University of Michigan Law School. He has edited *Harming Future Persons: Ethics, Genetics, and the Nonidentity Problem*, Springer (2009), *Quality of Life and Human Difference: Genetic Testing, Health Care, and Disability*, Cambridge University Press (2005), and *Genetics and Criminal Behavior*, Cambridge University Press (2001);

and has written extensively on disability issues, including (with Anita Silvers and Mary Mahowald) *Disability, Difference, Discrimination*, Rowman & Littlefield (1998) and articles in the *Journal of Moral Philosophy*, *Philosophy and Public Affairs*, and *Ethics*.

References

Albrecht, G. L. and Devlieger, P. J. 1999. The Disability Paradox: High quality of life against all odds. *Social Science and Medicine*, 48: 977–88.

Amundson, R. 1992. Disability, handicap, and the environment. *Journal of Social Philosophy*, 23(1): 105–19.

Asch, A. 2001. Disability, bioethics, and human rights. In G. Albrecht, K. Seelman, and M. Bury (eds.), *Handbook of Disability Studies* (pp. 297–326). Thousand Oaks, CA: Sage Publications.

Bickenbach, J. 1993. *Physical Disability and Social Policy*. Toronto and London: University of Toronto Press.

Buchanan, A., Brock, D. W., Daniels, N., and Wikler, D. 2000. *From Chance to Choice – Genetics and Justice*. New York: Cambridge University Press.

Cureton, A. and Brownlee, K. 2009. Introduction. In K. Brownlee and A. Cureton (eds.), *Disability and Disadvantage (pp. 1–13)*. Oxford: Oxford University Press.

Kahneman, D., Diener, E., and Schwartz, N. (1999) *Well-Being: The Foundations of Hedonic Psychology*. New York: Russell Sage Publications.

Kittay, E. F. 2005. At the margins of moral personhood. *Ethics*, 116(1):100–31.

2009. The personal is philosophical is political: A philosopher and mother of a cognitively disabled person sends notes from the battlefield. *Metaphilosophy*, 40(3–4): 606–27.

Kittay, E. F. and Carlson, L. (eds.). 2009. *Cognitive Disability and Its Challenge to Moral Philosophy*. Oxford: Blackwell.

Minow, M . 1990. *Making All the Difference: Inclusion, Exclusion, and American Law*. Ithaca, NY: Cornell University Press.

Nussbaum, M. C. 2009. The capabilities of people with cognitive disabilities. *Metaphilosophy*, 40(3–4): 331–51.

Parens, E. and Asch, A. (eds.). 2002. *Prenatal Testing and Disability*. Washington, DC: Georgetown University Press.

Parfit, D. 1984. *Reasons and Persons*. Oxford: Clarendon Press.

Rawls, J. 1971. *A Theory of Justice*. Oxford: Oxford University Press.

Roulstone, A., Thomas, C., and Watson, N . 2012. The changing terrain of disability studies. In N. Watson, A. Roulstone, and C. Thomas (eds.), *Routledge Handbook of Disability Studies* (pp. 3–11). New York: Routledge.

Scanlon, T. M. 1998. *What We Owe to Each Other*. Cambridge, MA: Harvard University Press.

Sen, A . 2009. *The Idea of Justice*. London: Allen Lane.

Shakespeare, T. 2006. *Disability Rights and Wrongs*. London: Routledge.

Silvers, A., Wasserman, D., and Mahowald, M. B. 1998. *Disability, Difference, Discrimination*. Lanham, MD: Rowman and Littlefield.

Wasserman, D. 2001. Philosophical issues in the definition and social response to disability. In G. L. Albrecht et al. (eds.), *Handbook of Disability Studies*. Thousand Oaks CA: Sage Publications (pp. 219–51).

World Health Organization (WHO). 2001. *Health and Ageing: A Discussion Paper*. Geneva: World Health Organization.

   2011. *World Report on Disability*. Geneva: World Health Organization.

1

Moral Worth and Severe Intellectual Disability – A Hybrid View

BENJAMIN L. CURTIS AND SIMO VEHMAS

INTRODUCTION

Consider:

> Case 1: You can save a normal adult human from a burning build-
> ing.[1] Should you do so?
> Case 2: You can save a normal adult dog from a burning building.
> Should you do so?

The ethical literature shows general agreement about the answers to the questions posed in cases 1 and 2, and general agreement about the reason for giving those answers. In case 1 you *should* save the human, and in case 2 you *should* save the dog. Why? Because both are morally valuable beings.

Now consider:

> Case 3: You can save *either* a normal adult human *or* a normal adult
> dog from a burning building, but not both. Given that both are morally
> valuable, which should you save?

Again the ethical literature evinces a general consensus, both about the answer to the question posed and about the reason for giving that answer. You should save the human and *not* the dog. Why? Because

---

[1] Assume further (both here and in the later cases) that there is no risk to yourself and little cost.

although both are morally valuable, normal adult humans are *more* valuable than normal adult dogs.

Now consider:

Case 4:Again, you can save *either* a normal adult human or a normal adult dog from a burning building, but not both. This time, however, the human is a stranger to you and the dog is *your* beloved dog. Which should you save?

Case 4 differs from case 3 only in that here you bear what we can term a "special relation" to the dog that you do not bear to the human. Once more, though, there is general agreement both about the answer to the question posed and about the reason for giving it. You should *still* save the human. Why? Because standing in a special relation to a normal, nonhuman animal does not raise the moral value of that animal to a level greater than (or even equal to) that of a normal adult human.

Finally, consider:

Case 5: Once more, you can save *either* a human or a normal adult dog from a burning building (with no risk to yourself and at little cost), but not both. This time, however, the human is not a *normal* adult human, but a human with a severe intellectually disability (or, as we shall say, a "SID"). Which one should you save?

When discussing case 5, agreement about the answer to the question evaporates. Two opposing camps exist, which we will call "the intrinsic property camp" and "the special relations camp." Those in the intrinsic property camp think that in most cases it is equally permissible to save either the dog or the human, and that in fact in some cases you should save the dog and *not* the human. Those in the special relations camp, by contrast, maintain that you should always save the human and *not* the dog. There is disagreement between these two camps about the answer to this question because there is disagreement between them about the moral significance of SIDs. Those in the intrinsic property

20

camp believe that the moral value of a human with a SID is equal to (and in some cases less than) the moral value of a nonhuman animal such as a dog. (They thus believe that the value of a human with a SID is *strictly less* than the value of a normal adult human.) Those in the special relations camp believe that the value of a human with a SID is *strictly higher* than the value of a nonhuman animal. (But they are not thereby committed to, but may nonetheless believe, that a human with a SID has equal moral value to a normal adult human.)

The questions we address in this chapter include:

1. Why do those in each camp hold the view that they do?
2. Which camp is right?

After discussing the first question in detail, we conclude in answer to question 2 that, in fact, *neither* is right. We suggest that one should join neither camp but that one should, rather, pitch one's tent somewhere in the middle. The position we favor, however, does produce an answer in case 5 that is in closer agreement with the special relations camp than the intrinsic properties camp. Our answer is that in all cases, unless the human with a SID is *wholly nonconscious*, it is the human with a SID that should be saved.[2]

We address questions 1 and 2 and examine the issues lying behind them by analyzing the debate between a notable member of the intrinsic property camp, Jeff McMahan, and a notable member of the special relations camp, Eva Feder Kittay. We take these two philosophers as spokespersons for their camps because they have written most extensively on the issues of contention between the two camps, and

---

[2] Our concern here is the issues that McMahan and Kittay raise, so we don't attempt to give a full list of all the philosophers who fall into each camp. But an excellent example of another prominent philosopher who falls squarely into the intrinsic properties camp is Peter Singer. Singer's views are expressed in many places, but to see the parallel between his views and McMahan's one can do no better than to consult Singer (1993). And an excellent example of a prominent philosopher whose views are similar in many respects to Kittay's is Martha Nussbaum (cf. Nussbaum, 2006).

have engaged in open debate with each other. Their debate is a fruitful basis for an examination of the issues because it unpacks them in detail and shows clearly that, ultimately, the disagreement between the two camps is about the very *foundations* of moral status itself. Roughly speaking, for McMahan and those in the intrinsic property camp, the intrinsic psychological properties of an individual are the basis of its moral worth, whereas for Kittay and those in the special relations camp, membership in a moral, human community is the basis of an individual's moral status.

We start with a summary of McMahan's position before turning to Kittay's disagreements. We then critically discuss those disagreements and develop our own view. We conclude by outlining why we believe our view to be superior to both McMahan and Kittay's.

MCMAHAN'S POSITION

McMahan on Moral Worth

McMahan makes a conceptual distinction between the moral worth of a being *itself* and the moral worth of that being's *life*. He argues that a being's life, at each particular point in time, is intrinsically valuable insofar as it is constituted by a pleasurable experience at that time. But, he maintains, it is not in general possible to obtain the *overall* worth of a being's life merely by summing the intrinsic values of a being's life at each time at which it exists. A being's life, he argues, gains extra moral worth if its experiences are interrelated with past and future experiences by what he calls "prudential unity relations" – psychological relations that bind the lives of conscious beings together across time.[3] Any being whose experiences are linked across time by these

---

[3] Examples of the relations McMahan has in mind are "the relation between an experience and the memory of it, the relation between the formation of a desire and the

prudential unity relations, McMahan argues, has a life that is worth considerably more than the sum of its momentary values. As he puts it, the psychological unity within the lives of such beings gives "[their] lives as a whole a moral and prudential significance that the mere sum of [their] experiences lacks – or, to put it differently, that makes [their] lives as a whole significant units for moral and prudential evaluation" (2002: 76).

In some cases, McMahan thinks, the worth of a being is *identical* to the worth of its life, for example, for nonhuman animals such as dogs. From the foregoing, however, it should be clear the lives of nonhuman animals are not all equal. Rather, the moral worth of a nonhuman animal x is greater than that of another, y, if and only if the life of x has a greater level of psychological unity than the life of y. Thus, it is more wrong to kill a being with a greater degree of psychological unity in its life than it is to kill a being with a lesser degree.[4] However, this leads McMahan to a problem. He considers the following two individuals:

> *Bright:* "a person with exceptionally high cognitive and emotional capacities that [make] possible for him an unusually high level of well-being"
>
> *Dull:* "the same age as Bright but [is] constitutionally dim-witted and stolid. There [is] thus a range of goods – including engagement in rich, complexly and subtly layered personal relations, the experience of intense, refined aesthetic states, and so on – that [are] accessible to Bright but from which Dull [is] by nature excluded." (2002: 234)

experience of the satisfaction or frustration of that desire, and the relation between an earlier and a later manifestation of a belief, value, intention or character trait" (McMahan, 2002: 39). These relations hold both directly and indirectly, and with varying degrees and strength, across the lives of different beings, and typically they hold more strongly across days than across years.

[4] In fact, matters are a little more complicated than this. McMahan's account of the wrongness of killing a being may also require taking into consideration that being's "time relative interests (2002: 232–40). For the sake of this chapter, we leave out this complication. Nothing hangs on our doing so.

According to the account given so far, the *life* of Dull is worth less than the *life* of Bright (by virtue of Bright's life having a greater degree of psychological unity than Dull's). But McMahan wishes to maintain the strong intuition that *ceteris paribus* it would be *equally* wrong to kill Dull as it would be to kill Bright. Thus, he endorses the view that there is a threshold of moral worth beyond which "all worth is equal worth" (2002: 251). A being lies over the threshold, McMahan argues, if it has sufficiently complex intrinsic psychological capacities to be worthy of respect as an individual (he thus calls the threshold "the threshold of respect" (2002: 246). All beings above this threshold have a moral worth that outstrips the moral worth of their lives *because* they are worthy of respect as individuals. To kill such beings constitutes an ultimate moral wrong because it would violate the respect they are due. Thus, on McMahan's view, all beings above the threshold are equally morally valuable and the value that each has exceeds the moral worth of each of their respective lives.[5]

McMahan maintains that the threshold of respect coincides with the threshold of personhood. But what capacities make one a person? According to McMahan, such capacities are those associated with the traditional Lockean concept of a person. Locke maintained that a person is "a thinking intelligent being, that has reason and reflection, and can consider itself as itself, the same thinking thing, in different times and places" (1977: 180). The lives of beings of this sort possess great psychological unity in virtue of possessing highly developed *cognitive* capacities (i.e., those capacities to do with conceptual abilities, understanding, problem solving, and rational decision making). Throughout his work, McMahan emphasizes the

---

[5] Actually, he does not strictly endorse this view. Officially he remains agnostic between this view and the "time relative interest" view. However, it does seem that McMahan takes this view more seriously than the time relative interest view, and as we take this view to be superior to the time relative interest view (precisely because it solves the problem of Bright and Dull), for the sake of this chapter we take McMahan to endorse it.

importance of such developed cognitive capacities, and suggests that it is a necessary condition of a being's having sufficient psychological unity to place it above the threshold of respect that it possesses such cognitive capacities. Thus, he maintains, the possession of sufficiently developed cognitive capacities is necessary for personhood and, what amounts to the same thing, necessary for being above the threshold of respect.

We are now in a position to appreciate McMahan's view about the moral worth of those with SIDs. McMahan claims that normal human beings possess the person-making cognitive capacities, but that nonhuman animals like dogs do not. But, McMahan also claims, those with SIDs are humans whose "psychological capacities and potential are comparable [i.e., equal in all relevant respects] to those of an animal" (2002: 205). Thus, because McMahan thinks that animals are nonpersons, he also thinks that those with SIDs are nonpersons. And because he thinks that persons are worth more than nonpersons, he is thus committed to the view that those with SIDs have a lower moral worth than any normal adult human. Moreover, the worth of nonpersons depends on the worth of their lives, which can vary depending on the level of psychological unity within them. So McMahan is committed to the view that if a particular dog happens to have a greater level of psychological unity within its life than a human with SID, then that dog will be worth more than the human.

McMahan on Special Relations

A special relation is simply a relation that holds between individuals that has moral significance. McMahan acknowledges that special relations exist (he agrees, for example, that the parent/child relation is a special relation). However, he maintains that their presence does not alter the moral *worth* of individuals related by them. Rather, he maintains, they serve only to "strengthen or extend one's moral [obligations] to benefit or not to harm that individual in a way that is commensurate with or proportional to the moral significance of the relation" (2002: 223).[6] He argues that a mother would do something wrong in saving a stranger over her own son not because her son is more morally *valuable* than the stranger, but rather because the mother's *obligations* to her son are *strengthened* by her being his parent. We can summarize McMahan's position here as follows:

1. Intrinsic properties *alone* are worth constituters.
2. The *fundamental* source of obligations toward a being derives only from that being's moral worth.
3. Special relations are not worth constituters and so can only *fortify* obligations and not *generate* them.

Although McMahan agrees that the parent-child relation is a special relation of considerable moral significance, he is much more skeptical about the species membership relation. He admits that its being a special relation cannot be wholly ruled out, but he argues that if it is a special relation, it is one of only *minimal* significance. In particular, he thinks that it is not significant enough to generate an obligation to treat cognitively disabled humans better than nonhuman animals. Certainly, he thinks that the relation is not significant enough to fortify our obligations toward humans with SIDs to a level where they are commensurate with the obligations we have toward normal humans. So, he thinks that, even taking into account the fact that we are (or at

---

[6] McMahan used "moral reasons" rather than "obligations." Again, nothing hangs on our expressing McMahan's view in terms of obligations rather than reasons. We do not suppose that obligations are decisive, that is, we do not suppose that if one has an obligation to perform an action then one must perform that action. This is because there may be stronger countervailing obligations not to perform that action. Consequently we take it that one has a moral reason to do something if and only if one has an obligation to do that thing.

least might be) specially related to humans with SIDs, it is still true that we owe them less moral consideration than normal human beings and no more than any comparable nonhuman animal.

McMahan's views on the moral worth of those with SIDs and the significance of special relations to case 5 in our introduction is this: McMahan believes that whether you should save the dog or the human with a SID depends solely on the levels of psychological unity present within their respective lives. If the dog and the human with a SID have an equal level of psychological unity, saving either is permissible. If the dog has a greater psychological unity within its life, then you ought to save the dog.

KITTAY'S DISAGREEMENTS

Kittay has two basic disagreements with McMahan that define her position. The first is a disagreement about whether there really are any humans with mental lives *equal* to those of nonhuman animals. The second is a disagreement about the power of special relations to bestow moral worth upon individuals, and about whether the species membership relation is a morally significant special relation. We take these two disagreements in turn.

Kittay's First Disagreement: On Comparing Humans with SIDs to Nonhuman Animals

Kittay presents two arguments against McMahan's view that humans with SIDs are cognitively equal to nonhuman animals and so are not persons. First, she argues that the possession of sufficiently developed cognitive capacities is not *necessary* to being a person. She emphasizes that a number of other *noncognitive* psychological capacities are of vital importance to personhood and suggests that possession of them are also important in assessing whether a being is a person. The capacities she has in mind are:

> capacities that we would want to encourage in the members of a moral community, such as giving care and responding appropriately to care, empathy, and fellow feeling; a sense of what is harmonious and loving; and a capacity for kindness and an appreciation for those who are kind. (2005: 122)

Second, she argues that there is something wrong with comparing humans with SIDs to nonhuman animals in the first place.

> Comparisons always involve the positing of at least a partial identity. We compare by matching up features or aspects of something, and then regard those features that do not align themselves as the differentia.... As the cognitive psychologist Amos Tversky pointed out, the predicate "is like" is not symmetrical (Tversky 1977). When we assert that A is like B, we take B as the template – its features are salient – and the features of A not found in B lose their salience. That is, if B is characterized by the features x, y, and z, then we come to see A only in terms of its similarity with respect to x, y, and z, even if in other contexts A's features, a, b, and c, are the salient ones. The pernicious reductive comparisons between humans and nonhuman animals take such an asymmetrical form.... Thus, to respond to the challenge to articulate the differences between a human animal with significantly curtailed cognitive capacities and a relatively intelligent nonhuman animal means that one first has to see the former as the latter. That is the moment of revulsion. Relating with that stance to my daughter as my daughter is an impossibility. (2009: 612–13)

The idea here is that, to make the comparison between humans with SIDs and nonhuman animals, one *must* first see them as animals, and to do this is to ignore morally relevant features that they possess. In other words, Kittay suggests that making the comparison itself forces one to take up a perspective that misrepresents the nature of those with SIDs. If Kittay is right here, then not only are such comparisons useless in getting to the truth about the moral worth of humans with SIDs, but the very act of making such comparisons is morally inappropriate.[7]

An important aspect of Kittay's presentation of these arguments is that she makes use of emotionally charged, deeply personal, descriptions of her own daughter, Sesha, who is herself a human being with a SID, and who lives in a group home with five other such human beings. Here is one such description:

> [Sesha] is enormously responsive, forming deep personal relationships with her family and her long-standing caregivers and friendly relations with her therapists and teachers, more distant relatives, and our friends.... Not one [of her housemates] can even remotely be described as "entirely unresponsive to their environment or other people." I am greeted by smiles and acknowledgments of some sort when I arrive, and my daughter's passionate kisses exhaust both me and my spouse. All her roommates share her real appreciation of music: one, Billie, will "dance" in his wheelchair to rock music. Two others, Matt and Heather, love to sing along, and although they are incapable of speaking, they vocalize in just the right pitch. Tony will thrill to some music, while other music makes him weep, and he asks for his own mother when I come to visit. Nora is entranced by watching ballet and is a serious participant in the music therapy program.

> When treated to a concert of classical music, an audience of severely multiply disabled adults and children, many with severe to profound retardation, was more respectful and appreciative than many I have encountered in concert halls. Although not one will read Spinoza, the claim that these folks are incapable of deep personal relationships or deep aesthetic pleasures could not be further from the truth. For my own Sesha, "severely-profoundly" mentally retarded though she is, music is her life and Beethoven her best friend. At our home, listening to the Emperor's Concerto, she gazes out the window enthralled, occasionally turning to us with a twinkle in her eye when she anticipates some really good parts. (2005: 126–7)

[7] There is a parallel here with Bernard Williams's famous "one-thought-too-many" argument that Kittay herself notes. See Williams (1981: 1–19).

We quote this passage at length because the details are important. It, and the other passages like it, are supposed to illustrate each of the following points:

1. Many of those lacking highly developed cognitive capacities nevertheless possess highly developed emotional capacities and capacities for aesthetic appreciation (from here on simply "aesthetic capacities").
2. The emotional and aesthetic properties possessed by cognitively disabled humans like Sesha are distinctly *human* and so could *never* be possessed by any nonhuman animal – that is, these properties are *essentially* human.
3. There is also a distinct emphasis on *how* the quoted passage, and those like it, are supposed to illustrate these two points, namely, by *showing* that they are true. Kittay suggests that these deeply personal descriptions are the best she can do in this regard, but that they still fall short of doing the job perfectly. She claims that there is something about how her daughter and others with cognitive disabilities behave that is evident to those who meet and engage with them, and that clearly marks them out as utterly, and significantly, different from nonhuman animals, but that cannot be given by giving a mere list of capacities.

Later, we agree with the first of these three points, but reject the latter two.

Kittay's Second Disagreement: On Special Relations

Kittay believes, in opposition to McMahan, that the species membership relation *is* a significant special relation and that its presence justifies our giving equal moral consideration to *all* human beings, no matter how severely disabled. Unlike McMahan, she thinks that special relations are *fundamental* sources of obligation – that is, that standing in a special relation to an individual *generates* an obligation toward that individual that did not previously exist. But although this view is inconsistent with McMahan's view that special relations cannot generate obligations, it is *consistent* with McMahan's view that special relations are *not* worth constituters. To see this, consider that one might think that special relations generate obligations toward individuals *without* increasing those individuals' worth. However, although she never explicitly denies this view, Kittay seems not to hold it. Much of what she says suggests that her view is, rather, that special relations generate fundamental obligations *because* they increase the moral worth of the individuals that stand in them. Kittay thus seems to *agree* with McMahan that our fundamental obligations toward an individual derive from that individual's worth, but she disagrees that intrinsic properties *alone* are worth constituters. Rather she thinks that, *by* standing in a special relation, a being can *thereby* gain moral worth. This comes out most clearly when she quotes with approval a comment made by Naomi Scheman at the aforementioned conference. Scheman, in talking of adopting a feral cat, says the following:

> Once I adopted the cat she is no longer a feral cat, she is a different sort of being. It is not that you cannot now do certain things to her that you couldn't do before because it would hurt me, it's because you can't do certain kinds of things to her because *now she is a different kind of being.* (emphasis in original) (Scheman, quoted in Kittay, 2009: 625)

Kittay agrees with this sentiment and goes on to say:

> We human beings are the sorts of beings we are because we are cared for by other human beings, and the human being's ontological status and corresponding moral status need to be acknowledged by the larger society that makes possible the work of those who do the caring required to sustain us. That is what we each require if we are some mother's child, and we are all some mother's child. (2009: 625)

So, Kittay's view here is that standing in the species membership relation *bestows* upon all those who stand in it a special moral worth that generates the obligation to treat all with equal moral consideration. We call this view the "bestowment view." Kittay gives little more explication of the bestowment view than this, but we develop it in greater detail later in this chapter.

DISCUSSION

Comparing Humans with SIDs to Nonhuman Animals

Is Kittay right that comparing humans with SIDs to animals forces upon us a false viewpoint of those with SIDs? *Must* we view humans with SIDs as animals to make the comparison? Prima facie, the claim is incredible. Why can't we view those with SIDs and nonhuman animals as they are, and compare their respective features objectively? Why should the very act of making such a comparison force us to view those with SIDs as animals? And even if making a comparison is asymmetric in this way, why is it asymmetric in this direction, and not the other way around? Kittay, in fact, has no good answers to these questions and no good reasons for her claims. As we have seen, she cites Tversky's (1977) study to justify them. However, it is at best a misleading use of Tversky's study. First, nothing Tversky says suggests that there is anything *wrong* with asymmetric similarity judgments. Certainly nothing he says suggests that when we make such judgments we take up a false viewpoint of the things being compared. But second, there is no reason to think that the case in question *is* an asymmetrical case. Although the empirical results Tversky discusses do show that statements of the form "a is like b" *sometimes* have the asymmetry Kittay adverts to (i.e., they force an interpretation where the properties possessed by the referent term "b" are more salient than the subject term "a"), Tversky is clear that they certainly do not *always* do so. Whether they do so in a particular case depends on whether we would judge a to be more similar to b than b is to a. To conclusively establish whether this is so in any particular case requires empirical research. But there is an a priori test that can be used (it is one that Tversky himself uses successfully in his study). The test is to consider two sentences of the following form:

1. a is like b. (Or: Fs are like Gs)
2. b is like a. (Or: Gs are like Fs)

If the first sentence strikes one as more natural than the second, or the second more natural than the first, this is a good indication that asymmetry is present in the case in question. If the sentences strike one as being as natural as each other, then this is a good indication that no asymmetry is present. For example, consider the following sentences:

1. Red China is like North Korea.
2. North Korea is like Red China.

Here we think it is clear that 2 is more natural than 1, and indeed in Tversky's studies an asymmetry was seen to exist in comparisons between Red China and North Korea (again, we stress, there is no suggestion that there is anything *wrong* with the comparisons for this reason). But now consider:

1. Nonhuman animals are psychologically like cognitively disabled human beings.
2. Cognitively disabled human beings are psychologically like nonhuman animals.

After careful reflection it seems to us that these sentences are as natural as each other, which strongly suggests that in this case there is no asymmetry.[8] So, without any further reason to think that there is an asymmetry in this case, we simply have no reason to accept Kittay's claims. Consequently, there is no reason to think that comparing humans with SIDs to nonhuman animals involves taking up a viewpoint that ignores morally relevant features of the former. And it follows from this that there is no reason to think that such comparisons are themselves morally inappropriate in any way. It may be a psychological fact about Kittay herself that in order to make such a comparison she must first see cognitively disabled human beings as animals, but there is simply no reason to think it is a general truth of psychology.

We now turn to Kittay's claim that there are a number of *noncognitive* psychological capacities, the possession of which are important when assessing whether a being is a person. Kittay's claim here is not that there are some isolatable noncognitive capacities that are also sufficient for being a person, but rather that one simply *cannot give* a list of capacities that express sufficient conditions for personhood. Her descriptions of Sesha are supposed to illustrate, albeit imperfectly, that there is something more to being a person than a mere list of capacities, and that any list of features and capacities will necessarily fall short of capturing the essence of personhood. However, we demur. Why? In short, because we find Kittay's descriptions of Sesha entirely convincing. They convince us that Sesha possesses psychological

---

[8] Objection: "After careful reflection? This is no argument! You need something more than this here." No. Tversky's paper is about semantic usage. We are competent users of the English language and as such our semantic usage is likely to map onto the usage of others. This is the very bread and butter of armchair conceptual analysis. If there's something wrong with our rejection here, then there's something wrong with vast swathes of analytical philosophy. Maybe there is something wrong with vast swathes of analytical philosophy, but the onus is surely on those who think this to demonstrate it. At any rate, we here rely on the very weak assumption that analytical philosophy is in good order. In the very same way that we can rightly reject the traditional Tripartite account of knowledge in light of Gettier cases without extensive empirical work, we can reject the supposed asymmetry in this case.

capacities that no nonhuman animal possesses and that place her *well above* the threshold for being a person. And they do so precisely by giving a description of capacities that she possesses. Now we do agree with the epistemological point that Kittay raises regarding Sesha, viz. that her cognitive capacities may be far more developed than it is possible to judge. So, for all anyone knows, Sesha may well have cognitive capacities sufficient for her being a person. But for the present point this is not relevant, for importantly the key descriptions of Sesha that convince us that she is well above the threshold of personhood are those that make *no mention* of cognitive capacities at all. So even if we suppose that Sesha *is* equal to a nonhuman animal such as a dog with regard to her *cognitive* capacities, we are convinced by Kittay's descriptions that she nevertheless possesses sufficient psychological capacities to count as a person. Because the descriptions given by Kittay that convince us involve only the attribution of emotional and aesthetic capacities to Sesha, we think that Kittay's descriptions thereby do enough to establish that the possession of emotional and aesthetic capacities *alone* are sufficient for personhood. And this, we think, is enough to refute McMahan's view of the necessary conditions for personhood.

Do Kittay's descriptions of Sesha *really* do enough to refute McMahan's view of personhood? Isn't something more than mere description needed? We think not. We know what persons are, and Kittay's descriptions describe a person. There is a further important point here about Kittay's descriptions, however. As we have seen, she insists that the descriptions she gives are attempts to *show* us that her daughter possesses those psychological features that are, in some way, essentially human. However, we reject both the showing claim *and* the claim that they are essentially human.

Why do we reject the showing claim? In fact, the reason is simple. That Kittay's descriptions convince us that Sesha is a person has nothing to do with them somehow *showing* us that Sesha possesses some hard to describe psychological features that are relevant to personhood. Rather, they convince us precisely because they manage perfectly well to *describe* those features. In other words, the emotional and aesthetic capacities that Kittay thinks Sesha possesses and nonhuman animals do not, far from being hard to describe, are demonstrably *describable* – Kittay herself describes them.

Why do we reject the essentiality claim? For the simple reason that we can't understand how it could be true. In order for a property to be *essentially* human it must be metaphysically impossible for anything but a human to possess it. But how could it be metaphysically impossible for a nonhuman to possess the psychological properties of a human? There is, of course, a weak sense in which it is impossible for anything at all to possess the psychological properties of any other thing – my happiness is *my* happiness and so cannot be possessed by *you*. But this, we take it, is a mere *de dicto* impossibility on a par with the *de dicto* impossibility of *you* owning *my* coat (for if you did, it would be *your* coat and not *mine*). Similarly there is a *de dicto* impossibility of any *human* possessing a *nonhuman* psychology and any *nonhuman* possessing a *human* psychology, but this *de dicto* claim is too weak to sustain the metaphysical impossibility claim. What is needed is that the psychological properties possessed by humans with SIDs are of a radically different *nature* to the psychology of nonhuman animals, and that their very nature guarantees that they can only be possessed by humans and not by nonhuman animals. But what sort of nature *could* the psychological properties possessed by humans with SIDs have that guarantee this? Perhaps Kittay's point about *showing* is supposed to come into play here. The psychological properties in question are supposed to be *displayed* by those with SIDs; they are supposed to *show* themselves in their behavior and their interactions with other humans. Perhaps the nature of these properties and the fact that they are *essentially* human can only be fully appreciated by spending time with those with SIDs. Perhaps. But we are unconvinced. Whatever behavior it is that those with SIDs partake in, and however they interact with other humans, we simply cannot see why it is metaphysically impossible for nonhuman animals to *also* partake in the same behavior. To say that the properties, whatever they are, are *essentially human* because they flow from sharing in a *human form of life*, does not help. To share in a human form of life can be nothing more than to perform particular actions that humans perform and to engage in patterns of behavior that humans engage in. How could it be *impossible* for nonhumans to engage in the same sort of behavior? Without an answer to this question we simply have no reason to believe that the properties in question are essentially human.

Of course, some of the actions performed by humans require that one possesses a human body, but we cannot see how this in itself can be relevant to the performance of the required actions. If it were, then those who have physical impairments and moved around by crawling or with a wheelchair would lose the ability to share in a human form of life.[9] Whatever a human form of life is, and whatever psychological properties are displayed in the behavior of humans with SIDS, nothing that Kittay says justifies the claim that it is *impossible* for nonhuman animals to likewise display them.

Despite the fact we think it is metaphysically *possible* for nonhuman animals to possess those emotional and aesthetic capacities possessed by Sesha, we think that *in fact* no nonhuman animal possesses them.[10] But it is important to realize that this is not an important point in the current context. Even if we are wrong about this and some nonhuman animals do possess emotional and aesthetic capacities equal to those possessed by Sesha, this would not degrade the key point that Kittay convinces us of. The key point that Kittay convinces us of is *not* that Sesha is necessarily psychologically superior to all nonhuman animals. Rather, it is that Sesha is a person by virtue

---

[9] The history of disability provides various examples where untypical ways of, say, mobility are seen to suggest animal-like behavior.

[10] But this, of course, does not make these properties *essentially* human any more than the fact that all presidents of the United States have been male makes being the president an *essentially* male property.

of possessing developed emotional and aesthetic capacities. If as a matter of fact we are wrong about there being no nonhuman animals that also possess those properties, that does not thereby show that Sesha is not a person. Rather, it shows that some nonhuman animals are persons too.

Our agreement with Kittay regarding which psychological capacities are sufficient for personhood points to a key mistake in McMahan's position, viz. his view that the possession of developed cognitive capacities alone is sufficient for personhood. But this turns out not to be a major problem for McMahan's basic position. He must, of course, redraw the boundary marking the threshold of respect. All those above the threshold will still be persons, but some persons will now be humans with SIDs (and perhaps some persons will now be nonhuman animals). He will also have to admit that a great many humans with SIDs are not psychologically equal to nonhuman animals such as dogs. But he can still maintain that *some* humans with SIDs are. Nothing that Kittay says has any bearing on this. As convincing as Kittay's descriptions are in demonstrating that *Sesha and those like her* are persons, they do nothing to show that there are *no* humans with SIDs who are psychologically equal to nonhuman animals that are nonpersons.

We conclude this section, then, by agreeing with Kittay that the conditions of personhood are far broader than McMahan allows. However, unlike Kittay, we believe that describable emotional and aesthetic capacities exist that are sufficient for personhood. The upshot is that McMahan is wrong in thinking that a large proportion of humans with SIDs are nonpersons and so not worthy of respect as individuals. However, Kittay is wrong to think that we cannot compare humans with SIDs to nonhuman animals, and wrong to think she has shown that *all* of those with SIDs are persons. Given the vast range of SIDs, it is still plausible that at least *some* of them will be psychologically equivalent to nonhuman animals that are nonpersons, and so must be nonpersons too.

Is the Species Membership Relation a Significant Special Relation?

We now turn to the issue of whether the species membership relation is a significant special relation. We argue, in agreement with Kittay and against McMahan, that it is. Let us start by introducing the notion of a "special obligation," which is an obligation toward a being that derives from that being standing in a special relation. With this notion in hand we can express the view that special relations can only generate "agent-relative" moral reasons as follows:

> AR: If an individual A stands in a special relation to set of individuals S, this can only generate special obligations toward A for the individuals in S.

Now consider the following representative passage from McMahan that expresses an argument that crops up again and again in his writings:

> [T]he claim that radically cognitively impaired human beings are specially related to all other human beings would not give Martians a moral reason to treat these human beings any differently from animals, except perhaps an indirect reason deriving from their reason to respect those human persons to whom the impaired human beings would be specially related. Martians might, that is, be morally required to accord the radically cognitively impaired special treatment for much the same reason they would be required to give special treatment to people's pets. Otherwise it would be permissible for them to treat the radically cognitively impaired in the ways in which we treat animals, assuming that our treatment of animals is consistent with what is demanded by respect for their intrinsic natures.... *This alone is sufficient* to show that the appeal to co-membership in the human species as a special relation is of limited significance even if it is true that this relation is a source of agent-relative moral reasons. (2005: 360) (emphasis added)

McMahan is wrong to think that *this alone* is sufficient to establish his conclusion, for this argument only goes through if AR is assumed. Nevertheless, what this does show is that if one is to maintain that the species membership relation is a special relation, one must reject AR and argue that special relations can give rise to special obligations that hold *objectively*, that is, independently of the evaluation of any particular moral being. The only possible way to reject AR is to accept the kind of view that Kittay accepts, viz. the bestowment view. It is this view that we defend here.

In getting a feel for the bestowment view and how it applies to the species membership relation, it is useful to consider its application in another area first. Imagine a piece of great artwork created by an artist, and an atom-for-atom qualitative duplicate of the piece created wholly by chance by some (improbable) cosmic accident. The two pieces are, by hypothesis, qualitatively identical. So they share all of their intrinsic properties. Yet it is overwhelmingly plausible that the original is more valuable than the duplicate. And it is also overwhelmingly plausible that the original is *objectively* more valuable than the copy, that is, that its having the value that it does is independent of who is evaluating it. If we ask *why* the original is more objectively valuable than the copy, the obvious answer is that the original is more valuable *because* it was created intentionally by an artist (i.e., because it stands in various relations to the artist who created it) while the duplicate was not. Of course, here the value in question is not a moral value, and so cannot give rise to any obligations. And, no doubt, the overwhelmingly plausible view that the original artwork is more valuable than the duplicate can be contested. But the view is very plausible, and if it is true it can *only* be true if it is possible for value to be bestowed upon a thing by its standing in relations to other things.

The bestowment view, then, is the view that objective value can be bestowed upon an individual by its standing in a relation to something else. Once bestowed, that value then functions to bind *all* evaluators, not merely those who stand in the bestowing relation to it. In a case where these values are *moral* values, their being possessed can then give rise to obligations that hold objectively. Is there any reason to think that this view is incoherent? We think not. Any temptation to think that the view is somehow incoherent, we think, arises from confusing the *source* and *object* of a value. Just because the *source* of a value lies outside of an individual, it is no bar on that individual being the object of it. Perhaps one thinks that "objective value" is a synonym for "intrinsic value" and that therefore an object cannot have an objective value that depends upon its *extrinsic* (i.e., relational) properties. But this too is a confusion. The term "intrinsic value" *is* often used as a synonym for "objective value," but it is also often used as a synonym for "the value an object has in virtue of its intrinsic properties," and these two uses are *distinct* (see O'Neill (2003) for more on this). Consider the last tiger in existence. Plausibly this tiger is intrinsically valuable in the first sense because of its *rarity*, but this is an extrinsic property and so the value it has because of it is not an intrinsic value in the second sense.[11]

That the bestowment view is Kittay's view is strongly suggested by her endorsement of Scheman's comments and the comments she makes in addition to them. The view those comments suggest is that human beings become bestowed with moral value by being born to and cared for by human beings within a human community. We think that this view is true, and that the worth bestowed upon any human who stands in the relation to the rest of the human community is strong enough to generate obligations toward him or her that are as

---

[11] For other examples from the art world, consider the value ready-mades have (e.g., Duchamp's *Fountain* – an upturned urinal) compared with qualitatively identical items used functionally. Perhaps it is in the fact that these items stand in a certain relation to the art world itself, rather than the artist, that they have their value. Perhaps. But if so, we think, this is grist to our mill. Then these items are valuable once more, not because of their intrinsic properties, but because of the relations in which they stand to other things. There is no reason to think the value they have is thereby not objective. This is to confuse the source and object of a value once more.

strong as the obligations we have toward any person. We believe this because it is the view that best explains our considered moral judgment that even if a human with a SID is psychologically equal to a nonhuman animal who is a nonperson, that human being is still more morally valuable than the nonhuman animal. We return to this point at the end of this section. Before this, however, we need to deal with an important point. We approach this point by considering that, even if McMahan were to concede that special relations can bestow value upon a being and thus give rise to objective obligations, his argument for thinking that the species membership relation is not a special relation still stands. What is that argument? It is, in fact, contained within one short paragraph:

> If the relation of parent to child, stripped down to its purely bio-
> logical component, is morally significant, perhaps the relation of
> membership in the same species is as well. This possibility cannot, I
> think, be wholly excluded. But if membership in the same species is
> an intrinsically significant special relation, it is surely one with only
> minimal moral significance. It can hardly have more significance,
> for example, than membership in the same race, which is a similar
> kind of biological relation. And it almost certainly has less signifi-
> cance even than the relation of a pet owner to his or her pet, which is
> at least a personal relation, involving a history of shared experience
> and companionship. (2002: 226)

In fact, if the special relation in question is viewed as purely biological, we agree with McMahan on this point. But we think that this
misconstrues the nature of the special relation in question. Although,
up to this point, we have referred to it as "the species membership
relation," it should be clear from our agreement with Kittay that it is
not a biological relation, and that it would be better to call it something like "the human community relation." Precisely what this relation amounts to is *genuinely* difficult to describe. It is the relation that
each of us stands in to each other by being a member of the human
community. It is the relation that holds between a human and the rest

of the human community when he or she is born of human parents, brought up and cared for by humans, and in general, treated *as* a human within the human community. We don't intend the brief list in the previous sentence to be taken as anything like a list of necessary conditions. The relation holds between different individuals and the rest of the community in different ways. It holds between you and the rest of the community because you participate fully within in it. For example, you vote, work, and pay taxes, as well as engaging in emotional and social interactions with other humans. It holds between humans with SIDs and the rest of the human community in a different way. They cannot vote, work, and pay taxes, for example, and *some* we think (although perhaps very few, and certainly not those like Sesha) cannot engage in emotional and social interactions either. Consequently, it is not *required* that those who are related to the human community *participate* within the human community, in the sense of partaking in those activities that normal human beings take part in. All that is required for the relation to hold is that an individual is *taken into* the human community: that he or she is *treated* by the community as human. For this to happen, however, it does seem to us to be required that the individual is capable of *some* kind of reciprocation, however minimal. In other words, for an individual to truly *be* taken into the human community requires not only that the community treat the individual in a certain way, but also that the individual is able to *receive* that treatment. Thus, we think that it is required of an individual, if he or she is to stand in the human community relation, that he or she has some sort of viewpoint on the world, has some level of consciousness, and is capable of some level of well-being. A table has no viewpoint, no consciousness, no level of well-being. One cannot care for it or be cruel to it. So one cannot genuinely treat a table as a human (the best one could do is *attempt* to treat it as a human). We admit that the idea here is a little opaque, but we think the basic point is clear enough and surely correct: no wholly *nonconscious* being can enter into the human community relation. Consequently, we think a tiny minority of human beings cannot enter into the human community relation – namely those human beings such as anencephalic infants who *are* wholly nonconscious. These human beings represent an exception to the rule. They truly are worth less than a normal person. In fact, because of their complete lack of psychological properties, they are worth less than any nonhuman animal too.

Now, we have already rejected Kittay's claim that the psychological properties possessed by humans are *essentially* human. Likewise we reject the claim that it is *only* humans who could be treated *as* humans within a human community. A dog who was *truly* brought up and treated as a member of the human community would also stand in a special relation to the human community. And we also reject the claim that all humans are *necessarily* part of the human community. A boy who was *truly* brought up by wolves would *not* be a member of the human community.[12] This is to say, those who have value bestowed upon them by being taken into the human community have that value contingently. In a similar vein we do not wish to ally ourselves here too closely with the Wittgensteinian camp. We are not here endorsing the obscure point about there being *forms of life*. We rely only on the claim that there is such a thing as *the human community* and *being a member*

---

[12] Is this claim *really* plausible? If we were to meet such a boy would we not immediately recognize it as a human being and treat it as such? Does this not show that the boy possesses objective features that mean it is already a member of the human community even before any human comes across him? We think not. Of course if we were to meet such a boy and take him into the human community, *then* he would be part of the human community. But he cannot be a member of the human community before, and thus cannot have any value *bestowed* upon him while he lives with the wolves. But remember that on our view the vast majority of human beings possess intrinsic psychological capacities that are sufficient for personhood. A boy brought up by wolves, despite being brought up by wolves, would still possess these capacities, so would *already* be more valuable than the wolves. This entails, for example, that even though the boy is not a member of the human community, it would still be morally worse for a hungry hunter coming across the pack containing the boy to shoot the boy than it would be for her to shoot one of the wolves.

of it, and the claim that human beings with SIDs fall into the latter category while nonhuman animals do not. We should also emphasize that one should not make too much of the claim that it is possible for a nonhuman animal to be taken into the human community. It is *possible*, but not likely to ever happen. We do not think that *any* animal is ever *truly* treated as a member of the human community. Dogs may well be doted on by their owners and loved a great deal (more, perhaps, than some human children are loved), but being treated by their owners in such a way is not the same as being taken into the community as a whole. And anyway, to love a dog is not to treat it *as* a human. No matter how much a dog is loved by its owner, it is still usually made to sit under the table in the local pub.

McMahan does, in fact, consider the bestowment view toward the end of his article in the *Journal of Ethics* (2005). He objects to it on the following grounds:

> On this [view], the moral status of the radically cognitively impaired is conferred or bestowed by our practices. The mere fact that it is our practice to regard the radically cognitively impaired as having a higher status than animals is sufficient to make it so. But this cannot be right. It would make whatever we collectively do automatically self-justifying. It implies that when, in the relatively recent past, the radically cognitively impaired were for the most part abandoned to neglect and social invisibility in dismal institutions, their moral status was lower than it is now. In the past when our practice was to hide them away and ignore them, they were, on this interpretation, less our fellow creatures and made a weaker claim on us than is the case now. But that conclusion is plainly unacceptable.

But McMahan misconstrues the bestowment view here, and his claim that it makes whatever we collectively do automatically self-justifying is false. It is not that we treat other humans as *valuable* that bestows value upon them, but rather that we treat them as *human* that does so. McMahan seems to think that treating someone as human on the bestowment view is *the very same thing* as treating them as being valuable. But nothing could be further from the truth. Treating someone as human does not mean treating them well. The example given by McMahan in this very paragraph shows just this. When, in the not-so-distant past, humans with SIDs were abandoned to neglect in dismal institutions they were still treated *as* humans (better: *mis*treated as humans). The phrase "to be treated like an animal" is well worn, but it is not to be taken too literally. No Victorian judge ever contemplated sending a human to Battersea any more than he contemplated sending a dog to Broadmoor. The conditions that prevailed in Victorian asylums have been exaggerated, but even in the worst of them the inmates were still treated as humans (i.e., they mostly wore clothes, slept in beds, etc.). On the bestowment view, to take an individual into the human community is not thereby to *treat* that individual as valuable, even though it is what bestows value upon the individual.

Finally, then, we return to the question of *why* we believe that the bestowment view is true, and that the human community relation is a significant special relation that bestows value upon those who stand in it and generates obligations toward them that are as strong as any obligation we have toward any person. In light of the previous sections of this chapter, however, we think little explicit argument is needed. The reason we think the view is true is simply this: the position is a coherent one that makes more sense of our considered moral judgments regarding the moral status of human beings with SIDs than any other available view. After careful reflection, we believe that a human with a SID, even if he or she were psychologically equal to a nonhuman animal such as a dog, is worth more than the dog. The bestowment view explains why this is so whereas other views cannot. This is the best argument that one could have for a moral position. Of course, if there were some other persuasive reason for thinking that the view is false, or for thinking that McMahan's view is more plausible, then we would have to reconsider. But, as we have argued, nothing McMahan says is persuasive, and we can think of nothing else that suggests the bestowment view is incorrect. So, it seems to us that the question is not "What reason is there to believe this view?" but rather "What reason is there to doubt it?"[13]

CONCLUSION

We have argued in agreement with Kittay that the conditions an individual has to meet to be classed as a person are significantly wider than McMahan allows. It is not only cognitive capacities that are relevant, but also emotional and aesthetic capacities. Consequently, many of those human beings with severe psychological disabilities that McMahan would class as nonpersons are in fact persons. As a matter of fact we do not think that any nonhuman animal possesses person-making capacities to also be classed as persons, but we admit that we may be wrong about this and so do not strongly commit ourselves to the claim. We do strongly commit ourselves to the claim, however, that *most* nonhuman animals, such as dogs, do not possess person-making capacities. And we strongly commit ourselves to the claim, in partial agreement with McMahan, that some human beings are psychologically equal to those nonhuman animals, and so are nonpersons too. The agreement is only partial, however, as our disagreement with McMahan over what capacities are person-making capacities leads us to the view that the number of human beings who are psychologically equal to nonhuman nonpersons is likely to be very small, whereas

[13] As we have indicated, on this view, wholly unconscious human beings such as anencephalic infants are not worth more than any animal. The considered moral judgment of many, including Kittay, is that they are. If this is also your considered moral judgment, then the bestowment view is not for you, for it cannot explain this judgment. But, in all honesty, we do not share this opinion. After consideration we think that there is a big difference between a human being with no consciousness and a human being with consciousness. We thus consider it to be a further point in its favor that our account explains why this is so.

McMahan believes that the number is very large (i.e., it includes most, if not all, of those *diagnosed* with SIDs).

We have also argued in agreement with Kittay that the human community relation is a significant special relation that bestows moral worth on those individuals who stand in and generate obligations toward them that are as strong as any obligation we have toward any person. Most human beings are already deserving of the highest moral consideration in virtue of being persons. But even the few humans with SIDs who are nonpersons should be treated with equal moral consideration in virtue of their standing in the human community relation. Because no non-human animal stands in this relation, those human beings with SIDs are thus worth more than any nonhuman animal (except, of course, those nonhuman animals, if there be any, who are persons). We are thus happy to accept McMahan's three-tiered hierarchy of moral worth, and we are happy to accept that all persons are level-three beings. But we reject his claim that the threshold between level two and level three *coincides* with the threshold of personhood, because on our view there are two ways to make it into level three: one way is to be a person and the other is to stand in the human community relation.

Our view falls neither into the intrinsic relations camp nor the special relations camp, but rather somewhere in between. But we think it is superior to any view that falls solely into either camp. It makes sense of our deeply held convictions about humans with SIDs in a way that is not open to criticism from any quarter. It allows that all of those diagnosed with SIDS except the *most* severely afflicted are persons, but still allows us to maintain the view that those who are not persons are more morally valuable as human beings than any nonhuman animal.

References

Kittay, E. F. 2005. 'At the Margins of Moral Personhood'. *Ethics* 116(1): 100–1.
2009. 'The Personal is Philosophical is Political: A Philosopher and Mother of a Cognitively Disabled Person Sends Notes from the Battlefield'. *Metaphilosophy* 40(3–4): 606–27.

Locke, J. 1977. *An Essay Concerning Human Understanding* (London: Everyman).

Maulik, P. K., Mascarenhas, M. N., Mathers, C. D., Dua, T. & Saxena, S. 2011. 'Prevalence of Intellectual Disability: A Meta-Analysis of Population-Based Studies'. *Research in Developmental Disabilities* 32: 419–36.

McMahan, J. 1996. 'Cognitive Disability, Misfortune, and Justice'. *Philosophy and Public Affairs* 25(1): 3–35.

2002. *The Ethics of Killing* (Oxford: Oxford University Press).

2005. 'Our Fellow Creatures'. *Journal of Ethics* 9(3–4): 353–80.

2008. 'Challenges to Human Equality'. *Journal of Ethics* 12(1): 81–104.

2009a. 'Cognitive Disability and Cognitive Enhancement'. *Metaphilosophy* 40(3–4): 582–605.

2009b. 'Radical Cognitive Limitation', in Brownlee, K. and Cureton, A. (eds.), *Disability and Disadvantage* (Oxford: Clarendon Press), 240–59.

Nussbaum, M. 2006. *Frontiers of Justice: Disability, Nationality, Species Membership* (Cambridge: Harvard University Press).

O'Neill, J. 2003. 'The Varieties of Intrinsic Value', in Light, Andrew and Rolston, Holmes (eds.) *Environmental Ethics* (London: Blackwell), 131–42.

Proctor, R. 1998. *Racial Hygiene: Medicine under the Nazis* (Cambridge: Harvard University Press).

Quinn, W. 1984. 'Abortion: Identity and Loss'. *Philosophy and Public Affairs* 13: 24–54.

Schalock, R. L., Borthwick-Duffy, S. A., Bradley, V. J., Buntinx, W. & Coulter, D. L. 2010. *Intellectual Disability: Definition, Classification, and Systems of Supports*, 11th edition (Washington, DC: AIIDD).

Singer, P. 1993. *Practical Ethics* (Cambridge: Cambridge University Press).

Tversky, A. 1977. 'Features of Similarity'. *Psychological Review* 84: 327–52.

Williams, B. 1981. *Moral Luck* (Cambridge: Cambridge University Press).

2

"Something Else"? – Cognitive Disability and the Human Form of Life

BARBARA SCHMITZ

> "Something else" does not only look differently than all the oth-
> ers – he has a big head and blue skin – but he also behaves dif-
> ferently: he paints pictures with forms and patterns others do not
> understand; he holds the badminton racket in the wrong way, i.e.,
> downwards, and he unwraps his lunch packets such that they fall to
> the ground. "Something else" wants to be like others but he never
> succeeds. "You are not like us. You do not belong," others say. "You
> are something else." "Something else" becomes sad and starts to
> live a lonely life, excluded on a high mountain. One day another
> something else turns up who has a nose like a trunk and uses the
> badminton racket like a guitar. The two become friends and play
> in their own way.

"Something else" is a figure from a picture book written for children to help them develop tolerance toward people who are different.[1] Probably "something else" has a kind of cognitive disability that
makes it impossible for him to act like others. Seen in this way, the
book mentions several aspects of the life of cognitively disabled human
beings: first, it shows that cognitively disabled human beings want to
participate and interact with others. Second, it points out that there
might be problems with this and that the recognition of differences in
acting makes it difficult for cognitively disabled human beings. Third,

---

[1] Cave and Ridell (1994).

it shows that the reaction of others might be exclusionary and stig-matizing, and this is very painful for cognitively disabled people. And fourth, the book mentions the value of friendship for them, their need for sharing activities, and their need for emotional support.

Viewing cognitively disabled human beings as "something else" is an understanding of them that is probably often found in the daily opinion of people. The most striking feature of cognitively disabled persons seems to be that they are different from others. Depending on the kind and severity of the disability, this difference can be more or less pronounced. The description of cognitively disabled human beings as "something else" is even more prominent in philosophy. If one looks at the history of philosophy one realizes that cognitively disabled human beings mostly have been seen and treated as radi-cally different, as creatures alien to philosophical thinking, as some-thing one cannot understand properly.[2] The result is often complete exclusion. The reason for this is easy to grasp: cognitively disabled human beings seem to lack exactly the feature philosophy is based on – reason.

However, in recent decades there has been a growing interest in philosophical questions related to disabled human beings, mainly in bioethics. This seems to be the result of the development of genetic testing and engineering that lead to various questions about dis-ability in general, such as the question of whether disabled people can have a good human life. Some questions, however, are spe-cifically related to cognitive disability, and some of these turn out to be very difficult. Most important among these is probably the question of whether cognitively disabled human beings have the same moral status as other human beings – a question the answer to which has important consequences. It is not just that our whole

---

[2] For a detailed description of the place of the cognitively disabled in philosophy and of the reasons for this, see the material in Kittay and Carlson (2009).

attitude toward cognitively disabled human beings may rely on this answer. The answer may also decisively influence political and bio-ethical decisions. Sometimes the question of moral status is seen as a new question that bioethics brought up, but it is in fact an old one in philosophy. The same problem arises with respect to the question of how to ground human dignity, and since Kant that question has been prominent in philosophical thinking. It is striking that the answers of modern philosophers in bioethics resemble those of the philosophical tradition.

In my chapter I want to take up several questions related to cognitive disability. As the considerations here show, four main tasks seem to be of vital importance: first, we need a proper understanding of cognitive disability. Is seeing the cognitively disabled as different from others a good approach, or should we try to establish a different view? Second, how might a human life for cognitively disabled human beings look? Third, how should we answer the question of their moral status? And last, how can we avoid exclusion and stigmatization of cognitively disabled human beings? In this chapter I say something about all of these questions, but my remarks will be scattered rather than comprehensive. This is the result of the fact that I want to propose an approach to the cognitively disabled that can be called "the human form of life approach." I think that by introducing the concept of a "human form of life" we can get a better understanding of cognitively disabled persons, their good life, and their moral status. Moreover, I think this approach can also show what philosophy can learn from taking into account cognitively disabled human beings.

As the notion of the human form of life is central, I first explain what I mean by the term and what kind of consequences this has. Then I apply this idea to cognitively disabled human beings and reconsider the question of whether they should be mainly characterized by means of differences. Third, I come back to the question of moral status. I end with some concluding remarks.

THE IDEA OF A HUMAN FORM OF LIFE

The notion of the human form of life has been made popular in philosophy by Ludwig Wittgenstein's late philosophy.[3] The main idea he wants to express with this term is that there is a kind of agreement that forms the background of language and thought and this agreement is our framework for understanding and meaning. Only in the context of a human form of life can words and other expressions have meaning: "To imagine a language means to imagine a form of life" (Wittgenstein, *Philosophical Investigations* §7). As he describes it, a human form of life consists of shared practices, customs, convictions, habits, and institutions. It means a totality of activities human beings develop.

However, this is not the whole task of the concept. The idea is also used to stress the fact that human beings share some prelinguistic ways of behavior, and these shared ways of behaving form the background for learning a language and for developing advanced practices of various kinds. An example of this is the notion of pain and the place of human pain behavior in our language of pain. Why do we understand someone who is in pain? Wittgenstein asks frequently in the *Philosophical Investigations*.[4] His answer goes against a model that would take our understanding of pain behavior as the result of a cognitive step or perhaps of analogical reasoning consisting in some kind of rational consideration: he acts like I do when I am in pain, therefore he must feel the same that I feel.[5] In contrast to such approaches, Wittgenstein develops an account according to which our understanding of the pain behavior of another human being rests on a kind of

---

[3] Wittgenstein is not the first to use the concept "form of life" even though it is not clear where he has taken it from. It can be found in the German tradition with philosophers like Herder and Hegel. However, Wittgenstein stresses some ideas that could also be found in Aristotle. Wittgenstein uses the term only a few times in his work, mainly, for example, *Philosophical Investigations* §§ 7, 19, 23, II p. 226.

[4] Ibid., §§ 243 ff.

[5] See, for example, ibid., §§ 293 ff.

agreement in instinctive reactions.[6] Our understanding is not built on cognitive reasoning, but is much more spontaneous and direct. If someone is crying because of pain, normally our helping and comforting reactions occur without question. A prelinguistic and precognitive way of understanding is the result of agreement in reactions. It rests on the fact that we share the same form of life, that we as human beings behave in certain ways. This fundamental agreement is the basis for developing practices, customs, and habits.

The form of life of a being is dependent on its species.[7] Therefore, for us human beings the human form of life plays the most important role. It is this life form we know from ourselves, and from our lives with others. We cannot share the life form of a different species, even though we might achieve some external understanding and give a description of how another living being is living. But any kind of inside knowledge is impossible, and because language rests on sharing the life form, we would not understand, for example, a speaking lion.[8] The underlying agreement in behavior, in constitution, and in practices would be missing.[9]

---

[6] Ibid., §§ 272 ff.

[7] In Wittgenstein scholarship there is a debate regarding whether Wittgenstein talks about different cultural life forms or whether he means an anthropological notion. I agree with Newton Garver that the latter interpretation is correct; see Garver (1994), 237ff. Apart from questions concerning the interpretation of Wittgenstein, this understanding is certainly more fruitful when it is applied to other contexts, for example, ethical ones.

[8] Wittgenstein, *Philosophical Investigations*, II, 568.

[9] More needs to be said about the accessibility of the form of life of an animal than can be done here. Even though it cannot be said that we can understand the form of life of, let us say, a dog, we can still have some kind of knowledge from the outside, on the basis of similarities to elements of our own form of life. But my issue in this chapter is not the understanding of animals and their moral status. I only want to deal with cognitively disabled human beings. This focus mirrors as well my thinking that the close link between animal ethics and considerations of cognitive disability easily leads to distorted results for the latter because it is often presupposed that we understand animals and the cognitively disabled in the same way.

This agreement, which is fundamental for the human form of life, is partly described by the fact that human beings have human capacities and human needs – an idea not directly found in Wittgenstein, but which for the purposes of ethical investigation can easily be built into the notion of a human form of life. It belongs to a human form of life that human beings have certain capacities and abilities like laughing, thinking, singing, expecting, and hoping. And it also belongs to a human form of life that humans have the need for food, shelter, and companionship, and the need to avoid pain. If we want to describe the human form of life, we need to say something about all these different elements. Wittgenstein answers the question of whether one such element is an important part of the human form of life by asking: What would be changed if we took this element away from a human life? In the case of pain, he asks us to imagine a tribe of humans that do not have our pain behavior, that do not see pain as something bad to be avoided, but who laugh and are happy when they are in pain. With respect to this tribe, he replies that we would have to imagine a different life for them, and that we are so far from creatures like them that we could not understand them. They would behave in many situations so differently from us that they would go beyond our understanding. This shows that if an agreement in one of the most fundamental aspects of the human form of life is lacking we get to the limits of our understanding.[10]

One important aspect of these elements of the human form of life is their interwovenness. The elements we pick out when we describe forms of life – a capacity, a need, a way of behaving, a practice – cannot be meaningfully seen as isolated. If one wants to understand the meaning and value of an element one has to show the role it plays in the context of other practices, other capacities, other needs, other ways of acting. Similarly, it is not possible to describe the human form of life by means of an isolated life of a single human being. It is always a

---

[10] In German Wittgenstein uses for this impossibility to understand the phrase "Wir können uns nicht in sie finden," Wittgenstein, *Philosophische Untersuchungen*, 568.

shared life form, and only with this social background do the practices, customs, and institutions have meaning.[11]

This picture of the human form of life is my starting point for investigating the questions about cognitive disability I mentioned at the beginning of this chapter. I want to show that this picture affords a view of cognitive disability that is different from what is prevalent in philosophy these days. This new view concerns many different aspects; I want to mention only five of them here.

First, an important function of the life form concept is that it stresses the underlying agreement among human beings. As mentioned, this agreement is not reached through a cognitive step or a particular decision, but it is a background from which we behave and act. We find this agreement in the capacities and needs of human beings, and it makes it possible for human beings to develop customs, practices, habits, and institutions. Taking agreement as a starting point is contrary to taking difference as a starting point. When we apply the form of life approach to cognitive disability, we should not start by describing the cognitively disabled as essentially different from us, as "something else," but rather as human beings like others. From this basis it can be asked afterward, in a second step, how they differ and what kind of role this difference plays.

Second, the notion of a human form of life stresses a plurality of capacities, needs, and practices. A human form of life is not characterized by a single capacity or by a few capacities, but is about a variety of them. This points to the fact that there are many more capacities of human beings than the capacity to reason, which philosophy often takes as its main focus. Besides reasoning, the human form of life includes capacities for humor, for playing, for hoping, for sensing, for running, and for jumping. The notion of the human form of life widens the scope of what we see in human beings. Cognitively disabled

---

[11] In Wittgenstein's philosophy this is of course clearly expressed in the Private Language Argument, cf. *Philosophical Investigations* §258 ff.

human beings, depending on the kind of disability they have, may have many of these capacities and could teach us something about them.

Third, related to the second point, talking about a human form of life means certain capacities and needs have to be seen in the context of a larger background of shared practices and should not be viewed in isolation. This approach stands in contrast to others that start with a single capacity and try to derive ethical consequences from the existence of this capacity alone. The meaning a capacity has for a human being will become clear only when we look at all the different practices this capacity has its place in. A comparison of one capacity across different forms of life is not meaningful. For a squirrel, climbing on trees is important because it could otherwise not satisfy its need for food, it could not build a safe nest; for a tiger, this is not important because it has other practices of getting something to eat. The question of the value of a capacity has therefore to be seen from this point of view.

Fourth, there is a strong connection between the human form of life and the good life for a human being. To explain human flourishing one needs to take the human form of life into account. What it means for a living being to have a good life cannot be viewed independently from the form of life the being belongs to. One reason for this is that every life form includes needs that are requirements to live this life form. Their satisfaction will always be of great importance. A good life will always mean that at least the most important needs of the life form are met. And because of this holism, these needs are linked to capacities and practices. Therefore, to develop the idea of a good human life from a human form of life account would mean to talk also about which capacities have to be developed, which needs should be satisfied, which practices are important to participate in.

Fifth, the notion of the human form of life can give us some help to answer the question of moral status. It is a presupposition of our form of life that another human being qualifies as being a human being. And it is part of the human form of life that we treat the others as human beings, that is, decently and with dignity. This does not need an extra reason like pointing to a special capacity or to a feature that grounds belonging. I spell out this argument later in this chapter. Now I will apply the notion of a human form of life to cognitively disabled human beings.

THE APPLICATION OF THE IDEA OF THE HUMAN FORM OF LIFE TO THE COGNITIVELY DISABLED

Although I have already mentioned how the idea of the human form of life can help us to view cognitively disabled human beings in a different light, at first glance it may seem counterintuitive to make this attempt. By introducing a human form of life I seem to be claiming that there are capacities and needs all human beings have and should have if they want to participate in the practices of the human form of life. However, disability in general is characterized precisely by the lack of some of the capacities or features a human life normally has. Deaf people do not have the capacity of hearing; tetraplegics do not have the capacity of walking; and cognitively disabled people do not have the capacity of reasoning. As this last capacity is so important for many practices that human beings see as important for their life, the cognitively disabled cannot be included in these practices. From this it is only a small step to exclude cognitively disabled human beings from certain practices that they could participate in. And, even more dangerous, it seems to follow that cognitively disabled human beings do not have the same moral status as us, the ones who are not cognitively disabled. They seem exactly to lack the main features of a human form of life.[12]

To answer this objection, more needs to be said about how we should understand cognitive disability. It needs to be pointed out that cognitive disability is an individual deviation from the human form of life. To do

[12] The problem mentioned here is one that is met by all universalistic and objective theories of the good human life. If one puts up a list of characteristics necessary for a good human life one always has to face the question of what do to with

this more needs to be said about the particular guises the human form of life can take. In some way this is obvious: we never find the human form of life just in itself; we only find concrete, particular forms of human life. The human form of life is found only in specific cultural contexts and in particular individual combinations of capacities and needs.

Human needs are the needs a human being has qua human being, such as the need for food, shelter, and companionship. However, each human being lives in a particular context with specific features. Each need, therefore is shaped by cultural and other specific forces. The cultural forming can be due to climatic circumstances, cultural background assumptions, or religious convictions. This means the need for food can take a specific cultural form because of the climate people are living in, or because their religion forbids them to eat certain types of food.[13] One can see the forming of a human need most clearly in the need for companionship. Cultures have developed a wide range of forms of having emotional and practical ties. These relationships may belong to a large family or to a tribe at large or to a religious group, or they manifest as friendships, as it often is nowadays in our culture.

human beings, like disabled human beings, who do not have these characteristics. Proponents of universalistic and objective theories use various strategies to answer this challenge; for example, Martha Nussbaum claims that there is an imperfection with disabled human beings. I return to this later. Other approaches to the good human life have, interestingly enough, fewer problems with integrating cognitively disabled human beings. Both a hedonistic approach and a preference-based account can claim without problems that cognitively disabled human beings can have a good human life. Only some forms of preference accounts – the ones that focus on rational or informed preferences – will be inclined to deny this.

[13] It goes beyond the scope of this chapter to discuss it in depth here, but the role of needs for various questions of political philosophy and ethics can hardly be overestimated. Human needs as the necessities of the human form of life can serve as a basis for human rights and for questions of justice. An ethics that focuses on needs may as well be a good general guideline for answering ethical questions of disability even though there is a tension in disability ethics to avoid the term "special needs" because it sees disabled human beings mainly as dependent and needy. I think the answer to this objection must be that a general theory of needs for all human beings is needed in ethics. A fruitful attempt to do this can be found in the work of Soran Reader (2007).

The individual forming of needs is dependent on the capacities of a human being as well as on the specific circumstances someone is in. Thus, a pregnant woman has different needs for food from a woman who is not pregnant. In the case of disability, the individual forming of needs can be of great importance. The need for food, shelter, movement, and companionship can all look different in the case of a disability. However, it is important to note that people with disabilities also have general human needs. Human needs, rather than particular needs, form the starting point of ethics. Sometimes the satisfaction of a need may take a different form in the case of cognitive disability, but that does not mean the person does not have that human need. Human needs are the basis for practical purposes even though for individual human beings these needs may have different consequences.

Individual forming also applies to capacities. A diminished or lacking capacity, for example, in one of the main senses, will affect the other senses as well. Sometimes, different practices may arise from this. All these practices, however, can be viewed as variations of human practices. They are all part of the human form of life, and recognizing that there are various particular human forms of life helps us to appreciate the practices of cognitively disabled persons. It is not simply the case that these people lack capacities or needs; these capacities are also often differently formed. One example is the capacity for humor. Human beings are creatures who laugh. Laughing results from thinking something is funny, from being able to see a comic feature in events or people or situations. What people actually laugh at can vary depending on cultural norms and individual abilities to see funny situations. Cognitively disabled human beings often have a very special sense of humor. My daughter, who has a severe learning disability, can laugh about situations very easily. She seems to pick up the funniness of situations quite quickly. Another girl, Lilli, who has a very severe cognitive disability and who cannot speak or control her tongue, laughs when she has crinkling paper around her. Here we see the capacity to laugh and for humor in different ways, but these ways are understandable for us simply because we all share the ability to laugh.[14]

If we take into account differently formed capacities and needs, we can see the large area of agreement with cognitively disabled human beings. The individual deviations from the most common features of the human form of life can in fact only be understood if we take the human form of life as a starting point. The agreement makes the understanding possible. The agreement is not always easily accessible, and the individual formings of a capacity or a need are not always easily understandable. There are many cases in which it takes time to learn to see the individual differences and to understand cognitively disabled human beings.[15] One needs to share a practice with them to achieve a clearer understanding; one sometimes needs to live a long time together with a cognitively disabled human being to get a kind of understanding by developing practices with him or her. But in all these cases, the human form of life, the agreement, forms the basis for the understanding. The individual forming is in some way always the second step, and not the first one. Only given the agreement can the difference be seen – and valued.

Some of these differences – not all of them – may even be important for us because they teach us something new about the human form of life.[16] We may see how our practices can be varied or formed differently,

---

[14] Another example can be found in Eva Kittay's work. She shows how much her severely cognitively disabled child has a sense for music and aesthetic pleasure. See Kittay (2005) and (2009).

[15] This fact is also the reason it may often be more appropriate to tell a story about how life with a cognitively disabled human being is instead of giving a simple argument. The difference between these two ways can be seen in the exchange between Singer and Kittay; see Kittay (2009).

[16] Here we can be reminded of the argument sometimes raised against a difference model of disability, which mainly sees disability as difference with the implicit claim that difference is something positive and valuable. However, difference in itself is neither positive nor negative. It is always a question of whether the different option or feature is positive or not. However, to acknowledge that there is a difference can often mean to open one's eyes and to widen one's view.

for example, in the case of friendship. Instead of just having the picture of friends as two autonomous, independent persons, one might get a new picture of friendship for which dependency if one starts a friendship with a cognitively disabled human being. Hans Reinders shows in his book how the notion of friendship itself and the often unrecognized bias of autonomy in our friendship can be changed when one starts a friendship with a cognitively disabled human being.[17]

But even if it is true that disability often consists in variation, deviation, and difference of the human form of life, one might still wonder whether we do not also have to speak about the lack of certain capacities. Are cognitively disabled human beings not lacking that which in the history of philosophy has always been seen as the main feature of human beings, namely the capacity of reason? Is cognitive disability not a deficiency of thinking? And is this deficiency not so serious – given the prominent role thinking plays in our form of life – that we would in the end doubt whether cognitively disabled human beings share the human form of life at all?

The answer to these questions must be complex, I think. First, it has to be recognized that when one looks more closely, cognitively disabled human beings hardly ever show a complete lack of reasoning capacity. If one understands reasoning not as an all or nothing ability, then a multiplicity of abilities can be properly called reason and thinking. Some cognitively disabled persons certainly have reasoning capacity; some have it to a lesser degree, some have differently formed reasoning, and of some it may be said that they lack reasoning entirely. According to what is the case with a specific cognitive disability, some practices may be differently formed, some may not be accessible at all. And both the different forming and the lack of a practice may be serious or not. Because of the interwovenness of a capacity with other capacities and needs, the general form of life of a cognitive disability may be seriously influenced or not. Therefore, I think, it is important

[17] Reinders (2008).

that we not only see that there is difference, but also that imperfection of a human life might follow from cognitive disability. Humans have a way of living that suits them, that gives them a certain way of flourishing. If there is a serious difference there, like in the case of a severe cognitive disability, this means that the difference is an imperfection. And such imperfection may be tragic and sad. It may lead to the exclusion from practices; it may lead to feelings that certain things are not possible for the disabled person like they are for others. However, it is important to see this kind of imperfection as a task, as a challenge to find ways to have a good human form of life. And what this good human life consists of will always be judged by taking into a account what a good human life in general consists of. There is no separate notion of their good life, but what their good life consists of must be derived from the human good life together with a recognition of their individual forming of needs and capacities.

However, one might ask now whether individuals can exist who are biologically human but who do not share the human form of life like, for example, the most severely mentally handicapped people; those who maybe do not have a brain. Do we here also talk about the human form of life or is there finally a criterion when someone belongs to the human form of life? Does it break down at some point? Are there cases where we want to say there are so many profound differences that we will in the end not recognize the human form of life anymore? I think it seems extremely unlikely we will reach that point.

THE QUESTION OF MORAL STATUS

Finally, after these considerations about the possibility of understanding cognitively disabled human beings and the practical implications this might hold, I want to come back to the most difficult question when one deals with cognitive disability in philosophy: the question of moral status.

Why should cognitively disabled human beings have the same moral status as all other human beings? What kind of reason can be given for this? For answering this questions I think it is important that the most intuitive answer seems to be: well, because they are human beings. This intuitive "pre"-philosophical answer reveals something which is interesting: our common understanding refers to the "human being", the human form of life as guideline. I will come back to this later.

Several bioethicists, mainly those with a utilitarian background, like Peter Singer and Jeff McMahan,[18] strongly question the idea that we could take the human form of life as a starting point. They would claim that to derive a particular moral status from a human form of life involves an unjustified speciesism, as moral claims cannot be grounded in belonging to a certain species. Taking the belonging to a species as morally relevant is merely a prejudice. Instead of taking a prejudiced notion like the human form of life as starting point, one should look at capacities and ground the moral status of an individual in them. In practice this leads to a comparison between the capacities of human beings and other animals, and to the question of which moral claims would follow from this.

As I said in the introduction to this chapter, this position bears a strong resemblance, both in its questions as well as in its answers, to traditional discussions about human dignity. Most theories in the philosophical tradition ground dignity in a particular capacity, mainly the capacity to reason, to judge, to think and act reasonably, to be an autonomous person. The exact formulation of the decisive criterion can vary, but they all point in the same direction: dignity is ascribed to persons who have some kind of capacity to think, to reflect, to be autonomous. We find the same solution with modern bioethicists. Peter Singer sees the ability to make future plans as a criterion; Jeff McMahan states

---

[18] That this position is raised by philosophers with a utilitarian background is not surprising. Utilitarianism has as one of its main presuppositions that it should be an overall maximizing of happiness, regardless of individual differences or belonging to a species.

that the threshold for moral status is a Lockean concept of a person, namely an entity with the abilities of "reason and reflection."[19]

Common to these two approaches is, first, that they rely heavily on the cognitive side of human beings. This can of course be questioned if we look at the plurality and multitude of capacities human beings have. Why should one favor the one-sided picture that philosophy gives us here about human life? A human form of life is certainly much more than its cognitive aspects. Their approaches take for granted that there is one single capacity that can be viewed in isolation and that is the ground for moral status. But is this really sound? Why should one capacity have this kind of value? How can a capacity have this value?

Here the notion of a human form of life can help us because it reminds us to ask first: Who should a capacity have value for? Only after we answer that question can we ask: Why does it have value? Both questions can only be answered if we think of the form of life of a living human being. A capacity only has value because it matters in the form of life of that particular human being. To talk about the value of capacities without taking this context into account is meaningless.

In the human form of life the value is not decided by the particular capacity of reasoning in isolation, but must be seen holistically. Reasoning must be viewed together with all the capacities and needs and practices that are characteristic for this particular life form. If we do not take this background into account, picking out a capacity will always be arbitrary or the result of some prejudice.[20] Whatever this criterion is, it will always be one-sided and forget the richness of a human form of life in all its aspects. Besides that, it seems far less clear that there is a capacity that has value in itself that cannot be used in

---

[19] See Singer (1993) and (2009) and McMahan (2009).

[20] This consideration also leads to skepticism toward approaches that speak about the enhancement of capacities, such as, for example, that of Jeff McMahan. Any answer to the question of whether human life would be better by enhancing certain capacities must take a huge range of considerations into account; it must look at many different ways of how a particular capacity is interwoven with other capacities.

morally problematic ways. Instead of taking one criterion, one ability as the ground for moral status, one should take a more complex notion like the human form of life for which a multiplicity of capacities matters, not a single one.

However, more can be said about this alternative way of grounding moral status. It may be helpful here to mention three attempts to ground moral status – all three alternatives to grounding it in one single capacity.

First, one could ground the moral status of a being, not on a capacity, but on needs and dependencies. At first, this approach seems attractive because it is less exclusive. All living beings have needs. Second, it is attractive because needs are the reference point for the issue of what needs to be protected by recognizing moral status. Because we have needs and are vulnerable, we need the notion of moral status. If we were not vulnerable, the question of moral status would have no meaning.

Does this mean that our vulnerabilities can ground our moral status? I do not think so. If we think about the function of a foundation of moral status – telling us why a being has a status, finding something positive that distinguishes the being from other beings – it is of no help. On the contrary, it leads to completely overshooting ethical demands: all living creatures would have moral status because they all have needs. All would have to be protected by us.

A second attempt is found in the work of Eva Kittay and other thinkers. She claims that there is no special individual capacity that is nonrelativistic or that can ground moral status, but that only relational characteristics can do so. Her argument is that the feature of belonging is the relevant criterion. She compares belonging to the human species to belonging to a family. She points out that to belong to a family no special capacity is needed. Similarly, no capacity is needed to ground why it is that belonging to the human species confers a special moral status. The special relation we have to someone in our family generates fundamental obligations and increases the moral value of the individual. The same is true, Kittay argues, for belonging to the "family of human beings."

Kittay's view avoids the problems of the capacity view. In many respects, it comes close to the human form of life account. Yet the comparison between belonging to a family and belonging to the human species is misleading. It is also far from clear whether belonging to a family gives the kind of special relationship she requires for her account. That belonging to a family creates special obligations can be due to several things: because family members know and love each other or because society's structure and values see family ties as important. In both cases, however, only a limited value is given to family relationships. In both cases, it is possible that family relationships do not exist; either because there are no personal relationships between different family members or because the structure of the society is one where family ties do not play a large role. In fact, the duties generated by family membership are not very strong any more in our Western societies. For example, it is not clear why I should have special duties toward an uncle I have never seen and do not care about. It is a subject of cultural change that may give family relationships its special importance.

Problems arise, therefore, when trying to compare belonging to the family and belonging to the community of human beings. First, I cannot explain my belonging to the community of human beings by mentioning special personal relationships I have. I neither know nor love all other human beings. Second, no cultural background tells me that the relationship to other human beings is of special importance and gives value to the individual. Maybe the argument behind this comparison is that all human beings have the same status as the result of a special recognition or decision. Maybe it is fundamental in a deeper sense. This is suggested by the third alternative of dealing with the question of moral status.

The third alternative can be found in Bernard Williams's discussion of "the human prejudice."[21] Williams proposes the following thought experiment: imagine Martians come and rule over our world. The Martians are extremely clever, have much higher cognitive capacities,

[21] Williams (2008), 135–54.

and are wholeheartedly good willing. Because of their traits they come to the conclusion that it would be better for the world if human beings were extinguished. How would we react to that? Williams suggests that some of us might wish to be collaborators who accept the judgment of the Martians and their higher moral status. Most human beings would not do so. They would defend themselves as the community of humans. The question "Whose side are you on?" would be answered by "on the human side." They would not need an argument for being on this side, their own side, the side that takes the human form of life as the important framework.

Williams does not develop his argument in the context of cognitive disability. It can, however, easily be transferred. The main point about it is that we do not need a reason why humanness matters for us. We do not need to point to capacities. It is simply a presumption of the human form of life that we care about us as human beings. We do not need a reason why as human beings other human beings matter. We have no reason for this; it is a presupposition of what it means to lead a human life. It is one of the fundamentals of our human life that we cannot simply abandon.

But does this answer the question of the grounds of moral status? One needs to look more closely at what is meant by the idea of moral status and what we want to express with this notion. I think the main idea about moral status is the need to treat others decently (with all the implications this has, both in the private and public spheres), and this can mean a variety of things and may form practices in different ways. In this way the idea of moral status is already implicit in our human form of life. It is not something we give or transfer to someone by a decision, but it is a fundamental part of our living together, for developing practices together. It is part of our whole view of seeing someone as human.[22] Of course, one might say at this point that

---

[22] A comparison of Wittgenstein's treatment of whether we know that a human being has a soul can be helpful here. How do we know that other human beings have souls, that they are living human beings and not just automatons? Wittgenstein criticizes all approaches that look for a special criterion here or that employ analogical reasoning

there are thousands of examples of violations of the rules of decent treatment of human beings, and that the history of the treatment of cognitively disabled human beings shows this all too well. When this happens, however, the perpetrators first try to convince themselves that those they harm do not really belong to the human form of life. They convince themselves that these are not really human beings; they try to establish a picture of them as completely different, as something else. Therefore it is so important to have the notion of a human form of life as a background. And in daily life we express this quite well when we are tempted to react to situations in which abusive and nondecent treatment happens: but this is a human being. We do not need a further argument. And this is particularly why our intuitive answer – being a human being grounds moral status – is so important. It reveals something we already hold as implicit in our form of life.

CONCLUDING REMARKS

I started this chapter by pointing out that cognitive disability and philosophy stand in a difficult relationship. The results of my arguments can now be summarized by looking at each side and asking what is the result for the cognitively disabled and what can philosophy learn. If we look at the questions about cognitively disabled human beings I raised at the beginning, some answers have become clear: the picture of them as "something else" is profoundly misleading. They *are* like all of us human beings. Like all other human beings, they share the human form of life. This means that no extra step of tolerance is needed to include them among us. They share the same form of life with us, and their difference to other human beings is one that rests on difference

from myself to others. He moreover describes it as such a fundamental attitude we have toward others that it lies at the heart of our language games; it is a certainty. The talk about moral status must be viewed in the same way.

inside the human form of life. The good human life for them is the same as the good human life for us and rests on the possibility of the satisfaction of human needs, even though these may be differently formed in the case of cognitively disabled human beings. The question of moral status cannot be decided by using a single criterion, but it is an implicit presupposition that cognitively disabled human beings have the same status as other human beings. The question of exclusion is, however, a serious issue, because the practices we have developed, particularly in our Western worldview with its focus on freedom and autonomy, make it hard for cognitively disabled human beings to participate in many practices. Our society takes exactly those practices as central and valuable that cognitively disabled persons are limited in. One needs to ask how at least some practices can be changed or made accessible for cognitively disabled human beings. How this inclusion might work in practice is a question that reaches beyond the scope of this chapter.

What can philosophy itself learn from the arguments put forward here? If we think that an important question of philosophy is "What is the human being?" philosophy is well advised not to see cognitively disabled human beings simply as "something else" that should be excluded, but as human beings who are in their individual forming of the human form of life more or less different from us. And because of this difference we can learn something from them. The main limitation experienced by cognitively disabled people lies in the realm of reasoning, the one feature philosophy often takes as the most important capacity. Taking cognitive disability into account will help philosophy to avoid one-sidedness in its thinking. Values and practices may be seen in a different light – and sometimes one-sidedness will be seen – when we realize that cognitively disabled human beings show what it means to be human. We might become aware that dependency and vulnerability can be valuable for us. And we might learn about other practices that are possible in the human form of life. We can learn about the plurality of capacities and needs, we can learn to build up new practices, we can learn to question our own value systems, we can learn to see the world and the human being in a new way. Such learning may not always be simple and easily accessible – but it is certainly worth it.

References

Cave, K., and Ridell, C. (1994). *Something Else*. Lynnwood: Mondo Publishing.

Garver, N. (1994). *The Complicated Form of Life: Essay on Wittgenstein*. Chicago, IL: Open Court Publishing.

Kittay, E. F. (2005). "At the Margins of Moral Personhood." *Ethics* 116 (1): 100–31.

(2009). "The Personal Is Philosophical Is Political: A Philosopher and Mother of a Cognitively Disabled Person Sends Notes from the Battlefield." *Metaphilosophy* 40 (3–4): 606–27.

Kittay, E. F., and Carlson, L. (2009). "Introduction: Rethinking Philosophical Presumptions in Light of Cognitive Disability." *Metaphilosophy* 40: 307–30.

McMahan, J. (2009). "Cognitive Disability and Cognitive Enhancement." *Metaphilosophy* 40 (3–4): 582–605.

Nussbaum, M. (2006). *Frontiers of Justice: Disability, Nationality, Species Membership*. Cambridge, MA: Harvard University Press.

(2009). "The Capabilities of People with Cognitive Disabilities." *Metaphilosophy* 40 (3–4): 331–51.

Reader, S. (2007). *Needs and Moral Philosophy*. London: Routledge.

Reinders, H. (2008). *Receiving the Gift of Friendship: Profound Disability, Theological Anthropology, and Ethics*. Grand Rapids, MI: Eerdmans Publishing.

Singer, P. (1993). *Practical Ethics*. Cambridge: Cambridge University Press.

(2009). "Speciesism and Moral Status." *Metaphilosophy* 40 (3–4): 567–83.

Williams, B. (2008). *Philosophy as a Humanistic Discipline*. Princeton, NJ: Princeton University Press.

Wittgenstein, L. (1953). *Philosophical Investigations*. Eds. G. E. M. Anscombe and R. Rhees, trans. G. E. M. Anscombe. Oxford: Blackwell.

Wittgenstein, L. (1985). *Philosophische Untersuchungen*. Frankfurt a.M.: Suhrkamp.

3

Disability (Not) as a Harmful Condition: The Received View Challenged

THOMAS SCHRAMME

It is almost commonplace to see disability as an instance of harm. For instance, John Harris claims that disabilities are "physical or mental conditions that constitute a harm to the individual, which a rational person would wish to be without" (2000: 98). Tristram Engelhardt holds: "to see a phenomenon as … a disability is to see something wrong with it" (1996: 197). The received view contends that to be disabled means to have suffered a kind of loss, to be disadvantaged in certain respects, or to be in a deficient physical or mental condition. Many different terms can be utilized for these kinds of negative evaluations of disability, though generally they all follow the same pattern, as they all state that disability is bad for the person who has it. Though many people would agree that it might offer a secondary gain for a person, that is, either an instrumental value such as securing financial or medical support from society or a long-term gain such as a more serious perspective on one's life, disability as such is hardly ever seen as neutral or even in a positive light.

This received view regularly clashes with the viewpoint of people with disabilities. At least some of them claim that they are not harmed by their condition. For instance, Mark Zupan, a quadriplegic rugby player, maintains: "My injury has led me to opportunities and experiences and friendships I would never have had before. And it has taught me about myself. In some ways, it's the best thing that ever happened to me" (Ebert 2005). A psychiatric patient gives the following account:

"Gee, you know, they're telling me this is a disease. If it's a disease, this is the one I want to have.... I look at myself as privileged to have had the experiences I had, the experiences they call pathology" (Farber 1993: 95). It is easy, on the basis of the received view, to read such statements as rationalizations of disastrous events, as an attempt to find meaning in senseless harm. But I believe that it is a truthful, indeed rational, point of view. To see this, we need to better grasp the notion of disability on one hand and of well-being on the other, because the conflict about assessments of disability is either based on different definitions of disability – most commonly a medical versus a social model – or due to contrasting interpretations of what is bad for people, which, again, is based on different conceptions of well-being.

In this chapter, I focus on disability in relation to well-being. I aim to show that the conflict between the received view and the perspective of many persons with disabilities has to do with a difference in their outlook. Whereas the received view makes a comparative assessment, the challenging evaluation is based on a non-comparative point of view. Because both perspectives are reasonable and, in the final analysis, compatible, my aim is also to show that the apparent conflicts stand at cross-purposes.

To put my cards on the table as regards the concept of disability, I believe it is important to distinguish the physical or mental condition of impairment from disability. *Impairment* refers to a pathological condition of an organism that has a certain chronicity, that is, is not a passing process like a disease. Whether a condition is an impairment depends on objective criteria regarding the natural functions of an organism (Boorse 2010). However, it is important to realize that impairment need not necessarily result in disability. The latter is present when impairment has systemic impacts that result in lack of abilities, such as the ability to walk, hear, or see, as well as to recognize, memorize, or imagine. *Disability* is first and foremost dis-ability, that is, lack of ability, where *ability* need not be restricted to intrinsic features of the agent, but involves aspects of opportunities as well. Impairments lead to disabilities within certain environments, hence the latter are also significant causal features. I don't want to go so far as to claim that just any impairment could be present without actually implying disability, even in the case of more severe impairments. For instance, when someone is intellectually impaired but lives in a community where advanced cognitive capacities are not required to get along, we might want to say that he or she is nevertheless disabled, because he or she cannot do certain things that human beings can normally do. As I said, I don't want to take sides in this quarrel for the purposes of this chapter. However, this aspect will later become important when we consider whether disability is necessarily a harm to the person who has it. Certain impairments might necessarily go along with harm to the affected person.

Because disability is due to both impairment, that is, intrinsic features of the affected organism, and to the environment, that is, disabling circumstances such as documents written in a complicated style of writing, in various degrees of combination, there can be some debate as to whether disability is a medical concept – because of the basis of impairment – or a social concept – because of environmental conditions. Of course, this debate has continued for many years regarding the notion of disability, and has resulted in the development of a medical versus a social model of disability. The whole dispute, however, is somewhat fruitless, as obviously disability is regularly due to both aspects (cf. Shakespeare 2006).

The quarrel regarding the definition of disability forms a backdrop for the debate about the evaluation of disability in terms of its effect on human well-being. Since many people seem to agree with the received view and tend to see disability as by definition a condition of harm, a common strategy to undermine the negative evaluation is challenging the classification of certain conditions as disability. In a similar vein, some maintain that if disabling aspects are merely due to environmental conditions, it cannot be a disability. I take it that this is, for instance, implicit in Jonathan Wolff's definition, which states that "to be disabled is to be in a position where *one's internal resources* do not provide one with sufficient genuine opportunities for secure functionings" (2009: 125, emphasis added).[1] Although I agree with this general viewpoint regarding the concept of disease, I should insist that the concept of disability does not seem to be logically restricted to instances of impairment, which are at least partially causally responsible for disability. If we would subscribe to a less restricted perspective, we could identify disabilities that were due only to external circumstances. It is, of course, doubtful, whether such an expansive notion should be deemed a medical, or medicine-related, concept. I would insist that it wouldn't be a sensible expansion, but this is not the topic of this chapter, and I want to insist that there is nothing in the logic of the word itself that forbids us from using a more expansive notion. Here I simply want to say that the more social aspects are involved in the causation and perpetuation of disability, the less people are inclined to regard it as a disability.

But be that as it may, I believe the conceptual debate, again, is in reality concerned with a different issue than classification, namely the problem of evaluation, as the more important question seems to be whether a disability is necessarily bad for the affected person. This has to do with the assessment of human abilities in relation to our well-being (cf. Kahane and Savulescu 2009). In philosophical parlance, the question is whether and which abilities are of prudential value.[2] It seems pretty obvious, at least to me, that Zupan, the quadriplegic rugby player, has a disability – he cannot walk – but this does not say anything about the general prudential value of walking, or about the assessment of not being able to walk from the individual perspective

---

[1] This quote is taken out of context and I don't want to insist that it represents Wolff's general point of view. Indeed, he seems to hold that environmental aspects are as important as internal ones. However, the perspective expressed in the quote is a common one.

[2] Everything that bears on people's interests can be of prudential value. The expression is repeatedly used in Griffin (1986) and has become standard.

of Zupan. Only if we have already agreed with a definition such as Harris's would the question of evaluation be decided by classifying a condition as disability.

But is it really possible, or reasonable for that matter, to doubt that disability is harmful? It might be possible to query the conceptual point, that is, that disability is bad for the affected person *by definition*, but disability as a phenomenon in people's lives seems nevertheless to be evaluated negatively in each and every instance – at least if one is truthful and reasonable. A supporting argument for this viewpoint stems from a debate in bioethics. It concerns the prohibition of causing impairment, for instance to a fetus (McMahan 2002: 280ff.). It seems that if disability were not to be disvalued, it would be allowed to actively cause it. But that would be imprudent, to say the least. Similarly, it would be perfectly reasonable to reject possible cures or scientific studies to find cures for disability, as we normally want to cure what we believe is bad for us. It is therefore common to challenge people with disabilities who argue that they are not harmed by their condition by asking what they would decide if they were granted a wish by a fairy, or if there were a magic bullet for curing disability. It seems that if they would choose the obvious they would take the perspective of the received view.

In contrast, I wish to show that they can happily desire a cure for disability without agreeing that disability is necessarily bad for them. The fact that there is no incoherence involved in these two judgments is due to the distinction between a comparative and a non-comparative perspective on disability. Disability can be comparatively worse than a contrasting condition, for instance without impairment, but it need not be bad for the affected person as judged by itself. This also works the other way around. Many people without disabilities, or who have recently become disabled, commonly assess their condition, or the hypothetical condition of being disabled, in a negative way, hence they see it as harmful. But we know from empirical studies about the so-called disability paradox (Albrecht and Devlieger 1999) that this assessment might change after a while.[3] People tend to be subjectively happy once they have adapted to the impacts of a medical impairment, even though they might have had fairly negative things to say about a possible disability some time before, and of course even though many other people within their environment see the condition as harmful. My explanation of this apparent paradox is that people tend to take a comparative point of view shortly after they have, for instance, suffered an accident, or if they are asked to imagine themselves in a situation of being disabled, but that they take a non-comparative perspective after a while, where they don't compare their current condition to a former or a hypothetical one. They simply assess their life as it is, not as it might have been or could be. This also allows for an explanation of the common differences regarding the evaluations of people with congenital disabilities, in contrast to people with acquired disabilities. For the former group of people, in contrast to the latter, an alternative condition to being disabled has never been an actual or experienced reality.

But before I elaborate on the two different evaluative perspectives I want to introduce different theories of well-being. The notion of well-being, or the good human life, is a traditional philosophical idea. However, as we will see, it is neither well defined what it means – and in fact scholars advocate diverse theories of well-being – nor is it clear what it implies for the evaluation of disability. Again, the received view is therefore not as straightforward as it might seem.

---

[3] This paradox goes back to Brickman, Coates, and Janoff-Bulman (1978), who hold a different view on explaining the data than the one I want to develop. Whereas I see it as based on two different evaluative perspectives, a comparative as opposed to a non-comparative perspective, they endorse the so-called adaption level theory, which roughly holds that everyone has his or her own standard of well-being based on prior experiences: a standard that might change because of habituation of new experiences. As far as I can see, they held that we always assess our lives in a comparative way; that's what makes happiness a relative notion to them. I discuss this claim, that is, that we always make comparative evaluations, later in this chapter.

THEORIES OF WELL-BEING

It has become common for philosophers to start debates about human well-being with a tripartite distinction of theories that Derek Parfit provided in an appendix of his book *Reasons and Persons*. According to this description, three kinds of theories exist: hedonism, desire fulfillment theories, and objective list theories. As will become clear, this is an inadequate distinction. Still, it is a valid starting point for discussions of well-being.

Hedonism is an account that has a long pedigree and was for a long time the dominant point of view. It was explicitly endorsed by Epicurus (1940), who held that something can only be good for us if it is experienced, and later supported by Bentham (1996) and Mill (1969), the founding fathers of utilitarianism. Pleasure and the absence of pain are, according to hedonism, the only constitutive elements of human well-being or happiness. What causes pleasure can of course vary, though whether something indeed causes pleasure in us is not for us to decide. Desire fulfillment theories were developed to deal with theoretical problems of hedonism that have to do with its lack of "worldliness," as it were. Hedonism allows for something to be of prudential value simply because it pleases, for instance when someone enjoys a hot bath. Some pleasures, however, are not at all based on reality; they are merely imagined or artificial, for instance, because of drug abuse. We would not normally say that something can be good for someone if it is not real. Desire fulfillment theories deal with this proviso by basing prudential value on facts about the world, namely whether a desire is fulfilled or not. Again, this allows for individual varieties of desires, but the criterion of something being good for us simply is that it fulfils a desire. Many modern utilitarians as well as many economists believe in this theory. As just described here, it has been deemed in need of qualifications, though. It seems that people often desire strange and irrational things, such as remembering the first 500 digits of the number pi by heart, which then calls into doubt whether it would actually be good for them if the desire were fulfilled. The desire fulfillment theory has accordingly been developed to include certain normative criteria that every desire has to meet, such as being voluntary, informed, and rational. Objective list theories take a different stance; they deem things good for us because they are objectively good, meaning that their value is not due either to our subjective experiences or desires. Objective list theories also go back to ancient philosophy; Aristotle is regarded as their founding father.

Parfit's distinction has become influential, and it is therefore not surprising that the most general distinction philosophers usually draw between different theories of well-being is to classify them into subjective as opposed to objective accounts. Hedonism and desire fulfillment are regarded as subjective in contrast to the objective list theory. We will see shortly, though, that there is an important ambiguity in the subjective-objective distinction. But it is nevertheless helpful to use this general distinction. An element of our well-being can accordingly be due to some subjective stance or pro-attitude of a person, or it can be good for her without her appreciating it as such. In the former case, it depends on the person herself what constitutes her well-being, so it is in a way her invention; in the latter case, it is something that can be discovered. A fitting way to describe the distinction is to call the subjective account the "taste model" and the objective account the "perception model" (Griffin 1996: 20ff.). Either something is valuable because it is desired (taste model), or something is desired because it is valuable (perception model). It is obvious that within the taste model the elements of human well-being differ widely, and it is this very fact that makes it plausible, as people indeed differ in their tastes and what they regard as good for them. Still, some elements of human well-being are universally valued and could for this reason be called objective values – though in this case it would be more adequate to call them intersubjective values. Intersubjectively valued elements of human well-being are not the same as objective ones, because the latter are not up to our choices, or tastes, for that matter. It is the source of value that is important for this distinction, and for an objectivist about well-being the source is not found in individual persons but in objective facts about humans more generally, or indeed external sources, such as a deity or a natural order. A good example, which is also pertinent to our topic, is health. Many theorists maintain that health is an element of human well-being, and that this fact is not due to our evaluating it thus; health is regarded as valuable in itself; it is good for us in virtue of facts about ourselves. Other examples that people deem objective elements of well-being include friendship, enjoyment, and knowledge.

But now let us have another look at hedonism. Is it really a subjective theory? It seems subjective because pleasure is a subjective experience. Philosophers may call it ontologically subjective because the value has to be instantiated in the conscious experience of a person. Pleasure, hence hedonistic value, only exists subjectively. However, what is pleasurable to us is not up to us to decide, but due to our nature. Again, this can vary; there can be individual "natures" of individual persons, but there might also be universal pleasures, for instance the pleasures of sex and eating. We cannot simply decide what to find pleasurable. It seems, therefore, to be a matter of discovery what is good for us according to hedonism, and consequently in this respect it would be wrong to call it a subjective account. In fact, we might want to call it an objective list theory with one element on the list, namely pleasure (and possibly absence of pain as a second element). An ontologically objective theory bases well-being on the external life circumstances of a person and her available resources, such as income or shelter. This approach has been commonly used in economics, especially as regarding a basis of welfare and development assessments of nation-states.

So theories of well-being can be ontologically subjective or objective, but we need another subjective-objective distinction that is not ontological but evaluative.[4] Theories are evaluatively subjective if they deem it up to persons themselves to decide what is good for them. The desire fulfillment theory is evaluatively subjective. A contrasting theory has already been mentioned. Theories of well-being that assume a kind of essence, or nature, of human beings, which then determines what is good for them – such as Aristotle's theory of *eudaimonia* or flourishing – are evaluatively objective.

Altogether we now have four possible combinations of ontologically or evaluatively subjective or objective accounts. The problem with Parfit's classification is that it restricts objective theories to evaluatively objective ones, which are then additionally required to list items – supposedly constitutive elements of well-being – though this seems hardly true even for a theory that most clearly falls into this category, namely Aristotle's. He rather gives a general description of *eudaimonia*, which is roughly to live in accordance with the virtues. In addition, Parfit does not allow for ontologically objective theories and he restricts ontologically subjective theories to hedonism, though there can certainly be alternatives, which might not see pleasure as the decisive conscious experience, but, for instance, religious experiences.

So the first version of accounts of well-being are "experience theories." These are ontologically subjective, and obviously hedonism is the best-known variant of this version. The second group of theories can be called "state-of-being" theories. They are ontologically objective as

---

[4] There is, in fact, a third way of drawing the subjective-objective distinction. A theory of human well-being can be epistemologically subjective if it sees the person as the only expert about her well-being. Theories that allow for errors about what is good for a person are epistemologically objective, as there is a kind of truth or right account about what is valuable for a person. Desire fulfillment theories are objective in this respect, as people can be misinformed about what things will actually fulfill their desires. Nevertheless it is the fulfillment of the desire itself that constitutes individual well-being, and hence the account is evaluatively subjective. What makes something good for us is due to our pro-attitudes, though which things causally lead to this result is not.

they focus on objective facts of the life of human beings or their life circumstances, including such things as resources, opportunities, or income, generally speaking items that John Rawls called primary social goods (1971: 90ff.). The third variant is the well-known and widespread desire fulfillment theory. Well-being, for its proponents, is a life according to one's own desires and ideals. It is therefore an evaluatively subjective approach. Finally, "essence" or "genus" theories base well-being on an objective standard of basic or necessary elements of the good human life. This is an evaluatively objective approach.

Obviously I don't want to claim that I have identified all possible theories of well-being. The main point of introducing this classification is first to stress that there is no unified approach, and hence no clear single basis for assessing disability in respect to human well-being, and second to provide such a rational basis for evaluation that does not beg the question regarding its standard of assessment. So the next step in the argument is to look at disability from the perspective of each of the four mentioned types of theories.

DISABILITY IN RELATION TO WELL-BEING

According to experience theories, disability is bad for the person if it is experienced as something bad, for instance as something painful. It is obvious that there can be no generalization regarding the badness of disability; it cannot be said that disability is always bad for the disabled person. If a person does not experience it thus, we have no basis for saying that her disability impairs her well-being. A possible rejoinder is the already mentioned disability paradox (which in fact does not seem to be a paradox). A variant of it can be found in John Stuart Mill's discussion of the "satisfied fool" (1969: 212), which states that people might be content with being cognitively and intellectually "foolish," but that this does not mean that they are deemed to be happy. The rejoinder accordingly insists that people sometimes experience something as pleasurable, or fail to experience it as harmful, because of the circumstances, such as mental adaptation to a harmed state of being. However, this thesis generally challenges the adequacy of experience theories, not merely the assessment of disability on its basis. The challenge implies that human well-being cannot only be based on ontologically subjective elements, but requires a standard of how people should normally experience certain things or aspects of their life. On the basis of experience theories alone, it seems nevertheless unlikely that we can claim that disability is always bad for the disabled person.

On the basis of state of being theories, we can argue that disability is bad, because it prevents opportunities, leads to lower income, or generally hinders one in the pursuit of resources. I believe it is especially the value of opportunities or options, and the claim that disabled people lack a normal range of opportunities (Daniels 1985: 27ff.), that heavily influences the discussion about the evaluative assessment of disability. It seems obvious that disabled people indeed do have fewer options within their lives than nondisabled people. The very term *disability* contains the notion that there are fewer abilities, hence fewer options, for people with disabilities. Therefore, disability seems clearly and in every instance a harmed condition. But there are at least two objections to this straightforward view. First, the theory itself is less convincing than it might seem. State of being theories focus on resources and generally the external life circumstances of a person, but not on the significance resources have in the life of persons. It can lead to a kind of "resource fetishism" (Sen 1980: 216) that tends to ignore the individuality of human beings. Disabled people might have exactly those opportunities and resources they deem of significance. Whether they could have more options if they were nondisabled might not be important to them. To insist that they are nevertheless harmed seems to ignore their individual point of view. Surely I don't want to assert that disabled people are always happy with the options they have, but at the moment I am concerned with the opposite generalization and want to challenge it. Second, and related, many restrictions in the opportunity range of disabled people are due to environmental conditions – hence societal decisions – not to the physical or mental condition of a person. So even if there is harm involved in the state of being of a person, it is not always due to the disability, and the harm can actually be overcome. This is, of course, a point that proponents of the social model of disability have put forward several times.

Desire fulfillment theories result in a view that disability is bad, if it is undesired, and similarly for experience theories. Again, there can be no generalization regarding the assessment of disability, as it is based on individual desires. There is also a similar rejoinder found in the literature that we can apply to the assessment of disability. We know from empirical research that people often adapt their preferences according to their real situations. If they cannot reach a certain good they might normally desire, they might solve the problem by adapting their preferences accordingly, like how the fox in the well-known fable dismisses the grapes he cannot reach as inedible. The rejoinder regarding adaptive preferences can therefore be called the "sour grapes" objection. We could then claim that people with disabilities who assert they are not harmed fall foul of a similar sour grape preference, or rationalization, as it is often considered. However, just as in the case before, this objection points at a general problem of the theory under scrutiny. It seems that it is based on an implicit standard of what human beings should desire and strive for.

The repeatedly mentioned reference to standards of normal happiness or desire fulfillment speaks in favor of a nonsubjective theory of well-being. Essence theories offer such an evaluatively objective account. According to this perspective, disability is bad because it prevents or restricts basic elements of the good human life, for instance, self-determination, liberty, and independence. It is indeed plausible to say that many people regard restrictions of disabilities as bad because they see them as undermining basic human capacities, such as seeing, hearing, speaking, walking, abstract thinking, remembering, and so on. So they seem to endorse an essence theory. This also ties in with the fact that many people do not see minor impairments, such as a missing finger or lack of any imagination, as disabilities, although they can have a considerable impact on some people's lives. But even if common sense seems to be in congruence with essence theories, this does not mean that they share the same philosophical basis. Common sense seems to be just that, a sense that is common, whereas essence theories would need an argument as to why certain characteristics of human beings are necessary requirements of the good human life. This is much harder than identifying a widespread agreement and what people find important. Indeed, many philosophers would see it as a hopeless task, as it seems to commit an is-ought fallacy by determining what is required for a good human life through an account of human nature. Only the philosophical argument, though, would reject as wrong the judgments of people with disabilities who challenge the received view and do not see their disability as harmful. Otherwise these people would simply have an unusual point of view that clashes with common sense. But even if such a philosophical theory were to succeed, it would only bear on severe impairments, that is, conditions that restrict essential elements of the good human life, and would not allow for a sweeping claim such as the one by Harris quoted earlier.

In this section I have looked at disability from the perspective of four different types of theories about well-being. All accounts provide reasons to call disability an instance of harm, but none seems to allow for a general claim about the impact of medical impairment on the quality of life of individual human beings. There cannot be a straightforward identification of disability and harm on the basis of these theories. In the next section, I add even more reasons as to why this identification fails. I argue that although disability might always be worse than a medically normal condition, this is not the same as stating that it is harmful in absolute, that is, non-comparative, terms.

COMPARATIVE VERSUS NON-COMPARATIVE
PERSPECTIVES

Human beings can be affected in their well-being in two different ways. Something that impacts their well-being can be harmful in itself, such as a life-threatening disease or the experience of pain. But harm can also be present when someone's situation is worsened, for instance when a fire destroys the house of a person. Here, whether something is harmful depends on a comparison with the situation a person was in before an event happened. It is important to realize that a comparative harm need not always be a case of non-comparative, that is, absolute harm. When a person loses money in a gamble she is worse off than before, but she is not necessarily harmed in an absolute way by the loss. The latter would likely be the case, though, if her financial means fall below a standard of sufficiency because of the loss.

Comparative harm is certainly something we deem negative and unwanted. We normally don't want to be worse off in any aspect of our lives, especially if we cherish the aspect that is affected. We value different things, of course, as we have already seen in the discussion of different theories of well-being. Someone might lose a stamp from his collection and would be worse off than before, but might not be bothered about it at all. For someone else, this loss might be deemed a considerable worsening of his situation. Hence, whether something is a comparative harm seems to depend on subjective evaluations.

In terms of conditions of health, disease, and disability, which are more pertinent to our topic, similar situations arise. Almost anyone will, for instance, prefer not to be allergic to certain substances – say, garlic – and hence deem such an allergy to be a comparative harm. But there can even be pathological conditions that people are neutral about, such as being dyslexic in an environment where written communication is obsolete, or being short-sighted in a community that secures access to glasses or contact lenses. So the evaluative assessment of comparative harms depends not only on our subjective preferences, but also on the circumstances we live in, that is, whether a particular disease or disability poses a real disadvantage. For some people, it would not be a sufficient compensation of the comparative harm of short-sightedness to wear glasses, for instance because they cannot anymore do the job they want to do.

Regarding disability, I believe it is plausible to claim that normally people prefer to be healthy and hence deem disability a case of comparative harm. I should think that even people with disabilities who claim that they are not in a harmed condition could agree with this, because it is not the kind of harm they refer to. They do not worry about the comparative worth of a disability but about its absolute impact on their well-being. But just as not everyone needs to see it as a harmful condition in absolute terms if he cannot eat garlic, not everyone needs to see a disability as harmful, absolutely speaking. I would claim that we deem these conditions or situations as harmful to us in absolute terms that we cannot identify with. To be harmful in its own right, a condition will be assessed as such, not in comparison to another condition, such as being healthy. Now to be absolutely harmful, a condition need not be experienced as harmful, that is, painful, but it needs to be something the affected person cannot endorse or see as part of herself; it is something the person wants to be rid of. Note that this is different from an assessment in comparative terms. A man can certainly claim, for instance, to prefer not to be bald, but still insist that he does not think the condition of being bald is harmful to him in its own right. This is because being bald can be part of his identity.[5]

I readily admit that my description of the source of seeing something as non-comparatively harmful in terms of not being able to identify with it is rather vague (but see Edwards 2005: 97ff.). But the

---

[5] For the purposes of this chapter, I take a very naive view concerning identity. I simply mean aspects of our lives that we see as constitutive elements of who we are. Even baldness can be such an element.

notion of identity is helpful, I believe, because disability almost by its nature is, or can become, a part of a person's identity. Disability is different from a passing disease. It is a condition a person was born with or will be in for a long time, maybe the rest of her life. This helps us to explain the apparent paradox that most people would deem disease absolutely harmful, though not everyone sees a disability, which can be described as a kind of chronic disease, as harmful in this way. This is because a chronic condition can become a part of one's identity, whereas this seems more difficult with passing diseases. It also provides a plausible explanation as to why people with congenital disabilities more regularly deny the absolute harmfulness of the disability than people with acquired disabilities. This is because for them the medical impairment has always been a part of their identity. For others, disability needs to become a part of their identity before they can make the same claim. This finally allows for an explanation of the apparent disability paradox. Well-being is closely related to one's identity, and it is therefore to be expected that once a disability has gradually become "internalized," its absolute harmfulness also gradually decreases.

So altogether we can say that disability might always be a comparative harm. It might always be worse to be disabled than to be healthy. This accounts for the common description of disability as making us worse off, being a detriment, or posing a disadvantage. These are all comparative notions. The comparative aspects of disabilities can often be mitigated such that they don't necessarily have permanent (comparative) harmful effects. The most discussed example in this respect is the compensating effect of sign language for deaf people.

Although we can agree that disability might be considered harmful in comparative terms, what is more important is whether it necessarily is a harm in absolute terms. I have argued that this is not the case, because disability can become, or often is, part of a person's identity. This means that it is an individual matter whether disability is bad for the person affected; hence the received view, which maintains that disability is generally a harmed condition, is false.

Someone might object that the difference between a comparative and non-comparative evaluation is less important than I have claimed, indeed, that we can always turn the absolute perspective into a comparative one if we include alternative, hypothetical situations. The person who had an accident or who was born blind *could* have had another life, or he *might* be cured in a conceivable world. We simply need imagination to do this kind of comparison. I believe this is correct and I haven't claimed that we cannot perform this kind of change of perspective. I merely defended the argument that often people do in fact take a non-comparative evaluative stance toward aspects of their lives, and that this might differ from a comparative one because of the fact that the particular aspect is regarded as an integral element of who they are. To take a comparative perspective regarding this particular aspect is certainly still possible and it can indeed lead to a form of ambivalence in the evaluation of disability that we often find in people with disabilities. My main claim in this chapter was to reject arguments that tend to ignore the non-comparative evaluation and only focus on comparative aspects.

There is a final twist in the argument that I won't be able to deal with adequately here, but which is worth mentioning. Some defenders of the received view might want to claim that although I might have been able to show that many people with disabilities do in fact not deem themselves absolutely harmed for good reasons, they *should* nevertheless not identify with these conditions. Such an argument might rely, similarly to the essence view, on a threshold that renders all disabilities instances of objective absolute harms after all. Although I see some merit in this view, and would myself argue along this line for certain significant disabilities, such as the lack of any way to communicate, I don't believe it is adequate. Some of the reasons for rejecting it as an account about disability *tout court* have already been mentioned, for instance the philosophical problems of any objective account of human well-being.

CONCLUSION

I have argued that to have a disability is (other things being equal) comparatively worse than being healthy. Hence, the argument from the prohibition of causing impairment is plausible, but cannot establish more than the comparative claim. This is important to notice, because to counter other claims about the evaluation of disability of the received view, the comparative aspect need not be denied by people with disabilities, for instance by pointing out specific benefits that their disability brings. Whether these are present or not does not matter for the absolute evaluation of disability. Accordingly, to accept that disability is comparatively worse than being healthy does not imply that one has to view disability as an instance of absolute harm.

If we confuse the two perspectives on well-being and harm, we are discussing at cross-purposes. I believe that the non-comparative perspective is indeed the focus of many people with disabilities, especially with congenital impairments, whereas for many defenders of the received view it is enough to focus on the comparative claim. But they would need a separate argument as to why disability necessarily needs to be evaluated as harmful even in absolute terms. To simply claim that disability is bad per se is not a good enough argument.

I believe that one main problem of the debate about disability and well-being is that too many generalizations are used – on both sides of the argument. Our discussion of theories of well-being and their different assessments of disability has shown that the whole issue is diverse and should be dealt with accordingly. Not all disabilities are the same; not all people with disabilities are the same; not all societies in which people with disabilities live are the same. In consequence, how limiting, if at all, disability is, and hence how it is evaluated and is to be evaluated, depends on all these variables. Whether disability is to be considered harmful depends on the person with a disability, the kind of medical impairment (especially whether it is acquired or congenital), the life circumstances of a person, a particular theory of well-being used as a backdrop of assessment, and, finally, whether we take a comparative or non-comparative perspective. Most of the debate so far has been at cross-purposes. We need to make a fresh start.[6]

References

Albrecht, Gary L. and Devlieger, Patrick J. (1999), "The disability paradox: High quality of life against all odds," *Social Science and Medicine* 48: 977–88.

Bentham, Jeremy (1996), *An Introduction to the Principles of Morals and Legislation* [1789], ed. by J. H. Burns and H. L. A. Hart. Oxford: Clarendon Press.

Boorse, Christopher (2010), "Disability and Medical Theory," in D. Christopher Ralston and Justin Ho (eds.), *Philosophical Reflections on Disability*. Dordrecht etc.: Springer, 55–88.

Brickman, Philip, Coates, Dan, and Janoff-Bulman, Ronnie (1978), "Lottery winners and accident victims: Is happiness relative?" *Journal of Personality and Social Psychology* 36 (8): 917–27.

Daniels, Norman (1985), *Just Health Care*. Cambridge: Cambridge University Press.

Ebert, Roger (2005), "Sundance #3: Of Heart and Humor," http://rogerebert.suntimes.com/apps/pbcs.dll/article?AID=/20050125/FILMFESTIVALS05/501250301/1023 (accessed: 30 July 2012).

Edwards, Steven D. (2005), *Disability: Definitions, Value and Identity*. Oxford: Radcliffe.

Engelhardt, H. Tristram, Jr. (1996), *The Foundations of Bioethics*, Second Edition. Oxford University Press.

Epicurus (1940), "Letter to Menoeceus," in Whitney J. Oates (ed.), *The Stoic and Epicurean Philosophers*. New York: The Modern Library, 30–4.

Farber, Seth (1993), *Madness, Heresy, and the Rumour of Angels: The Revolt against the Mental Health System*. Chicago and La Salle, IL: Open Court Publ. Co.

Griffin, James (1986), *Well-Being: Its Meaning, Measurement and Moral Importance*. Oxford: Clarendon Press.

(1996), *Value Judgement: Improving Our Ethical Beliefs*. Oxford: Clarendon Press.

---

[6] I'd like to thank Franziska Felder, Steve Edwards, and the participants of a conference on "Disability and the Good Life" in Basel for valuable comments.

Harris, John (2000), "Is there a coherent social conception of disability?" *Journal of Medical Ethics* 26: 95–100.

Kahane, Guy and Savulescu, Julian (2009), "The Welfarist Account of Disability," in Kimberley Brownlee and Andrew Cureton (eds.), *Disability and Disadvantage*. Oxford: Oxford University Press, 14–53.

McMahan, Jeff (2002), *The Ethics of Killing: Problems at the Margins of Life*. Oxford: Oxford University Press.

Mill, John Stuart (1969), Utilitarianism [1861], in *The Collected Works of John Stuart Mill*, vol. 10. Toronto: University of Toronto Press.

Parfit, Derek (1984), *Reasons and Persons*. Oxford: Clarendon Press.

Rawls, John (1971), *A Theory of Justice*. Cambridge, MA: Harvard University Press.

Sen, Amartya (1980), "Equality of What?" in Sterling McMurrin (ed.), *The Tanner Lectures on Human Values*, vol. I. Cambridge: Cambridge University Press, 197–220.

Shakespeare, Tom (2006), *Disability Rights and Wrongs*. London: Routledge.

Wolff, Jonathan (2009), "Disability among Equals," in Kimberley Brownlee and Andrew Cureton (eds.), *Disability and Disadvantage*. Oxford: Oxford University Press, 112–37.

4

Nasty, Brutish, and Short? On the Predicament of Disability and Embodiment

TOM SHAKESPEARE

INTRODUCTION

According to the World Health Organization, there are 1 billion disabled people in the world, of whom somewhere between 110 million and 190 million are adults with very significant difficulties in functioning (WHO 2011). This prevalence estimate begs the question of what counts as disability. WHO's answer to that question is found in the *International Classification of Functioning, Disability and Health* (WHO 2001), from which voluminous catalog we learn that *disability* refers to the negative aspects of the interaction of a person with a health condition and that individual's contextual factors – environmental and personal. Perhaps surprising from a disability activist perspective, we are not far from the UN Convention on the Rights of Persons with Disabilities, which states that "disability results from the interaction between persons with impairments and attitudinal and environmental barriers that hinder their full and effective participation in society on an equal basis with others."

The Convention on the Rights of Persons with Disabilities (CRPD), which came into force in 2008, marks an important stage in the growth and globalization of the disability rights movement and in the changing societal responses to disability. At the time of writing, 101 states had ratified the CRPD, meaning that they were bound by international law to uphold and implement the fifty articles, and by so doing remove those attitudinal and environmental barriers that hinder persons with disabilities from full and effective participation. Because it is a treaty that focuses on participation of existing persons with disabilities, the CRPD barely discusses prevention of health conditions or impairments associated with disability. The sole exceptions are Article 25, Health, and Article 26, Rehabilitation. According to the CRPD, and in line with previous human rights statutes, persons with existing impairments have the right to access the health and rehabilitation services they need. They should be protected from the secondary conditions that are a consequence and complication of their primary condition, and they should be protected from co-morbidities that would also reduce their state of health or functioning. However, the CRPD does not address the issue of nondisabled people's right to be protected from acquiring impairments and becoming disabled people.

The emphasis on barriers in the CPRD is congruent with the social model of disability, about which I have written at some length elsewhere (Shakespeare 2006). For the global social movement of people with disabilities who campaigned for the CRPD, and whose leaders were part of the process of drafting it, the CRPD is the best global mechanism available for equalizing opportunities and reducing disadvantage by eliminating social barriers and unfair treatment. For many in the international disability rights movement, impairments are not the problem: society is the problem, as the social model highlights (Oliver 1990). On this account, if social and environmental barriers are removed, impairment is no longer a disadvantage. It becomes a neutral characteristic. By way of evidence, disability advocates can point to the full and rich lives led by many people with a diverse range of health conditions and impairments, at least in high-income countries. They can also draw on the testimonies of disabled people about their quality of life.

I want to start this chapter by accepting and providing evidence for this disability rights argument, namely that life with what I would prefer to refer to as the "predicament" of impairment (Shakespeare 2006) can be a good form of life. Next, I argue that, notwithstanding this possibility of a good life with impairment, preventing health conditions and impairments remains desirable. Third, I explore the implicit contradiction this entails: If life as a disabled person is so good, why would anyone want to avoid it? In conclusion, I make some broader points about human existence and suggest that our ideas about disability would be richer and more balanced if we adopted a pessimistic materialism about existence in general.

LIFE WITH IMPAIRMENT CAN BE GOOD

Impairment seems, on the face of it, a very unpleasant phenomenon, which most people in their right mind would prefer to avoid. Philosopher John Harris reflects this intuition when he offers a definition of disability as "a negative state which people have a reasonable preference not to be in" (2000). The popular idea that it would be better to be dead than to be disabled is only a more extreme version of this attitude. In general, disability is a very negatively valued condition, which is one reason many people with impairments are very reluctant to identify as disabled (Shakespeare, Thompson, and Wright 2010). Disability, in everyday thought and language, is associated with failure, with dependency, with not being able to do things.

Stepping back from these surely distorted judgments, what is wrong with having an impairment? According to the *International Classification of Functioning* (WHO 2001), disability entails decrements in functioning: disabled people cannot do everything the average human being can do. Often, health conditions leading to disability involve some degree of pain and suffering and indignity. Sometimes, these health conditions result in a shortened lifespan. On top of this, as disability advocates themselves report, disabled people face widespread discrimination and prejudice. As the *World Report on Disability* (WHO 2011) proves, they are excluded from education and employment, receive worse health care, and are denied the rehabilitation and assistive devices they need. Disabled people are disproportionately vulnerable to violence and abuse.

However, these agreed facts do not have to lead to the extreme conclusions cited earlier. The standard disability rights argument is that much of the disadvantage associated with disability stems from social arrangements, environmental barriers, and social oppression. Even pain and suffering arising from a health condition can be mitigated if the individual gets access to appropriate health care. That is to say, the disadvantage is not a necessary consequence of the underlying health condition or impairment. The thrust of the *World Report on Disability* (WHO 2011), the Convention on the Rights of Persons with Disabilities (UN 2006), and many other national and international initiatives is to make it easier for disabled people to live full lives of high quality. It seems plausible that life for disabled people will indeed improve in the future, in the same way that it is hoped that the situation will improve for the world's women and children and indigenous people and so on.

Notwithstanding the impact of a health condition, and even in a world that is not designed to facilitate well-being, let alone full participation, of people with disabilities, the empirical evidence and anecdotal testimony shows that for many people with disabilities, life is surprisingly good. In a now classic paper on what they call "the disability paradox," Gary Albrecht and Patrick Devlieger (1999) marshal the evidence that reveals that people with disabilities consistently report a quality of life as good as, or sometimes even better than, that of nondisabled people.

What reasons can be found to explain the disability paradox? Some would cast doubt on the reports of good quality of life. Bioethicists sometimes describe these self-reports in terms of the "happy slave" idea: people think they are happy because they do not know any better. People with disabilities are simply not telling the truth, it could be claimed. Perhaps these cheerful people with disabilities are deluding themselves and others. It may be just too humiliating to think of one-self as inferior and suffering, or it may be impossible to incorporate the damage into a positive sense of self. Therefore people are in denial. Or perhaps people with disabilities secretly really do feel that disability is awful, but they are not prepared to admit that to others. They do not want to be thought of as inferior or to be pitied, and therefore they dis-simulate about their own lives. Perhaps in private they admit to misery, while in public they put on a brave face. These explanations do not seem fair or reasonable. They seem extremely patronizing, not to say insulting. Psychological research has supported disabled people's self-reports of good quality of life, rejecting the skepticism of, for exam-ple, bioethicists (Amundson 2010). So we need to find better ways of understanding what is going on.

First, it appears that human beings are capable of adapting to almost any situation, finding satisfaction in the smaller things they can achieve, and deriving happiness from their relationships with family and friends, even in the absence of more worldly success. This account offers a less demeaning explanation of the psychological processes that go on in the mind of a person with disability. Christopher Murray (1996) distinguishes three related process of adaptation, coping, and adjustment. *Adaptation* means finding another way to do something: for example, the paralyzed person might wheel places rather than walk places. *Coping* is when people redefine their expectations about func-tioning over time. They decide that a stroll of a half a mile is fine, whereas previously they would have only been content with a ramble of ten miles. *Accommodation* is when someone learns to value other things: they decide that rather than going for walks in the country with friends, the really important thing in life is being able to go to great restaurants with them. Note, however, that none of these explanations implies that being paralyzed, for example, is not a negative experience: adaptation, coping, and accommodation merely explain how someone may come to terms with their limitation over time. For a notion like Disability Adjusted Life Years to work, Christopher Murray and his cohorts have to believe that impairment is always and consistently a burden: they also have to ask their panel to focus on the impairment and estimate its impact on life, rather than asking panel members to think of people with impairments whom they know, and ask about their quality of life, which would produce very different results (Amundson 2010).

Second, it appears to be the case that our appraisal of life with impairment may have less to do with actuality than with fear, ignorance, and prejudice, all of which make the experience appear worse than it actually is. That is to say, we have a distorted view of disability, one made more graphic by the ways cultural representations of disability play on our fears of impotence, incapacity, and dependency (Shakespeare 1994). Catriona Mackenzie and Jackie Leach Scully (2008) warn us of the dangers of relying on our imagination when it comes to disability: we tend to exaggerate, project, and mistake what life is really like for people with disabilities. We wrongly assume that difficulties for people result in misery for people (Amundson 2010).

Third, even to the extent that health conditions and impairments do entail suffering and limitation, other factors in life can more than compensate for them: for example, an individual with access to resources, such as Philippe, the protagonist of the recent French box office sensation *Les Intouchables* (directed by Olivier Nakache and Eric Toledano 2011), can have an extremely good quality of life notwithstanding his tetraplegia. Even someone who is not lucky enough to be a wealthy Parisian aristocrat can enjoy the benefits of friendship, culture, or other interests, notwithstanding the restrictions that impairment places on him or her. By contrast, it is plain to see that someone can have a fully functioning body or mind and yet lack the social networks or the personality necessary for living a happy and fulfilled existence.

Fourth, most disabled people have the potential to enjoy much of what gives life meaning. For example, if modern humans might sum up their life goals in terms of "job, partner, family," there is every possibility of most disabled people experiencing those achievements.

Empirically, it is clear that many disabled people have sexual partners, become parents, and earn a living. It is certainly the case that they are less likely to achieve these goals, but it would be wrong to conclude these goals are impossible for them. The notion of disabled people being asexual and incompetent is certainly a myth.

People born with an impairment have nothing to which they can compare their current existence. Someone lacking a major sense has never experienced music or birdsong, visual art, or a sublime landscape. Someone born with restricted growth has always been that way: even if life is sometimes hard, they are used to being how they are. Somebody with intellectual disability may not consider themselves different at all, and may resist attempts to label them stupid or a second-class citizen. For people with congenital impairment, disability is part of their sense of self and becomes identity constituting (Edwards 2005). Only in rare cases, for example when a person has a degenerative disease, does an individual regret his or her form of embodiment. To want to be nondisabled is, essentially, to want to be a different person, which is a psychological and cognitive dissonance few human beings seem able to enter into. The weight of evidence from quality of life studies and from case studies and other autobiographical reports suggests that human flourishing is possible without a major sense, without legs, without average intelligence.

People who become disabled tend to go through a similar trajectory. Immediately after injury or disease has rendered them disabled, they may feel profoundly depressed, to regard their life as over, and even to contemplate suicide. Yet after a period of time, they adapt to their situation, reevaluate their negative attitude to the disability, and start making the most of their situation. Often they are driven to greater achievements than before. Usually, their quality of life returns to approximately what it was before the trauma struck. This phenomenon, which also explains why lottery winners revert to their previous state of happiness after the thrill of riches has worn off, is known as *hedonic adaptation* (Amundson 2010). For disabled people, impairment usually makes little difference to their quality of life. The research shows, for example, that overall levels of life satisfaction for people with spinal cord injury are not affected by their physical ability or limitations (Kennedy et al. 2010). Furthermore, the clinical fact of whether the spinal lesion is high or low, complete or incomplete – all aspects that affect functioning – has a weak and nonsignificant relationship with quality of life (Kreuter et al. 1998).

It seems reasonable to conclude that on balance of evidence, disability usually does not have to equate to exclusion from most of what makes life good. I can perhaps agree with Michael Oliver (1990) and other authors in the disability rights tradition when they reject the "disability as tragedy" assumption. I do not thereby feel compelled to accept the "disability as difference" or even the "disability as positive variation" argument. Most of the time, "disability as predicament" seems to me (Shakespeare 2006) a workable and balanced judgment. Life with impairment can be good, and certainly far less bad than ill-informed observers perceive. Ron Amundson's wonderful discussion of hedonic psychology highlights how human beings' attitudes to events or experiences, not the events or experiences themselves, result in happiness or misery (2010).

PREVENTING IMPAIRMENT IS GOOD

If life with impairment is so much better than our initial assumptions suggest, why then should we put any effort into avoiding it? Could governments reduce their public health budgets without denting gross domestic happiness? In this section, I offer arguments in favor of preventing impairment, using a range of arguments from different perspectives on the good human life.

One rejoinder is to say that disability is very diverse in ways that suggest that we have to qualify the claim that "disability is no tragedy." Not all, but some, health conditions and impairments undoubtedly involve greater degrees of misery and suffering than the average human should have to endure. We might think here of depression, which Lewis Wolpert (2001) labeled "malignant sadness." Being unable to feel happy or optimistic for long periods of time may undoubtedly render one's life bad, and may make one wish one had never been born. Here we see a reversal of Mackenzie and Scully's point about the outsider's moral imagination: an outsider might perceive a person with depression to have a good life, but the individual considers himself or herself to have a poor quality of life (Papakostas et al. 2004). Or consider a condition like epidermolysis bullyosa (EB), a painful inherited disease in which skin blisters develop in response to minor injury, and which is associated with pain, suffering, and early mortality. People who experience depression or EB will certainly have periods of happiness and fulfillment. They can enjoy many aspects of life. But overall, it is much harder to be sanguine about these forms of life than it is about impairments such as deafness. So the "disability paradox" might not apply to all disability. Indeed, discussions of the "disability paradox" are often qualified with the observation that impairments that involve considerable pain, whether physical or mental, are less compatible with a good quality of life (Albrecht and Devlieger 1999; Amundson 2010). We are reminded that disability is extremely diverse and heterogeneous and that generalizations – "disability is tragic" or "disability is just another form of difference" – are usually misleading.

A second point is that while many limitations experienced by disabled people are externally imposed restrictions arising from inaccessible environments and social discrimination, there are also often intrinsic limitations to individual functioning that can only be overcome through the assistance of others, and not always even then. This form of life may not mean suffering, may not be incompatible with a good life, but might entail not being able to do everything that a person might want or hope to do. If we want to maximize freedom and increase possibilities, then we might think it better to enable more people to enjoy more of what life has to offer: listening to music, seeing great art, playing sport, enjoying nature. Preventing people being impaired will help ensure that more people can enjoy these diverse experiences that give life meaning. Impairments are relevant factors affecting well-being and human flourishing.

More generally, disabled people usually have fewer choices than nondisabled people. Because of the limitations in functioning associated with impairment, and the less-than-perfect accessibility of most societies, the disabled person is likely unable to have a full choice of jobs to perform, cars to drive, places to stay, tourist attractions to visit. Additionally, the disabled person is more likely to rely on mechanical devices – elevators, wheelchairs, communication devices – that periodically malfunction, rendering the individual excluded or dependent. Most disabled people become inured to the frustrations of inaccessibility or breakdown, but it certainly makes life less predictable, more complicated, and less free than nondisabled people take for granted. When disaster or emergency strikes, and normal systems of distribution, support, and protection break down, the greater needs of the person with disability can expose them to additional risks and even increased mortality.

Moreover, the processes of adaptation, coping, and accommodation described by Christopher Murray take time. For example, even if a person who has a spinal cord injury eventually comes to terms with the situation, he or she is still likely to have a few years of misery immediately after the trauma. He or she will have to go through rehabilitation and learn to function as a paraplegic. The patient will have to adapt his or her house and car, and possibly find a new occupation. Evidence suggests such individuals have a higher likelihood of divorce, even though the prospects for a new relationship post injury are quite positive. Life may be enjoyable after paraplegia, but it is more complicated in some respects, and more limited in others. Therefore overall we might think it would be better for them if they did not have the struggle-followed-by-happiness trajectory, together with the complications of adaptation, coping, and accommodation.

For reasons like these, we can accept that disability is not always bad, may not be the worst thing, may even be completely compatible with a good life, but still do our best to avoid becoming disabled or having disabled children. Is this the contradiction that it at first appears? I have argued that on one hand, disability is not the bad thing many people fear. But on the other hand, health conditions leading to impairment are best prevented where possible. Why prevent a phenomenon that is not incompatible with a good life? In particular, is not prevention of impairment similar to preventing the birth of girls or efforts to eliminate homosexuality? Disability activists might claim that a social difference is being medicalized and pathologized, when it should rather be accepted, supported, and included.

One solution would be to try and prevent some forms of impairment, but not others. This demands that we refine our notion of disability and differentiate between conditions for which the response is prevention, and conditions where the response is barrier removal and antidiscrimination initiatives. We might examine all the different types of impairment and agree to concentrate on preventing and treating the really problematic forms of embodiment: conditions like depression and epidermolysis bullyosa, for example, which most people might agree are incompatible with a good quality of life. One imagines that this radical abbreviation of the public health mission might make the job of the World Health Organization considerably easier.

But we could also see that by creating a hierarchy of impairment this approach would alienate many people who live with these conditions, who feel a judgment is being made on their right to exist. Moreover, it would be very difficult to agree to any list of "really problematic forms of embodiment." Different people value different aspects of life. Some people would prefer to avoid physical pain at all costs. Other people would wish to avoid any form of mental limitation. For some, a short happy life would be acceptable, but others would be unwilling to accept any curtailment of an average lifespan.

Tackling the contradiction head on, another possible approach is to argue that even though a situation such as disability may not have a bad outcome for some people, that does not imply that it is not worth avoiding it, if possible. Another relevant example is teenage motherhood. There are many examples of young women who have babies at the age of fourteen, fifteen, sixteen, or seventeen who give birth to healthy children, who continue to study for the qualifications they need, who turn out to be good mothers, and both mother and offspring go on to have happy and successful lives. But the success of individual cases of teenage parenthood does not mean that young people should not be advised to wait a few years to reproduce, given access to contraception, or discouraged from reckless sexual activity. Being a teenaged mother is more difficult, on average, and outcomes are worse, on average, and therefore it would be better to avoid that route in life, if possible, even if many teenage pregnancies turn out well.

Another approach is to look again at some of the reasons for the resistance to preventing disability. The disability studies literature often makes an analogy between impairment, on one hand, and gender, ethnicity, and sexuality, on the other. All right-thinking people would object to measures that prevent the birth of people who are female, gay, or black. In the same way, some disability scholars and activists say, we should not try to prevent the birth of people with disabilities, and we should be concerned about measures to try and cure impairments. However – and here the difference from other disadvantaged groups like women, minority ethnic communities, and lesbian and gay people becomes clear – disabled people would still experience disadvantage after the social world was made inclusive. For example, equal opportunities in employment notwithstanding, many disabled people cannot work full time, and some disabled people cannot attain the literacy and numeracy most modern jobs require. As a result, after barrier removal, additional social protection is required. But even with these interventions, in this best of all enlightened, accepting, and supportive worlds, people with certain impairments are likely to remain significantly restricted. That is, there is an inextricable disadvantage consequent on having many forms of impairment that is far more profound from any minor diswelfares associated with membership in the other subaltern categories listed. The gender, ethnicity, and sexuality comparison is a false analogy.

The major challenge to this argument – and the case most frequently adduced against disability prevention – is Deafness. People who are born Deaf and who are part of the sign language–using community argue that Deafness does not entail suffering or health problems, should not even be defined as an impairment, but is simply a case of linguistic difference. Deaf people are thus a minority community who use a different language. The strengths of this argument are outside the scope of this chapter, but suffice it to point out that Deafness is unique in this respect, as a disability where the barriers are almost all social and cultural. Most other impairments are not like Deafness.

If the disability/gender/race/sexuality analogy is weaker than first appears, for most instances of impairment, then what might be a better comparison? Poverty springs to mind. Most people would seek to prevent poverty while not demeaning individual poor people. Poverty makes life harder, even though it can also generate solidarity and community. Many people from poor backgrounds have achieved great things, but we do not thereby think it is acceptable if people grow up in poverty and deprived of material goods. We can celebrate the lives of poor people, and enjoy their distinctive cuisine, music, or cultural achievements, while still wishing that they had not been poor in the first place. Life in poverty – or with impairment – can be good, but on average, life is more likely to be good in different circumstances.

The conclusion of hedonic psychologists appears to be that people's quality of life reverts to the mean, soon after what appears to be a very good event (winning the lottery) or a very bad event (becoming tetraplegic) (Amundson 2010). This is good news for disabled people, just as it is bad news for gamblers. But we surely cannot draw the wider conclusion that it therefore does not matter if people's lives are full of good things or bad things. Poverty is bad, even if poor people can lead happy lives. Impairment is worth preventing, even if disabled people often lead wonderful lives. Shortly before he died of AIDS-related disease in 1992, actor Anthony Perkins said that HIV had taught him about love, selflessness, and human understanding (Weinraub 1992). I would hope that nobody concluded from this positive spin on a dreadful disease that they should therefore stop researching cures and vaccines for HIV. The proven adaptability and stoicism of the average human being surely cannot lead to the implication that it does not matter what happens to people, because it will all be okay once they have come to terms with it and reverted to their underlying state of happiness.

Much of human progress has been driven by the effort to make life a bit easier, to make disease a little less common, and to enable people to avoid and overcome difficulties. While those individuals who would have been affected may be no more happy than they would otherwise have been, it is plausible to think that people's well-being would be improved if more cases of paraplegia could be prevented, if fewer people developed multiple sclerosis, maybe even if fewer babies were born with achondroplasia. This is the thrust of progressive politics in general, and public health in particular: to reduce the hazards and minimize the struggles human beings have to endure, but always tempered by respect for human rights and values such as informed consent. Creating situations that increase the possibility of a good life, or that offer the opportunity for flourishing, seems to me to be a more plausible aim of government than "life, liberty and the pursuit of happiness."

Is it contradictory to respect people with disabilities and promote their inclusion while trying to prevent the incidence of impairments leading to disability? Evidence is weak. It may be that the latter effort leads to disabled people being regarded as "failures of screening" and they or their parents are blamed for failing to follow public health advice. Despite experimental evidence (Marteau and Drake 1995) and stigmatization of, for example, obese people or others whose lifestyle causes their health problems, in general it seems plausible to conclude that prevention campaigns such as preconception care, immunization, and road safety do not contribute to negative thinking about disability.

Contradictions do arise when methods to reduce disability denigrate people with disabilities. For example, health promotion campaigns or campaigns against drunk driving may utilize the threat of becoming disabled to shock viewers into changing their behavior. In defense of the strategy, one could argue that this merely reflects the widespread public belief that "it is better to be dead than disabled." Young men, who are most likely to be injured, may not fear death and may believe themselves to be invulnerable. But they are likely to think twice at the prospect of being in a wheelchair for the rest of their lives. The QuadPara Association of South Africa, a disabled persons' organization, even runs a road safety campaign with the slogan "Buckle up! We don't want new members." However, the danger is that some of these public health strategies risk reinforcing the idea of disability as a tragedy and disabled people as useless, and thus go against efforts to promote positive attitudes toward disabled people. Great care with imagery and slogans is needed to avoid fueling prejudice.

For those who fear that it is in practice incompatible both to support people with disabilities and to try and reduce the incidence of disability, China is an example of a country that very actively adopts both strategies. Emma Stone (1996) has argued that Western criticisms of eugenic practices overlooked the progress made in supporting people with disabilities. China Disabled People's Federation, founded by the paraplegic son of Deng Xiaoping, is a quasi-governmental organization that promotes employment and participation in society with some success. While not endorsing the lack of informed consent and democracy in Chinese approaches, the example does demonstrate how policies of impairment prevention and disability rights can coexist.

CONCLUSION

In this chapter, I have deliberately not adopted a specific account of the good life. In some part of the argument, I have focused on the happy life, in the sense of people's reports of their own quality of life. This blurs the "hedonist" and "preference satisfaction" approaches to the good life. It is very clear from the empirical evidence that disability usually does not prevent a happy life. Even when difficult things occur to people, they still have resilience and adaptation and can be content. But I think it is also possible to defend the stronger claim, that disability need not always be an obstacle to the good life, defined in terms of "objective goods" (Edwards 2005). However, on average, and even with enlightened social policies and implementation of human rights, I think impairment can make it harder to have a good life, and in some cases impossible.

Because, on balance, disability makes it harder to have a good life, I have argued that measures to reduce the incidence of disability remain desirable and do not have to entail a contradiction (Durkin and Gottlieb 2009). We are compelled to do everything in our power to remove the barriers that prevent people with disabilities having good and happy lives (UN 2006). To the extent that my conclusions echo, for example, Dan Brock (2005), the originality of this chapter may lie less in what I have said and more in that a disability studies scholar has accepted arguments from mainstream bioethics: but therein may also lie its nuance. Balanced accounts of disability are required that avoid either the "disability as tragedy" danger or the other extreme, which is a Pollyanna-ish optimism about the lives of people with disabilities. Disability is rarely "just a difference," nor is it solely and simply a "social construction": it is real and material, and it often limits people's lives and choices. Removing social and physical barriers makes it much easier to live with disability, but disadvantages usually remain.

However, I would like to conclude by making the wider point that life for everyone involves disadvantages. Hamlet, listing reasons why death is to be preferred, highlights "the thousand Natural shocks … That Flesh is heir to."

The human condition, as Hobbes said, is "nasty, brutish and short." To be born is to be vulnerable, to fall prey to disease and pain and suffering, and ultimately to die. Although life chances have greatly improved for most people in Denmark and England since the six-teenth century, one wonders whether Hamlet or Hobbes would revise their opinions were they to return half a millennium later. Moreover, everyone experiences limited choices and restricted talents. The formal equality and freedom that liberal theory celebrates in practice conceals limitations that all, not just disabled people, endure. It is certainly true that there is on average physical and mental restrictions in the lives of many disabled people, but nondisabled people are neither invulner-able nor omnipotent, however much they might wish and think and pretend that they are.

This line of argument has long lineage: Lucretius in classical times, perhaps Sophocles too; Leopardi in the nineteenth century, particu-larly in his late poem "La Ginestra" (Timpanaro 1979); twentieth-century Marxist Sebastiano Timpanaro (1975); and indeed Friedrich Engels himself. Pessimistic materialism is by no means a miserable outlook, merely a realistic one. It achieves a balanced perspective on the frailty and brevity and precariousness of human existence, much as the Stoics did, not taking anything for granted, and not expecting good things to last. It also takes much more seriously the constraints of the natural environment.

The "disability as predicament" approach that I have espoused (Shakespeare 2006) counters the "disability as tragedy" tradition while not fully accepting the relativist "disability as difference" approach from radical disability studies. The point is that disability may make life more difficult – like poverty and teenage pregnancy – but it is in the nature of life to have difficulties. Even the good life contains difficulties. It would be fantastical to imagine a person whose life was free of any hardship. Sometimes, the part of life that is difficult brings other benefits, such as a sense of perspective or true value that people who lead easier lives miss out on. But we can at the same time seek to minimize those difficulties wherever possible.

When Timpanaro writes "'Physical ill' ... cannot be ascribed solely to bad social arrangements; it has its zone of autonomous and invincible reality" (1975: 19), it seems like a rejoinder to the social model approach in disability studies. Rather than the usual disability studies strategies of revalorizing disability, or trying to break the connection between disability and disadvantage, or being relativist about disability, the pessimistic materialist would instead point to the commonalities between disabled and nondisabled people. Disability is not defined by frailty and vulnerability, because life itself is about frailty and vulnerability. It is not necessary, perhaps, to redeem disability, merely to be realistic about ability.

ACKNOWLEDGMENTS

Thanks to Barbara Schmitz and Simo Vehmas for their useful comments on this chapter, to Simon Woods for his continuing wise advice, and to all the participants in the Basel seminar that launched this collection. This chapter was written while the author was a staff member of the World Health Organization. The author alone is responsible for the views expressed in this publication and they do not necessarily represent the decisions or policies of the World Health Organization.

References

Albrecht, G. L., and Devlieger, P. J. The disability paradox: High quality of life against all odds. *Soc Sci Med.* 1999, Apr. 48(8): 977–88.

Amundson, R. Quality of life, disability and hedonic psychology. *Journal for the Study of Social Behaviour* 2010, 40(4): 374–92.

Brock, D. Preventing genetically transmitted disabilities while respecting persons with disabilities, in D. Wasserman, J. Bickenbach and R. Wachbroit (eds.). *Quality of Life and Human Difference: Genetic Testing, Health Care and Disability*. Cambridge: Cambridge University Press, 2005.

Durkin, M. S., and Gottlieb, C. Prevention versus protection: Reconciling global public health and human rights perspectives on childhood disability. *Disability and Health Journal* 2009, 2: 7–8.

Edwards, S. *Disability, Definition, Value & Identity*. Oxford: Radcliffe, 2005.

Harris, J. Is there a coherent social conception of disability? *Journal of Medical Ethics* 2000, 26: 95–100.

Kennedy, P., Smithson, E., McClelland, M., Short, D., Royle, J., and Wilson, C. Life satisfaction, appraisals and functional outcomes in spinal cord-injured people living in the community. *Spinal Cord* 2010, 48: 144–8.

Kreuter, M., Sullivan, M., Dahllöf, A. G., and Siösteen, A. Partner relationships, functioning, mood and global quality of life in persons with spinal cord injury and traumatic brain injury. *Spinal Cord* 1998, Apr. 36(4): 252–61.

Mackenzie, C., and Scully, J. L. Moral imagination, disability and embodiment. *Journal of Applied Philosophy* 2008, 24(4): 335–51.

Marteau, T. M., and Drake, H. Attributions for disability: The influence of genetic screening. *Social Science and Medicine* 1995, 40(8): 1127–32.

Murray, C. J. L. Rethinking DALYs, in C. J. L. Murray and J. D. Lopez (eds.), *The Global Burden of Disease: A Comprehensive Assessment of Mortality and Disability from Diseases, Injuries, and Risk Factors in 1990 and Projected to 2020*. Washington, DC: World Bank, 1996.

Oliver, M. *The Politics of Disablement*. Basingstoke: Macmillan, 1990.

Papakostas, G. I., Petersen, T., Mahal, Y., Mischoulon, D., Nierenberg, A. A., and Fava, M. Quality of life assessments in major depressive disorder: A review of the literature. *Gen Hosp Psychiatry*. 2004, Jan–Feb 26(1): 13–17.

Shakespeare, T. Cultural representation of disabled people: Dustbins for disavowal? *Disability and Society* 1994, 9(3): 283–99.

Disability Rights and Wrongs. London: Routledge, 2006.

Shakespeare, T., Thompson, S., and Wright, M. No laughing matter: Medical and social experiences of restricted growth. *Scandinavian Journal of Disability Research* 2010, 12(1): 19–31.

Stone, E. A law to protect, a law to prevent: Contextualizing disability legislation in China. *Disability and Society* 1996, 11(4): 469–84.

Timpanaro, S. The pessimistic materialism of Giacomo Leopardi. *New Left Review* 1979, 1/116.

On Materialism. London: NLB, 1975.

Weinraub, B. Anthony Perkins's Wife Tells of Two Years of Secrecy, *New York Times*, 16 Sept. 1992.

Wolpert, L. *Malignant Sadness: The Anatomy of Depression*. London: Faber, 2001.

World Health Organization. *International Classification of Functioning, Disability and Health*. Geneva: WHO, 2001.

World Report on Disability. Geneva: WHO, 2011.

5

Recognizing Disability
HALVOR HANISCH

INTRODUCTION: IF IT WEREN'T FOR DISABILITY

Is there something wrong with society or is it just me? While disability scholars, practitioners, policy makers, and activists often disagree on where the emphasis should be put, their common denominator is the view that something *is* bad in the lives of most people with disabilities. Although there are empirical exceptions (such as disability pride), as well as theoretical exceptions (such as a minority paradigm or an affirmation model), this is a common ground. In this chapter, however, the purpose is neither to shed light on disabling processes nor to describe or explain why life with a disability is unnecessarily *bad*. Instead, the emphasis is on *the good life* with a disability.

With regard to the common notion that something *is* wrong, I make two main points: (1) Different understandings of disability *do* in fact provide imaginings of the good life, although the degree of explication varies greatly. (2) What is imagined is often a not-yet-disabled life, primarily postulated as the normal life.

By "understandings of disability," I am referring to four strands of thought: The UK tradition ("the social model of disability"), the U.S. tradition (with its emphasis on culture), the Nordic tradition ("relational model"), and finally the interdisciplinary WHO tradition, as it is expressed in the *International Classification of Functioning, Disability and Health* (ICF). The purpose is not to discuss whether any of these are preferable, as they have different purposes. Instead, the purpose is to demonstrate that certain presuppositions are pervasive by tracing them in all four traditions and then to discuss the implications of these presuppositions.

I first argue that we need to emphasize misrecognition if we are to understand disabling processes. If being taken into account, acknowledged, appreciated, or recognized is crucial to the goodness of life, misrecognition is equally crucial to the badness of life. Second, this chapter explores how recognition is crucial to promotion of the good life with a disability, be it in the form of interpersonal recognition, in the form of rights or policies, or in other forms. These two stages draw upon "arguably the most significant contribution to the theorization of identity and difference in contemporary political theory" (Arneil 2009: 218): Canadian philosopher and social theorist Charles Taylor's "The Politics of Recognition" (1992). Third, this chapter discusses the relation between different forms of recognition – which also is the relation between different ways of promoting the good life with a disability. This discussion draws upon the work of French cultural theorist and psychoanalyst Julia Kristeva.

Drawing on these two thinkers when discussing disability is no risk-free endeavor. Arguably, Taylor's work is "deeply problematic" and even "represents disabled people in a language which is both limiting and depreciating" (Arneil 2009: 219). Similarly, both Kristeva's arguments and her rhetorics have been questioned. It may be that they "reify dichotomies," or even "imply that vulnerability is a totalizing characteristic of the disabled experience," turning "the disabled/non-disabled distinction into an insurmountable barrier" (Grue 2012: 9–12). Nevertheless, I choose to give preference to describing the issues as accurately and in as well-informed a manner as possible. If this means engaging with a politically problematic framework, I trust the reader to emphasize the implications of my arguments rather than those of Taylor or Kristeva.

THEORETICAL CONCEPTUALIZATIONS OF DISABLING PROCESSES: IMPLIED HYPOTHETICAL REASONING

Before we start thinking seriously about disability – not to mention engaging with it personally or politically – it is clear that the concept of disability is rooted in a dichotomy: the disabled are defined in contrast to the nondisabled or the normal. As many scholars have demonstrated (Davis 1995: 23–49; Price and Shildrick 2002), the notion of normality is derived from the term *norm*, and is de facto normative. This normative hierarchy, which in itself often becomes a strain on the lives of people who are in some sense different, also engenders an analytical hierarchy: the lives of the nondisabled are thought to shed light on the lives of people with disabilities, rather than the other way around. This is why the good life, for people with disabilities, is often imagined by way of an asymmetrical *comparison* with a postulated normal life.

This asymmetrical comparison is, however, not disability specific. As Rosemarie Garland-Thomson has shown, the postulated normal subject ("the normate") is embedded in a multitude of such asymmetrical comparisons. For her, this "veiled subject position of the cultural self, the figure outlined by the array of deviant others" is formed not only by excluding people with impairments, but also by excluding people along the axes of gender, ethnicity, sexual orientation, and many others (1997: 8–12).

To understand the implied comparison, it is worth noting that most discourses on disability seem to share what can be referred to as *transitional thinking*: the lives of people with disabilities are not only described in contrast to the normal life, which is given a normative priority over life with a disability. Life with a disability is also described as a reduced or restricted version of a hypothetical life; as if people with disabilities have gone through some kind of negative transition that took away the normal life that one could have had. Lennard Davis describes this in this way:

> When one speaks of disability, one always associates it with a story, places it in a narrative. A person became deaf, became blind, was born blind, became quadriplegic. The disability immediately becomes part of a chronotope, a time-sequenced narrative, embedded in a story. (1995: 3)

This "placing" (which also entails asymmetrical comparison) is not only common in the social discourses scrutinized by disability scholars and activists. It is the main argument of this chapter that even our theoretical perspectives on disability share this three-stage chronotope:

- The lives of people with impairments are *made bad* by certain processes.
- The lives of people with impairments are ways of life that (in one sense or another) followed some kind of *original* or pre-disabled state.
- To the extent that people with impairments lead good lives, the "goodness" of this life can be determined by the convergence between their present lives and the original state(s).

This does not mean that most scholars argue that this pre-disabled state has *actually* existed, or that they argue that a nondisabled state could be achieved. However, they often tend to conceptualize the lives of people with disabilities – regardless if they emphasize its badness or the good life with a disability – *as if* this state was a valid and preferable point of reference.

In the UK tradition, transitional thinking has pervaded since the tradition's foundational phase. In the formative documents, such as the 1975 declaration *Fundamental Principles of Disability* by the activists in Union of the Physically Impaired against Segregation, this becomes quite explicit. Defining disability as "a particular form of social oppression," they juxtapose disability with "participation in the mainstream of social activities" (UPIAS 1976: 20).

However, this kind of reasoning is equally potent in today's less politicized climate, as in, say, Carol Thomas's work. In *Female Forms* (1999), she attempts to give a "social-relational" definition of disability to escape the shortcomings of the earlier social model. Restricting her interest to disabling processes, rather than presenting an ontology of disability, she changed the definiendum from "disability" to "disablism" in her 2007 book *Sociologies of Disability*. Within both of those scopes, disability studies remains widely reliant on her definiens:

> Disability is a form of social oppression involving the social imposition of restrictions of activity on people with impairments and the socially engendered undermining of their psycho-emotional well-being. (1999: 60, 2007: 73)

Translated into verbal nouns – *oppression, imposition*, and *undermining* – the temporal structures here presuppose some kind of state where disabled people were *not oppressed*. This does not mean, of course, that Thomas makes a factual claim about such a state. Instead, life with a disability (good or not) is imagined as a downfall from an a priori and undescribed state. Since life with a disability is contrasted with a non-disabled or normal life, the reader has no choice but to imagine the undescribed state as normal.

The Nordic tradition is often said to emphasize "interactivity between impairment and disabling modes of socio-economic organisation," rather than oppressive structures as such (Goodley 2010: 16). According to Dan Goodley, the Nordic relational model approaches the study of disability with three main assumptions: "(1) disability is a person/environment mis/match; (2) disability is situational or contextual; and (3) disability is relative" (2010: 16). At first sight, this tradition seems to conceptualize disabling processes in terms of (in) compatibility, rather than transitive thinking. In a grammatical sense, for instance, Nordic scholars tend to avoid verbal nouns derived from transitive verbs, such as *oppression* or *exclusion*, preferring *interaction* or *mismatch*. The latter is of particular importance.

The metaphor of *mismatch* implies a certain chronology. In the *Oxford Dictionary of English*, the noun *mismatch* is exemplified by an example from commerce. Furthermore, the noun *match* is exemplified by relations such as sports competitions, combining clothes or other material objects, war, or marriage. It is worth noting that all those relations deal with parties, be they competitors, enemies of war, or spouses, that *preexist* the relation. This would have been of less interest were it not for the analytical purpose that these metaphors serve, namely to investigate the social and contingent nature of disabling processes. In so doing, Nordic scholars often share the tendency to imagine disabling processes as transitions, which could either have not taken place (if past social developments had been different) or can be remedied or reversed (by social change, including policy reforms).

In the U.S. tradition, transitional thinking takes a much more historical direction. In his groundbreaking *Enforcing Normalcy*, Lennard Davis states:

> The social process of disabling arrives with industrialization and with the set of practices and discourses that are linked to eighteenth- and nineteenth-century notions of nationality, race, gender, criminality, sexual orientation, and so on. (1995: 24)

In this diachronic analysis, Davis claims that disabling processes were absent (not yet *arrived*) before specific changes in those social structures. This highlights how Davis's very influential work – which has also been decisive in increasing the dialogue between European and American research communities – roots the badness of life with a disability in historical changes or transitions.

How, then, does the work of Davis and others imagine the good life with a disability? The antithesis of disabling processes is circumstances in which people with disabilities were considered in some sense ordinary:

> If we rethink our assumption about the universality of the concept of the norm, what we arrive at is the concept that preceded it: that of the "ideal." ... The central point here is that in a culture with an ideal form of the body, all members of the population are below the ideal. (Davis 1995: 25)

However, it is important to acknowledge that the antithesis serves the critical interest in disability studies, rather than a descriptive interest in the good life and disability. He repeatedly emphasizes that people with impairments have always been different, and led more or less different lives. Hence, it seems, Judith Butler's critical interpretation of historiographical implications in "classical feminism" is just as applicable to disability studies.

> On occasion feminist theory has been drawn to the thought of an origin, a time before what some would call "patriarchy" that would provide an imaginary perspective from which to establish the contingency of the history of women's oppression. (1990: 45)

While Davis does not claim that people with disabilities should lead average lives in the literal sense, and nor did the second-wave feminists, he nevertheless fails to provide any other conceptualization of the *good* in the good life with a disability.

This is also the case in the ICF, where the outcome of disabling processes is defined as "participation restrictions":

> Participation restrictions are problems that an individual may experience in involvement in life situations. The presence of a participation restriction is determined by comparing an individual's participation to that which is expected of an individual without disability in that culture or society. (2001: 229)

This concept belongs to the core of the ICF. It replaced the term *handicap*, which was the most crucial disability-related term in the 1980

International Classification of Impairments, Disabilities and Handicaps,
which the ICF replaced in 2001 (ICF: 229, n. 25). There, *handicap* is
defined as:

> A disadvantage for a given individual, resulting from an impairment
> or a disability, that limits or prevents *the fulfilment of a role that is*
> *normal* (depending on age, sex, and social and cultural factors) for
> that individual. (my emphasis)

In the *Oxford English Dictionary*, *fulfillment* is defined as "the achievement of something desired, promised, or predicted." On one hand, this
demonstrates the purposes and strengths of the ICF: the classification
of disability aims to empower people with disabilities, and promotes
the good life with a disability rather than describing its shortcomings.
On the other, there is little if any room for the *goods* or qualities in life
that are important for people with disabilities but not equally important for nondisabled people.

By and large, we have seen that asymmetrical comparison – often
carried out by way of transitional thinking – is crucial to all four traditions. However, the pervasiveness of this thinking is not only a matter
of theoretical perspectives, it is also a matter of policies and practices.
According to Henri-Jacques Stiker, this "mode of designation" is not
only constitutive of understandings of disability, it is also constitutive
of practices and policies of rehabilitation:

> Phrases such as *la réadaption des handicapés*, "the rehabilitation
> of the disabled" [are] applied to congenital cases as well as to the
> adventitious. It implies returning to a point, to a prior situation, the
> situation that exists for the able but are only postulated for the oth-
> ers.... The lack is removed (words with negative prefixes in *in/im*
> are erased) and reference is back to the assumed prior, normal state.
> (1999: 122)

It is important to acknowledge that this argument is persuasive
for at least two good reasons. First, the social contingency of disability is hard to conceptualize – not to say address personally or

politically – without some kind of screen or canvas. To find a voice for these experiences, it is necessary (or at least very useful) to compare present experiences to *what could have been*. Furthermore, we must acknowledge that this comparing has facilitated improvements. Policies for inclusion in the labor market and measures to improve access, for instance, are measures to let people with disabilities *do what the others do, and go where the others go*, respectively. Similarly, there is little doubt that this way of thinking can point to important possibilities on a personal level. Nevertheless, we need to clarify what it means that we tend to define the good life with a disability with reference to a *hypothetical* life.

MISRECOGNITION AND RECOGNITION

In the UK tradition of disability theory, it is worth noting that the foundational UPIAS definition of disability grounds disabling processes in "a contemporary social organisation *which takes no or little account* of people who have physical impairments" (my emphasis). Furthermore, influential American scholars, such as Sharon L. Snyder and David Mitchell, ground disabling processes in "the rejection of people with disabilities" (Snyder and Mitchell 2001: 380).

The striving for recognition has been a common theme for activists, academics, artists, and individuals in the field of disability over the past decades. Not coincidentally, this corresponds historically to the positioning of recognition as a key issue in contemporary political theory. This positioning is perhaps best known from the work of Nancy Fraser, Axel Honneth, and Charles Taylor. Interestingly, they all argue that recognition is both fundamental and fundamentally diverse. Fraser, on one hand, has developed "a two-dimensional conception of justice that can accommodate both defensible claims for social equality and defensible claims for the recognition of difference" (2003: 9). Honneth, on the other, emphasizes that a critical theory – including a theoretical conceptualization of recognition – has to "be compatible with a diversity of reasonable visions for the good life" (2003: 223).

Fraser and Honneth both emphasize the public level. Taylor, on the other hand, combines these concerns with a strong emphasis on identity and valuing in dialogical relations. Given the theme of his book – the good life – his perspective is preferred for discussing both personal and political aspects of life. For Taylor, it is always important to combine these two "planes" in analysis and theoretical work:

> The importance of recognition is now universally acknowledged in one form or another; on an intimate plane, we are all aware of how identity can be formed or malformed through the course of our contact with significant others. On the social plane, we have a continuing politics of equal recognition. (1991: 49)

For Taylor, it is crucial to modernity that recognition is no longer distributed through "predefined" hierarchies (such as, for instance, nobility or slavery). As recognition and identity are increasingly fluid and "remain dialogical throughout our lives" (Taylor 1995: 231), the chances that recognition can lead to substantial social changes increase. In a society marked by "disembedding" and "reembedding" – to use Anthony Giddens's terms – much more is *at stake* in ongoing striving for recognition (1991: 10–34). Understanding recognition is not only necessary to understand *the good life* in the context of disability. We also need an understanding of recognition if we wish to analyze how the good life with a disability can be promoted further.

The background of Taylor's paper is quite simple: the politics of equal recognition no longer calls exclusively for universal recognition, but also for recognition of the uniqueness of groups or persons. Hence, late modernity has complemented the politics of equal dignity with a "politics of difference":

> With the politics of equal dignity, what is established is meant to be universally the same, an identical basket of rights and immunities; with the politics of difference, what we are asked to recognize is the

unique identity of this individual or group, their distinctness from everyone else. (Taylor 1995: 233)

With regard to the *policy* level in "the politics of equal dignity," Taylor emphasizes that "the content of this politics has been the equalization of rights and entitlements" (1995: 233). He exemplifies this equalization by groundbreaking social changes that hugely inform the field of disability rights, namely women's rights and the U.S. civil rights movement in the 1960s (1995: 251–2). With regard to the *policy* level in "the politics of difference," he often discusses issues of aboriginal populations and linguistic minorities (1995: 242–4).

Although some see these two forms of politics as a strong dichotomy, Taylor himself does not. He repeatedly insists that they provide "entries" for one another, because they often dovetail in policy. Furthermore, he also traces their intertwined roots in the history of philosophy. However, this commonality does not mean that Taylor sees these two forms of recognition as fully compatible:

> These two modes of politics, then, both based on the notion of equal respect, come into conflict. For one, the principle of equal respect requires that we treat people in a difference-blind fashion. The fundamental intuition that humans command this respect focuses on what is the same in all. For the other, we have to recognize and even foster particularity. The reproach the first makes to the second is just that it violates the principle of nondiscrimination. The reproach the second makes to the first is that it negates identity by forcing people into a homogeneous mold that is untrue to them. (1995: 236)

This "negation of identity" also constitutes social structures that are adapted to nondisabled people exclusively. This point – that universalist recognition may entail misrecognition – is as crucial to Taylor as it is to disabled people and disability scholars: "the supposedly fair and difference-blind society is not only inhuman (because suppressing identities) but also, in a subtle and unconscious way, itself highly discriminatory" (Taylor 1995: 237). The dichotomy between politics of universal dignity and politics of difference is not a matter of choosing one or the other, but it is rather a tension in all cultural and political phenomena that minority positions bring to the fore.

MISRECOGNITION: THE BADNESS OF LIFE WITH A DISABILITY

For people with impairments, social life is (*ceteris paribus*) a situation marked by misrecognition. This insight is explicated, for instance, in Carol Thomas's now widespread notions of "barriers to being" and "psycho-emotional disablism" (1999, 2007). This emphasis on emotional or existential "being," which is often harmed or turned inauthentic in social situations, is equally crucial to Taylor's analyses of identity and misrecognition:

> [O]ur identity is partly shaped by recognition or its absence, often by the misrecognition of others, so a person or group of people can suffer real damage, real distortion, if the people or society around them mirror back to them a conflicting or demeaning or contemptible picture of themselves. Nonrecognition or misrecognition can inflict harm; can be a form of oppression, imprisoning someone in a false, distorted and reduced mode of being. (1995: 226)

The importance of misrecognition (for badness of life) also points the way toward the good life. On many levels, the good life with a disability relies on a trajectory from misrecognition to recognition. To illustrate this trajectory with *Einfühlung*, I have chosen to make some emblematic reconstructions of the intrapersonal voice(s) that belong to different "modes of being":

Others can't look beyond my disability. It is obvious, but too crucial to be left unmentioned, that many disabling processes, not only in social interactions, but from intimate self-perception among people with disability to policy making, is rooted in prejudice. *Prejudice* should not be taken in the hermeneutical sense, where prejudice is both necessary and productive, but in the sense of wrongful presuppositions about the abilities and opportunities of others. Furthermore, these presuppositions are not only *inaccurate perceptions*, but wrongdoings that affect the fundamental (or, in psychological terms, *global*) self-perception of people with disabilities. Hence, this voicing is deeply intertwined with another painful voicing: *I am of less worth than many of my peers.*

This latter voicing is the mark of a particular misrecognition; people with disabilities are often disallowed their universal dignity. In the case of people with disabilities, this means that they are deprived of an equal position; not only before the law, but also in everyday interactions, in encounters with socio-material barriers, and in many other ways. This misrecognition is not only a misrecognition of the lives led by people with disabilities, even the potentials of these life situations are (mis) recognized as inferior. Misrecognition also implies, in Taylor's words, a disallowing of "a potentiality that is properly [one's] own" (1995: 229). Difference, be it different bodies, different modes of cognition, or different lives, is linked to inferiority rather than potentiality. Hence, it is no surprise that experience of this disallowing can be voiced as *I wish my life would be like the lives of others.*

This potentiality is not only a matter of *doing*, but also (not least according to Taylor) a matter of *being* and *voicing*. The voicing *I wish my life would be like the lives of others* is not only an experience of social barriers or a result of disallowing. It is also – arguably – a consent to a message often entailed in misrecognition of people with disabilities. The experiences of people with disabilities are often disallowed, a disallowing that de facto accuses them of *mauvaise fois: even though you say you are satisfied with your life, you should admit that you wish it were like ours.*

The latter voicing is not necessarily a form of misrecognition. To the extent that life with disability is *made different* from the lives of others – for instance, by reduced social participation because of disabling barriers – the wish for a normal life can be interpreted as an insight into those barriers. Nevertheless, the wish can be ambiguous;

it can be a consent to the social misrecognition of life with a disability. Nondisabled people are by no means the only ones to misrecognize people with disabilities and their lives. *I wish my life would be like the lives of others* can be misrecognition of life with a disability, be it one's own life or the lives of others with disabilities.

FROM MISRECOGNITION TO RECOGNITION OF UNIVERSAL DIGNITY

If the bad life is marked by social nonrecognition, then the good life is marked by social recognition. On the most fundamental level, the experience of prejudice (*others can't look beyond my disability*) is intertwined with a desire for recognition in a particular and literal sense. When encountering prejudice, which positions them as something *unknown*, most people with disabilities have wished for their prejudiced peers to recognize them as something *well known* and fairly normal.

This wish is often fulfilled, and is in fact a major factor in facilitating *the good life* for people with disabilities. This is important if we want to understand the good lives that people with disabilities *actually* lead: people with disabilities are – in a greater number of situations than one tends to assume – included as parts of a larger *we*. Recognition of universal dignity therefore often takes the form of recognizing persons or groups as "one of us."

Recognition of universal dignity is also crucial on a more intimate level. For many people with disabilities, the universalist recognition paves the way from *I am of less worth than many of my peers* to *I am just as valuable as my peers*. Not least of all, it paves the way for powerful policies that promote the good life for people with disabilities. There is little doubt that many policies, such as prohibiting labor market discrimination or taking steps toward inclusive education, *have* facilitated the good life for people with disabilities. It is also quite clear that these policies are (among other things) a way to implement recognition of universal dignity. Finally, it is also worth noting that even those reforms that do not lead to universal rights are often underpinned by universalist arguments. To a large extent, then, recognition of universal dignity engenders processes from *I wish my life would be like the lives of others* toward *my life is like the lives of others*.

By implication, given that the measure of the good life is the resemblance it bears to the hypothetical normal life, the *actual* life with a disability may be defined as a negative version of the ordinary normal life. If disability is considered a negative element in life (which it *should*, at least if we take most disabled people's own experiences into account), and the good life is not in some way connected with the disability specifically, then life with disability remains a *saddening exception*. The meaning of *my life is like the lives of others* can, de facto, be explicated as *my life is like the lives of others, with the exception of factor X*.

This voicing bears the mark of a very ambiguous form of recognition. On one hand, autonomy and potential is clearly recognized; it can criticize or deconstruct prejudice. On the other, it is not clear if one really recognizes "a potentiality that is *properly* [one's] own" (Taylor 1995: 229, my emphasis). Arguably, these forms of recognition of people with disabilities recognize a *hypothetical I* in a person with a disability, rather than really giving recognition to him or her.

This troubled recognition also frequently sets the stage for a race without any sign of a finish line, not least on the cultural and personal levels. As to cultural contexts, the hugely popular television show *Beyond Boundaries* (first produced by the BBC in 2002, and since then produced and televised in many countries) is emblematic. In this show, a number of persons with different impairments embark on an expedition through the wilderness. Footage from the expedition is cross-cut with interviews with the participants about social exclusion and psycho-emotional issues. Hence, the conquering of a mountain range, a river, and so on is positioned as conquering the badness of life with a disability in contemporary society. The BBC states that:

> Despite their disabilities they are determined to overcome any hurdles and prove something to themselves and the world. And all of them know the expedition will be a rite of passage experience, something that will change their lives forever.

In this quote, a certain "passage" (from the bad life to the good life) is outlined toward doing what others do (*"despite* their disabilities") by overcoming social and internalized prejudice (*"prove* something to themselves and the world"). As the *doing* in this case is closely linked to physical performance, strength, endurance, and so on, some would argue that overcoming impairment is given too much emphasis, regarding it as "tragedy to be triumphed over," and possibly even "reduc[ing] social issues to individual challenges" (Cameron 2010: 183–7). *Beyond Boundaries* indicates an important motif that pervades such diverse fields as public discourses, rehabilitation processes, and the labor market: the emphasis on personal *effort*.

On a personal level, the emphasis on effort is justified and fully understandable. Life with a disability *is* (regardless of all discussions about the socio-medical intertwinings) often demanding. Disability is seldom a lucky break, and the good life does not come for free in a situation marked by both impairment and disabling processes. However, the notion that personal effort (*proving something to the world*) can overcome misrecognition can pose a problematic personal demand that itself can engender misrecognition. This demand can be voiced as follows: *my life is like the lives of others, with the exception of factor X, which I need to minimize as much as possible.*

However, it is not self-evident that this problem – that implicit references to normal lives and universal notions of subjectivity may imply misrecognition of different lives or people with disabilities – is rooted in recognition of universal dignity. It might also be that humanism (including our societies' broader notions of recognition and universal dignity) "can find a chance to revitalize itself in the battle for the dignity of the disabled by constructing what is still sorely lacking: respect for a vulnerability that cannot be shared" (Kristeva 2012: 30). Nevertheless, this renewal does not take place without further ado. Even disability theories – which explicitly aim to interpret and counter misrecognition of people who are in some sense different – have trouble really recognizing the *good* in life with a disability.

FROM RECOGNITION OF UNIVERSAL DIGNITY TO RECOGNITION OF DIFFERENCE

To understand the importance of recognition in the context of disability, it can be viewed as a transformation in how life with disabilities is defined. By and large, the misrecognition of people with disabilities rests on the traditional tragic view of disability. This view implies a certain genus and differentia definition of life with a disability: *life with a disability is a tragic life, determined and destined by impairment.* First, this definition set people with disabilities apart from the normal majority: while it is mostly an open question if it will lead to a good or a bad life, the badness of life with a disability is taken for granted. Second, people with disabilities are separated from other tragic figures (such as the poor) by a specific differentia, namely impairment.

The first operation, whereby people with disability are located in a separate genus of the unhappy and unworthy, can be reversed by recognition of universal dignity. This form of recognition dissolves the separate genus and includes people with disabilities in the genus of the worthy. Nevertheless, the former differentia – impairment – remains a strictly negative element, and for very good reasons. However, there is a risk that this differentia ends up largely carrying the same negative meaning as the former genus: life with a disability would have been a normal life, if it hadn't been for the specific and utterly negative effects of impairment and disability.

Recognition of universal dignity is crucial to people with disabilities. Nevertheless, the implicit reference to a normal *hypothetical life* remains more problematic. More precisely, disability remains *(ceteris paribus)* a reason for misrecognition. If the definition of life with a disability is to describe (and, thereby, promote) the *good* life, this definition is insufficient. If the differentia is to carry other meanings than the negative meaning of the previous genus, the definition needs to encompass any *disability-specific* elements in the good life. Hence, it is necessary to have two differentiae:

> Life with a disability would have been a normal life, but is set apart by the negative effects of impairment and disability, as well as the specific resources and opportunities available in this situation. The second differentia accentuates disability-specific experiences and frames them within an experience of *the good life*, in at least four ways.

(1) First, it can accentuate *freedom*. On one hand, misrecognition often leads to exclusion from the social mainstream. On the other, Taylor repeatedly conceptualizes the wish for recognition as a striving for recognition of one's authenticity. In Taylor's perspective, this means that one actually seeks recognition for one's "*individualized* identity, one that is particular to me and I discover in myself." Hence, individual particularities *(ceteris paribus)* could perhaps engender recognition of authenticity by disembedding them from social boundaries. Just as disability can be a barrier to social participation, disability might also lead to individual freedom with regard to roles or identities (Hanisch 2011). This experience can be voiced – and appreciated – as following: *my life is different from the lives of the others; I am free from iron cages that frame so many of the others.*

(2) The good life with a disability can accentuate identity and community. Empirical research on disability and identity, for instance, suggests that this specific social situation (life with a disability) can lead to specific experiences that can be appreciated (Gabel and Peters 2004;

Hahn 2004; Swain and French 2000). Those experiences can engender the good life, giving rise to an affirmation model of disability:

> It is essentially a non-tragic view of disability and impairment which encompasses positive social identities, both individual and collective, for disabled people grounded in the benefits of life style and life experience of being impaired and disabled. (Swain and French 2000: 569)

There is little doubt that many people with disabilities value the specifics of these life experiences, and that many feel some kind of belonging to a "disability community." Although disability identity used to have negative points of departure (be it experiences of impairment or experiences of social marginalization), it is increasingly important. In particular, this kind of identity politics can point beyond the striving for a hypothetical life: *being a person with a disability, I lead a life marked by a specific and valuable community.*

(3) The good life with a disability can accentuate interdependency and love as qualities of a good life. Tom Shakespeare, among others, emphasizes that:

> dependency or at best interdependency is normal for human beings. The good life depends on caring solidarity, in which families, neighbours, and local services are able to care for each other and provide necessary support to those who need help and those who help them. (Shakespeare 2007: 52–3)

It is also frequently argued, especially by parents of disabled children, that living with a child with disabilities can bring on very valuable and meaningful experiences. Eva Feder Kittay, for instance, describes this as a true gift:

> I have received from my daughter Sesha a knowledge of, as Alasdair MacIntyre puts it, "the virtues of acknowledged dependency" and of the extraordinary possibilities inherent in relationships of care toward one who reciprocates, but not in the same

coin; one who cannot be independent, but makes a gift of her joy and her love.[1]

Although this recognition is mostly given to people with multiple and severe impairments, such as Kittay's daughter, the relevance goes wider: just as people with disabilities can be misrecognized with reference to their (inter)dependency, they can also be recognized with reference to the increased connectedness that increased interdependency can engender. On a personal plane, such recognition can be voiced as follows: *my life is not like the lives of the others, and marked by exclusion, but it is also marked by interdependence and love.*

(4) Impairment-related experiences can lead to insights beyond disability issues. If one accepts that impairment, disability, and vulnerability are aspects of *la condition humaine*, this suggests not only that people with disabilities should be recognized in universal terms. It might also suggest that people with disabilities – and perhaps even those who share their lives with people with disabilities – are less alienated from this aspect of *la condition humaine*. And, because alienation is key to modern notions of unhappiness, one could quite simply argue that they lead better lives. On an intrapersonal level, this way of reasoning can be explicated as follows: *my life is not like the lives of others, but it has given me a certain wisdom.*

The movement at stake in this chapter – from misrecognition to recognition of universal dignity to recognition of difference – is analytical, but often also deeply personal. This must not be taken as an argument for some kind of hierarchy. It is important to underline that the recognition of difference is not *more* emancipated, *more* empowering, or better than the recognition of universal dignity. To the contrary, they are often intertwined. Furthermore, the recognition of difference is perhaps more important to disability studies (and to disability policy) than in people's everyday lives. However, recognition of difference

---

[1] Eva Feder Kittay, "The Ethics of Care, Dependence, and Disability," *Ratio Juris*, 24(1): 49–58.

(or at least the possibility of it) is necessary to let the recognition of universal dignity reach its full potential.

RIGHTS AND RECOGNITION

To understand how to promote the social recognition of disabled people – and thereby, the good life with a disability – it is impossible to avoid the issue of *rights*. Being the chief implementation of recognition, disability rights are also crucial to its promotion. On a global scale, the chief source of human rights is the UN *Convention on the Rights of Persons with Disabilities* (UN 2006). Interestingly, the CRPD both raises and relies on notions of recognition. The overarching elements of the CRPD, such as the Preamble and the General Principles (Article 3), repeatedly underscore that countries "are to recognize" certain rights or "respect ... inherent dignity." Hence, two questions arise: (1) Which image(s) of the good life is at stake in the CRPD? and (2) What kinds of recognition are explicated (or implied) in the Convention?

It is obvious that the CRPD, like other UN conventions, seeks to promote the good life. Article 9 (on accessibility) states its purpose as following:

> To enable persons with disabilities to live independently and participate fully in all aspects of life, States Parties shall take appropriate measures to ensure to persons with disabilities access, on an equal basis with others, to the physical environment, to transportation, to information and communications, including information and communications technologies and systems, and to other facilities and services open or provided to the public, both in urban and in rural areas.

The good life imagined here seems largely the same as the image implied in the ICF: although the CRPD is an instrument for social and political change – while the ICF is not – these two instruments share the reference to a certain imaginary person. It is hard to distinguish the imagined subject doing "that which is expected of an individual without disability in that culture or society" (ICF) from a member of "the public" (CRPD).

Not surprisingly, given the importance of this "general" or pseudo-universal image, the CRPD seems to rely on recognition of universal dignity. With regard to Article 12, for instance, the guiding principle is defined as "equal recognition before the law." This emphasis is not only justifiable, but necessary. On a global level, recognition of universal dignity is by far the most important goal. If the recognition of equal dignity is scarce or even lacking – as it is in many countries across the world – appreciating recognition of difference is either secondary or hardly possible. Similarly, the strongholds of the politics of difference – such as academic disability studies, crip theory, or disability arts – depend on the recognition of universal dignity, which to some extent characterizes the situation in Europe and North America.

However, the notion of recognition in the CRPD is not restricted to recognition of universal dignity. To the contrary, the CRPD explicitly entails politics of difference, as well as the recognition of potential. The general principles of the Convention, like other documents that deal with disability rights and policy, integrate these notions of recognition (Article 3):

a. Respect of inherent dignity, individual autonomy including the freedom to make one's own choices, and independence of persons;
d. Respect for difference and acceptance for persons with disability as part of human diversity and humanity.

While general principle (a) relies on recognition of universal dignity, general principle (d) relies on recognition of difference. The CRPD demonstrates that the combining of the politics of universal dignity and the politics of difference is not only analytically important, but also politically powerful.

CONCLUSION: FORMS OF RECOGNITION, CONFLICTS, AND INTERTWININGS

Throughout this chapter, I have argued that disabling processes are signs of misrecognition, and that the good life with a disability therefore should be understood (and promoted) in terms of recognition. Recognition of life with a disability – as *a good life* – seems to depend on two forms of recognition. First, it depends on recognition of universal dignity, where disability is recognized as compatible with a good life. Second, it depends on recognition of difference, which recognizes the good in living a more or less *different life*.

However, these two forms of recognition may enter into conflict. This becomes clear if we, for instance, look at the increased prevalence of user-led service provision (cash for care) in many developed countries. In these policies, the entitlements to services (or at least the level or amount of such services) are individually defined. While non-disabled citizen X is not entitled to services, severely impaired citizen Y and less severely impaired citizen Z are entitled to different levels of service. This turn in policy lends sensitivity to the service provision, improving the quality of life for people with disabilities (both in itself and in optimizing services as promotion of the good life).

On the other hand, there is also a risk that this acknowledgment of difference in the designing of services could cloud the issue of insufficient *levels* of service provision. Without an easily understandable (and applicable) standard, it can become difficult to determine if the recognition is insufficient. If the lives of people with impairments differ from others by way of a characteristic marginalized position in society, it is not clear that recognition of difference always promotes *the good life*.

This is more than a policy matter. If the respect and acceptance of difference (as in general principle d) is not bridled, it can become a disguise for *lacking* "respect for inherent dignity" (general principle

135

a). And, conversely, an unbridled politics of universal dignity may overlook inherent dignity in favor of the dignity invested in normality.

Taylor sees the relations between the two forms as reproaches, *as if* in a political debate. However, the arguments presented in this chapter suggest that either one of the two politics remains impotent – even without *reproaches* – if they are not brought in connection with one another. Furthermore, the *personal* importance of recognition also suggests that it touches fundamental notions of subjectivity and politics, which cannot be properly understood if they are interpreted *as if* belonging to a debate on disability policies.

To conclude with these issues, it is useful to turn to Kristeva's work on disability, which largely draws on her work as chair of the Conseil National d'Handicap (the French national council for people with disabilities). According to Kristeva, recognition of people with disabilities should destabilize and change, not only expand, how we think politically. Hence, she has tried to rework the Enlightenment dictum (*liberté, equalité, fraternité*) into *liberty, equality, fraternity ... and vulnerability.*

Kristeva's crucial point, which this chapter draws upon, is quite simple: the recognition of people with disabilities must apply to difference (including interdependency and vulnerability), but must also place people with disabilities at the origin of the political consciousness. It is (according to Kristeva) important to stress that a *fraternité* of rational and normal agents is insufficient to recognize *anyone*, and that recognition of difference is necessary to renew humanism and modern democracies. Kristeva also underlines that the relation to vulnerability is decisive to the good life for everyone, not only for those who are particularly vulnerable:

> I am convinced that humanism – which has always been in search of itself, from its emergence in the past to its crises or revitalizations today and in times to come – can find a chance to revitalize itself in the battle for the dignity of the disabled by constructing what is still sorely lacking: respect for a vulnerability that cannot be shared. (2012: 30)

The term *humanism* can perhaps seem to suggest pity and empathy rather than fundamental recognition. However, this is not the case. Humanism is, at least for Kristeva, the fundamental ethos that characterizes the good life, not least through many forms of sharing. Rather, her point is that the general processes of sharing and solidarity is at their most utopian – that is, in their most intimate and radical form – in the context of disability. Therefore, she continues:

> My ambition, my utopia, consists of believing that this vulnerability reflected in the disabled person forms us deeply, or, if you prefer, unconsciously, and that as a result, it can be *shared*. (2012: 30)

According to Kristeva, recognizing disability as difference (an "incomparable exclusion," "a vulnerability that cannot be shared") is crucial to recognizing a universal element of human life (vulnerability).

Unlike activists and scholars searching exclusively for recognition of universal dignity, she insists that this sharing cannot be reached by *looking beyond* disability. She argues instead that recognition of difference can lead to processes of recognition that reach beyond the particular difference at stake. Her work also suggests that the two politics – of universal dignity and of difference, respectively – are perhaps not only complementary and equally necessary, but also inseparable if we wish to understand disability – and, not least, the good life with a disability – as dangerous, necessary, and interdependent.

References

Arneil, B. (2009). Disability, Self Image and Modern Political Theory. *Political Theory*, 37(2): 218–42.

Butler, J. (1990). *Gender Trouble: Feminism and the Subversion of Identity*. London: Routledge.

Cameron, C. (2010). *Does Anybody Like Being Disabled? A Critical Exploration of Impairment, Identity, Media and Everyday Experience in a Disabling Society*. PhD Thesis, Queen Margaret University.

Davis, L. J. (1995). *Enforcing Normalcy: Disability, Deafness and the Body*. London: Verso.

Fraser, N. and Honneth, A. (2003). *Redistribution or Recognition? A Political-Philosophical Exchange*. London: Verso.

Garland-Thomson, R. (1997). *Extraordinary Bodies: Figuring Physical Disability in American Culture and Literature*. New York: Columbia University Press.

Giddens, A. (1991). *Modernity and Self-Identity: Self and Society in the Late Modern Age*. London: Polity.

Goodley, D. (2010). *Disability Studies: An Interdisciplinary Introduction*. London: Sage.

Grue, J. (2012). Rhetorics of Difference: Julia Kristeva and Disability. *Scandinavian Journal of Disability Research*, iFirst artice, http://dx.doi.org/10.1080/150174 19.2012.660705.

Hanisch, H. (2011). Disabled Adolescence – Spaces, Places and Plans for the Future. *Alter*, 5(2): 93–103.

Kristeva, J. (2012). *Hatred and Forgiveness*. New York: Columbia University Press.

Mitchell, D. L. and Snyder, S. L. (2001). Re-Engaging the Body: Disability Studies and the Resistance to Embodiment. *Public Culture*, 13(3): 367–90.

Price, J. and Shildrick, M. (2002). Bodies together: Touch, ethics and disability. In *Disability/Postmodernity: Embodying Disability Theory*, M. Corker and Tom Shakespeare (eds.). London: Continuum.

Shakespeare, T. (2007). Disability, normality and difference. In *Psychological Challenges in Obstetrics and Gynecology: The Clinical Management*, J. Cockburn and M. Pawson (eds.). London: Springer.

Stiker, H.-J. (1999). *A History of Disability*. Ann Arbor: Michigan University Press.

Swain, J. and French, S. (2000). Towards an Affirmation Model of Disability. *Disability & Society*, 15(4): 569–82.

Taylor, C. (1991). *The Ethics of Authenticity*. Cambridge, MA: Harvard University Press.

Taylor, C. (1995) *Philosophical Arguments*. Cambridge, MA: Harvard University Press.

Thomas, C. (1999). *Female Forms: Experiencing and Understanding Disability*. Buckingham: Open University Press.

Thomas, C. (2007). *Sociologies of Disability and Illness: Contested Ideas in Disability Studies and Medical Sociology*. Basingstoke: Palgrave McMillan.

United Nations. (2006) *Convention on the Rights of Persons with Disabilities*. Geneva: United Nations.

UPIAS [Union of the Physically Impaired against Segregation] (1976). *Fundamental principles of disability*. Retrieved July 2012 from http://www.leeds.ac.uk/disability-studies/archiveuk/UPIAS/fundamental%20principles.pdf.

6

Understanding the Relationship between Disability and Well-Being

DAVID WASSERMAN AND ADRIENNE ASCH

INTRODUCTION

The relationship between disability and well-being is important both theoretically and practically. How philosophers, social scientists, and policy makers understand this relationship matters for the theories of welfare and flourishing we construct, the judgments we make about our lives on a regular basis, and the social and health policies we adopt.

Disability scholars have argued persuasively that it is not tragic or catastrophic to have a disability, even a major disability like quadriplegia or multiple sensory impairments (Asch 2003; Silvers, Wasserman, and Mahowald 1998). But is it disadvantageous or undesirable? What does it mean to claim that it is, and what implications does that claim have for the prevention and correction of disability? What sorts of evidence are relevant to assessing that claim, and is that claim more likely to be valid for some disabilities than others? These are among the questions we address in this chapter – questions on which scholars have written relatively little, and on which there may be considerable disagreement, even within the disability community.

Clearly, the relationship of disability to well-being depends on how disability and well-being are understood. If, for example, *disability* were defined as a property that reduces well-being, their relationship would be obvious and uninteresting. Guy Kahane and Julian Savulescu, who define *disability* in these terms,[1] recognize that their definition "prejudges the normative issue of the relationship of disability to well-being, making it tautological" (2009: 42). They argue, however, that their definition "shifts the normative question to where the action really is, the question of well-being" (42). Once we develop a satisfactory account of well-being, the question of what properties reduce it in what circumstances becomes a manageable empirical inquiry.

Without denying the value of this approach, we think "the action really is" in other places as well, and that in those places, an approach that defines disability in terms of well-being will not be very useful. An individual is deciding whether to undertake expensive and risky surgery to restore a function lost in an accident; a couple is deciding whether to continue a pregnancy with a fetus diagnosed with a genetically based health condition; a legislature is deciding how much money to allocate to competing injury prevention programs. In each case, the decision cannot await consensus, philosophical or popular, on an account of well-being. The legislature should recognize a plurality of reasonable accounts; the individual and couple may not have given the issue much systematic thought, even if they have strong beliefs or assumptions about what makes their lives go well. These decision makers initially encounter disability as a biological phenomenon – a sudden or gradual loss of functioning; a genetic condition with various health effects; a range of vehicular, recreational, household, and workplace injuries. Their concern is with the effect of disability, encountered this way, on lives they care about or are charged with protecting: their own, their future children's, or their constituents'.

To address the questions that confront these decision makers, we define *disability* for our present purposes in a narrow medicalized sense as an impairment, injury, or disease that involves or results in the absence, loss, or reduction of normal or species-typical function.

---

[1] As "a stable physical or psychological property of subject S that leads to a reduction in S's level of well-being in circumstances C" (2009: 25).

Although characterizing a function as normal or species typical may itself be a normative claim, this definition has no other normative content. It takes disability as it is usually encountered and understood in practical contexts, and leaves open its relationship to well-being.

In addressing the impact of disability, thus understood, on well-being, one thing is clear: over the past fifty years, the relationship between impairment, injury, disease, and various aspects of well-being – pleasure, satisfaction, participation, and achievement – has come to appear far more complex than it once did. Several factors may have contributed to this changed perception; we mention three. First, probably most familiar to readers of this volume, disability scholars and advocates have argued that many or most of the disadvantages associated with injury and impairment are attributable to mutable features of the environment: to structures built only for the healthy and normal, and to social attitudes and practices that exclude or marginalize the unhealthy and abnormal (Amundson 1992; Bickenbach 1993; Silvers et al. 1998; Wasserman 2001). Second, whole disciplines have emerged – hedonic psychology and happiness science – that find that normal functioning and health (as well as wealth and professional success) have far less effect on (self-reported) well-being than commonly assumed (Kahneman, Diener, and Schwarz 1999). Third, philosophical criticism of accounts of well-being based on single features – pleasure, desire satisfaction, or achievement – have lent support to a commonsense, if theoretically unsatisfying, pluralism best accommodated by objective list accounts (Crisp 2008; Griffin 1986, 1993). Well-being is many things, including but not limited to the candidates proposed by monistic accounts.

In part because of these developments, it is now widely recognized that disabilities need not have a substantial adverse impact on well-being, on any plausible account. The claim that people with severe disabilities can live highly satisfying and accomplished lives was once seen as a *reductio ad absurdum* of a theory of well-being (Sen 1980). Now, it is often regarded as a test of a theory's ability to accommodate diversity in human flourishing. Yet the relationship to well-being of variations in embodiment and functioning remains a matter of considerable uncertainty and debate. We do not want to foreclose these questions by adopting a definition of disability like Kahane and Savulescu's (2009) – one that stipulates rather than examines its relationship to well-being.

We begin by reviewing the standard contemporary accounts of well-being and exploring how those accounts accommodate disability. We observe the divergence between first- and third-person assessments of the adverse impact of disability on all these accounts, and suggest reasons for this. We then argue that despite appearances, subjective accounts based on pleasure or satisfaction are not necessarily better at recognizing the possibilities for doing well with a disability than objective or pluralistic accounts based on activity and achievement.

We then consider the apparent tension between the claim that lives with most disabilities can go as well as lives without them and the widely held view that it is desirable to prevent, correct, or mitigate disabilities, and generally undesirable to acquire one. These claims can be partially reconciled with three distinctions: (1) between the loss and the absence of a sensory, motor, or psychological function; (2) between disabilities as static conditions involving absent or limited function, and diseases as processes involving pain, functional decline and loss, or reduced life expectancy; (3) between the direct physical or psychological limitations imposed by a disability and the social and environmental exclusion to which an individual with those limitations is subject. Although loss, disease, and exclusion are associated with disability, that association is highly contingent, and much of the adverse impact on well-being claimed to arise from disability is attributable to those conditions.

Yet many would claim that even when these associated conditions are factored out, disabilities remain at least marginally disadvantageous; that all else being equal, lives go better without than with them, even if they involve no loss of prior function, no discomfort or pain, no disruption, no increase in health care needs or decrease in life expectancy, and no stigmatization. At the same time, others would claim that disabilities need not reduce well-being even if these conditions are *not* factored out. They argue that lives can go as well with disabilities as without them even if some of these conditions are present, as they typically are. Without denying that these conditions can be regarded as harmful, they would argue that they need not reduce the overall well-being of the individual who experiences or undergoes them. The final part of the chapter examines these two divergent, but not contradictory, responses.

In this chapter, we limit ourselves to physical disabilities, because the relationship between well-being and intellectual and psychiatric disabilities arguably raises distinct issues, such as the meaning and measurement of intelligence and the scientific basis of psychiatric classifications. These issues warrant more attention than we can give them here.

THEORIES OF WELL-BEING

Philosophers who debate questions about what makes a life go well generally recognize three distinct types of accounts. T. M. Scanlon distinguishes "experiential theories ... which hold that the quality of a life for the person who lives it is determined completely by ... its experiential quality"; "desire theories ... which hold that the quality of a person's life is a matter of the extent to which that person's desires are satisfied"; and "substantive-good theories ... which hold that there are standards for assessing the quality of a life that are not entirely dependent on the desires of the person whose life it is" (1998: 109ff.). The first two types of accounts are subjective, in that they define well-being as relative to the individual's experiences or desires, whereas the last theory is objective, assuming a substantive view about what makes life go well that may conflict with the judgment of the individual himself or herself.

Each of these various theories can take different forms, and philosophers find problems with formulations of each. Experiential or hedonist theories are bedeviled by the famous counterexample proposed by Robert Nozick, the "experience machine" (1974: 42–3). Suppose an individual can be hooked up to a machine that stimulates his brain to think and feel that he is "writing a great novel, or making a friend, or reading an interesting book." He has the experience of doing these things without really doing or having to do them. Would we say his life is going well, even if, as the example has it, he has no way to detect the simulation? Nozick takes it that most people would say no. Desire or preference theories confront the problem that individuals may have desires that they have no reason to have or, worse, desires that there are reasons for them not to have. Their desires may be based on misinformation or ignorance or bad logic, in which case they might not contribute to well-being. This has led some philosophers to propose a qualified version of the theory, a so-called informed desire account of well-being. On this view, well-being is constituted by the satisfaction of desires that one would have if one were fully informed, that is, about their genesis and consequences (e.g., Parfit 1984; Scanlon 1998). There are problems with this too, however. Some informed desires, such as the desire that astronomers find evidence of past life on Mars, may be too tangentially related to the course of our lives to contribute to our well-being when satisfied. And then, as Scanlon points out, we may wonder what role the notion of desire is really playing here. Suppose among my informed desires is to go to college: that is, this is what I would want if I fully appreciated what going to college would do for my life. But then isn't it what college would do for my life, not the fulfillment of my informed desire to go to college, that contributes to my well-being?

It is hard to resist the conclusion that one's well-being must depend to some extent on whether one's life contains objectively good activities, relationships, or achievements. Derek Parfit has coined the term "objective list theories" to refer to accounts that assess well-being in terms of such goods (1984: 493ff). Some of the more contentious questions about the relationship between disability and individual well-being concern what objective goods are indispensable for a good life and at what level of generality they should be described. Although that term may suggest a simple checklist, it is better seen as recognizing (i) that there is an irreducible plurality in the goods of life and (ii) that their contribution to well-being cannot be expressed in terms of a common metric, like utility. Martha Nussbaum, an influential objective list theorist, includes the following among her valuable capabilities and functionings: health, nourishment, shelter, sex, mobility; the ability to use one's senses and to imagine, think, and reason; family and other relationships, attachments, and love; living a life one has thought about and in some way chosen; laughter, play, and living in contact with the natural world (1998: 135–56). It is difficult to see what unifies all these different categories, but item by item there would probably be widespread agreement on their value.

Yet the significance of such agreement in establishing the centrality of these categories for well-being remains unclear. As Jerome Segal (1998) points out, most of us would agree that a life can go very well even without one or more of the capabilities Nussbaum regards as essential. The most successful lives of people lacking a single capability may go as well as the most successful lives of people with a standard complement of sensory and motor functions. Although a life could hardly go well without at least some of these capacities, we have no clear basis for establishing a minimum set.

Moreover, any plausible objective list theory must recognize that different people in different social and personal circumstances vary considerably in the weights they attach to these valuable items. It must also recognize that individual well-being is not an additive phenomenon but a holistic or organic one. That is, one should not be described as doing well in the requisite sense simply because one possesses valuable good

A *and* valuable good B *and* valuable good C, and so forth. Rather, what should be assessed is well-being as a feature of a whole life, and for this it is necessary to consider how the goods are combined and what sort of overall balancing of different goods the individual achieves. Thomas Hurka has argued that "when we think seriously about lives, the compelling ideal is surely of well-roundedness" (1987: 727–46). Similar views are found in the writings of philosophers who claim that an ideal life consists of some sort of harmonious achievement of different goods, an idea that hearkens back to Plato's *Republic*. What "well-roundedness" or "harmonious" or "balanced" achievement means, whether it is truly necessary for well-being, and how it is achieved are questions that require considerable philosophical elucidation.[2]

Even if it is necessary to introduce substantive goods or normative ideals into an account of individual well-being, it is not only the possession of such goods, or the achievement of such ideals, that makes a life go well. Also relevant is how a life seems to the person living it, and this reintroduces subjective elements. Common sense supports the view that individual well-being must have a subjective as well as an objective aspect; "two strands," as Jonathan Glover puts it (2006: chapter 3). Roughly speaking, well-being consists partly in having certain substantive goods and partly in being happy with (or being content with, or enjoying, or taking pleasure in) one's life. But these strands may not be readily separable: the subjective valuation of objective goods may

---

[2] A hybrid balance theory of well-being, according to which well-being is a holistic, not an additive, notion, and having a balance of substantive goods and being happy or satisfied with one's life are both necessary for well-being, would provide another promising way of thinking about the relationship between disability and well-being. Because questions about what constitutes a decent and rewarding *balance of goods* are distinct from questions about what constitutes an *optimal realization of each good*, considered individually, this sort of view may not have the same negative implications for persons with disabilities as other objectivist accounts, because a disabled person might fail to optimize a particular good but still achieve a rewarding balance of the remaining goods. To the best of our knowledge, however, such a hybrid account has yet to be developed.

be necessary for the possession of those goods to count toward well-being, or for their absence to count against it.

HOW DOES DISABILITY FARE ON DIFFERENT
ACCOUNTS OF WELL-BEING?

These rival accounts of well-being clearly have different implications for the bearing of disability on individual well-being. If, as hedonic experiential theories hold, well-being is a matter of having positive experiences, greater or lesser well-being will be a function of the degree of pleasure that a person with a disability enjoys in his or her life. On these theories, the self-reports of persons with disabilities carry considerable weight in assessments of well-being. With the exception of impairments defined in terms of pain, sadness, or frustration, people with impairments can have as much pleasure, happiness, or satisfaction as people without them, and research on subjective well-being suggests that they often do (e.g., Albrecht and Devlieger 1999). Indeed, some philosophers regard this as a reason for rejecting subjective accounts – they see the "happy cripple" as a *reductio ad absurdum* of hedonic accounts (see Crocker 1995; Sen 1980). Desire theories assess the well-being of persons with disabilities in terms of how having an impairment affects their capacity to satisfy their (informed) preferences. Self-reports will also have a great deal of authority on desire accounts, because individuals may be in the best position to know their own desires – if not always about their satisfaction. Self-reports will have the most limited and contingent relevance on objective accounts, because individuals will not always be in the best position to know how well they are doing in various physical, social, and professional domains. Self-reports will merely be evidentiary, even if they are often the best evidence.

The treatment of adaptation highlights some of the differences among rival accounts of well-being. Adaptation is the process whereby newly disabled people may change their habits, patterns of acting, and goals to accommodate their disabilities. It involves several distinct processes: developing new skills, changing comparison classes and goals, and habituating to pleasant or unpleasant experiences (Menzel et al. 2002). Although the first of these processes – the acquisition of new skills – might reflect a change in objective well-being, the latter two would not (unless feelings of satisfaction and pleasure are included on the objective list). But adopting more modest goals and habituating to unpleasant experiences might improve well-being under a hedonic account by making the individual feel more satisfied or more euphoric. Only on an objective account of well-being might goal downsizing and mere habituation not contribute to well-being.

Some disability scholars have been drawn to subjective metrics out of a concern that more objective conceptions of well-being place it beyond the reach of people with disabilities. We argue later in this chapter that this concern is exaggerated. First, however, it is worth observing that subjective accounts may offer only thin and dubious support for the claim that people with most disabilities are not handicapped in the pursuit of happiness. Many nondisabled philosophers and laypeople are inclined to doubt the veracity of high ratings of life satisfaction from people with disabilities – the so-called disability paradox. Some suspect that those ratings are deliberately overstated to take account of their expected discounting by nondisabled people. Others regard them less as self-reports than as directives against pity or sympathy. Even when they are accepted as sincere self-reports, they are seen as distorted by adaptation or response shift; by habituation to aversive experiences or a shift to more modest objectives or comparison classes (McClimans et al. 2013; Menzel et al. 2002; Murray 1996). They are not regarded as having much to tell nondisabled people about the prospects for living well with absent, lost, or reduced functions.

Moreover, the life satisfaction reported by people with disabilities does not appear to be based primarily on the experience of simple pleasures or the satisfaction of modest desires. It is instructive to observe that when people with disabilities seek to inform their nondisabled family, friends, or readers about how they are doing, they do not simply invoke their feelings of euphoria or satisfaction, if they mention them at all. Rather, they describe what they do with their lives. The extent to which the disability paradox can be explained without recourse to a subjective account of well-being is suggested by Connie Panzarino's self-description:

> At 42 years of age I am mostly paralyzed; have full feeling; I cannot swallow food unless it has been pureed in a blender, use a BiPAP for respiratory problems; use a puff 'n' sip wheelchair; take medication for my heart, stomach and body pain; and must be repositioned by my PCAs every 20 minutes. I also run my private psychotherapy/ art therapy practice; own my own home and van; serve on several boards; maintain my sexual relationship with my lesbian lover; pet my cat with my chin; take my blender out to dinner with friends (and blend lobster, or whatever I like); travel; show the artwork I make by mouth or computer; write; read; plant a garden, and on and on. I have made a choice to live as fully as I can. (1990: 7)

In this passage, there is no reliance on feelings of pleasure or satisfaction, no claim that those feelings are impervious to the biomedical realities of Panzarino's life. Rather, Panzarino provides a detailed description of activities and achievements coexisting with those realities. Panzarino's description of her life suggests that she should be regarded as having a high level of well-being because she is *doing* well, not, or not only, because she is *feeling* well, happy, or satisfied.

DISABILITIES AND OBJECTIVE LISTS

In understanding how severe disability may be compatible with high levels of well-being, understood in objective terms, it is helpful to distinguish intrinsic from instrumental value. An activity may be valued for itself, for example, seeing as a rich sensory experience; or instrumentally, for what it achieves or contributes to, for example, seeing as a means of finding an object. As intuitive as the distinction seems, it can be difficult to make clearly: first, there is deep disagreement about what is of ultimate value; second, it is possible to parse many activities and conditions indefinitely into instrumentally valued means and intrinsically valued ends, for example, making money or meeting friends can be seen as ends in themselves, or as a means to obtaining comfort and security.

The social model of disability encourages the parsing of activities in this manner, as Asch contends (2003, 327):

> Those who maintain that disability forecloses opportunity, and that any foreclosed opportunity diminishes life, focus too narrowly on the activity and do not see it as a means to an end, e.g., … walking instead of mobilizing or exploring; talking instead of communicating.

As Asch suggests, much of what we value in seeing, talking, and walking is instrumental; we value them as ways of achieving communication with other people, reading, and moving from place to place – activities we regard as valuable in themselves. (Of course, we also recognize that these activities have instrumental value as well, for example, for finding social partners and business opportunities.) None of these intrinsically valuable activities is precluded by deafness, blindness, or paraplegia; each can be achieved in alternative ways, by signing, reading Braille, or operating a wheelchair. This suggests that the instrumental value of species-typical functioning is greatly exaggerated, because its ends can frequently be achieved in multiple ways, many of which are available to people with fewer, impaired, or atypical functions.

Disability scholars do not deny that typical sensory and motor functions can have great intrinsic as well as instrumental value, but they argue that their intrinsic value is often understood too narrowly. If, for example, we see the intrinsic value in sight not specifically in visual experience, but in sensory and aesthetic experience, then that value is not precluded by blindness.

There is no point in claiming that such a broad characterization is appropriate for all purposes – clearly, it is reasonable to say that someone who cannot see or hear lacks experiences of great intrinsic value that are available to someone who can see or hear. It is in assessing the role of intrinsic value in how well our lives go that a broad characterization seems most appropriate. One obvious source of intrinsic value for standard sensory functions and activities, for example, is aesthetic – their beauty, richness, and complexity. But we do not regard color blindness, tone deafness, and impairments of smell or taste as inimical to well-being, although they preclude vast ranges of rich aesthetic experience. We generally assume that someone who has never had, or has long lost, those sensory functions (as opposed, say, to an artist or food critic who relies on them for her vocation) can lead a life as aesthetically rich and rewarding as that of someone who has those functions, despite lacking admittedly valuable experiences. This suggests that we cannot infer from the fact that there is great value in a function that those who lack it have lives that go significantly less well. It is only plausible to claim that a good life needs to contain certain kinds of valuable experiences and activities if those kinds of experience and activity are characterized very broadly.

One influential framework for understanding the role of valuable activities and experiences in well-being is Martha Nussbaum's capabilities approach, which attempts to delineate the distinct capacities essential for human flourishing. Over the past two decades, Nussbaum has modified her individuation of capabilities to recognize the high levels of flourishing achieved by many people with disabilities. Her capabilities have become more general, in part because the more broadly they are framed, the less they are precluded by specific impairments. Thus, Nussbaum has gone from making the ability "to use the five senses" a condition of human flourishing (1990: 225) – which would deny that blind or deaf people can flourish (see Crocker 1995) – to reconceptualizing the capability as "being able to use the senses, to imagine, to think, to reason" (2006), which she sees as encompassing experience from any combination of sensory modalities. This broader formulation makes human flourishing available to people who are blind or deaf.

THE "PARADOX" AND THE ASYMMETRY

It should be clear that there is no paradox in the life satisfaction people with disabilities report, or in the disparity between their evaluations of their own lives and the evaluations made by nondisabled people. Most plausible accounts of well-being can explain why life can, and often does, go as well for most people with most disabilities as for people without disabilities. There are unresolved issues about how broadly the categories of well-being can be framed without becoming so broad as to lose distinct content. But these questions may be less about disability than about objective list theories generally; about what Roger Crisp (2008) calls the enumerative and explanatory dimensions of a theory of well-being. What are the intrinsic goods for us, and how are they identified? Why do they enjoy this status?

A less examined concern, more specific to disability, is the apparent asymmetry between disability and characteristics like race and sex. The latter two characteristics are widely believed to be neutral with respect to well-being, once social exclusion is factored out. Disability has been included with these characteristics in antidiscrimination law; its inclusion is a tenet of the minority group model (Wasserman et al. 2011). But it has also been grouped with those characteristics by writers who argue, more ambitiously, that disability, like race or sex, is a neutral characteristic – one that, in the absence of social exclusion, does not make lives go any worse on average (Barnes 2009; McBryde-Johnson 2003) These writers do not deny that *becoming* disabled may make life go worse, at least for some time, but no more so than other wrenching changes, like losing a job, home, or loved one. In the former case as well as the latter, the bad or harm is in the transition – in the loss and disruption – not in the end state.

Yet these writers rarely confront a stubborn asymmetry in the case of disability that appears to distinguish it from race and sex and to challenge its neutrality: we generally seek to prevent individuals who are not disabled from becoming disabled, but not vice versa. We generally oppose measures to promote disability but support measures to prevent disability, if prevention can be accomplished without coercion, harmful side effects, or the loss or disruption of personal or narrative identity. Consider a form of prevention widely seen as unproblematic: taking folic acid during pregnancy to prevent spina bifida. Some governments mandate that certain food be enriched with folic acid. These mandates are controversial, but the controversy concerns the issues of involuntary medication and possible side effects rather than the intended preventative effect. Few, if any, disability advocates object to these mandates, any more than they object to the myriad safety measures imposed by the modern state, from requiring seat belts to restricting teratogenic drugs. Many object to the needlessly grim depiction of disability in some safety campaigns; few to the campaigns themselves (Emens 2012).

No such asymmetry exists for other allegedly neutral characteristics: there would be strong opposition to government measures to prevent them, alter them, or reduce their incidence. Imagine that a dietary supplement as safe as folic acid could alter the sex of the fetus or lighten its complexion. We suspect that most people would find it troublesome for pregnant women to take that drug voluntarily, let alone for the government to put it in the food supply. Or imagine a fluoride-like substance with a similar effect that could be safely added to the water supply. Fluoridation for female sex or dark skin would strike most people as offensive, even though it would not prevent the existence of anyone on the basis of a disfavored characteristic. The claim that women or people of color lead worse lives on average because of pervasive discrimination would be seen as at best an excuse, not a justification, for changing sex or race. Undertaken by an individual, it would be seen as complicit with sexism or racism regardless of its motivation; undertaken by the state, it would be seen as an egregious expression of racism or sexism. We doubt that fluoridation for disability would provoke similar objections.

Similarly, many societies now accept and subsidize sex-change operations for individuals who experience a mismatch between their gender identity and their biological sex. There is, as far as we know, no difference in the willingness of those societies to support sex change in one direction to sex change in the other (except differences based on cost or technical feasibility). In contrast, most qualified surgeons are willing to implant limbs for individuals who lack the standard complement, whereas very few are willing to remove limbs from individuals who regard the standard complement as excessive and encumbering.

In general, measures to alter other significant characteristics or conditions, including sex, race, ethnicity, and nationality would be considered objectionable or in need of special justification (e.g., to restore population balance or promote economic development), whereas measures to prevent disabilities are considered presumptively acceptable. We should note, however, that the contrast may not always be so sharp. For example, even societies willing to subsidize sex-change operations often view them with reservations, at least to the extent of imposing counseling and other requirements they do not impose on other types of elective surgery. But these requirements are imposed regardless of the direction of the sex change.

The contrast between sex and race, on one hand, and disability on the other, is especially striking in light of the fact that measures to alter stigmatized social identities are often regarded as more objectionable than measures to alter dominant social identities; for example, compare skin lightening to skin darkening. Just the reverse is true for disability. Giving deaf children cochlear implants is somewhat controversial; deafening hearing children would be considered criminal abuse. And this would be so even if the child were too young to have the self-conscious experience of hearing, had no other effects from being deafened, and faced no discrimination on the basis of deafness. Our aim is not to defend these contrasts, but merely to note how sharp and firm they appear to be. The question is whether the asymmetry with respect to disability prevention is compatible with the view that disabilities are neutral characteristics; that they do not make life go worse overall.

We have argued elsewhere that such "static impairments" as deafness, blindness, and paraplegia can be seen, in this respect, as akin to illiteracy: worth preventing although not intrinsically bad or harmful (Asch and Wasserman 2010). Parents who fail to prevent illiteracy, like parents who fail to prevent disability, are regarded as negligent, even by those who acknowledge that people could flourish without formal education or specific skills like reading and writing. There are striking parallels: first, the absent resources or capacities are clearly valuable. Like sight and hearing, literacy is a good thing to have. Indeed, it is often touted as opening up new worlds inaccessible to the unlettered. Second, despite the great value of literacy, lives can go as well without it as with it. There is little reason to doubt that the best lives of our illiterate forebears went just as well, or incommensurably well, on any plausible account of well-being, as the best lives of our literate contemporaries. It may be that our ancestors only fared as well as they did because illiteracy was so widespread. But their flourishing is enough to belie the claim that that condition is intrinsically bad. Third, as this population effect suggests, much of the bad or harm associated with illiteracy arises from demographic and social circumstances. To be illiterate in a literate society is to be excluded from many valuable social activities that do, but need not, require literacy, and to be shunned or pitied by many of the majority possessing that good.[3]

---

[3] Dan Moller argues that the comparison of disability to poverty and illiteracy actually favors disability, at least in the case of minor disabilities involving limited but not absent sensory and motor functions. He contends that the goods precluded by poverty and illiteracy are central or essential to well-being, understood in objective terms, whereas the goods precluded by minor disabilities are not. "A life of vast unrealized

Thus, on a reasonably pluralistic view of well-being, one can live as good a life illiterate as literate in many decent, hospitable environments. Yet we see literacy as a good and strongly support literacy campaigns and mandatory schooling. Are disability prevention policies based on the demands of specific environments that make disability, like illiteracy, locally harmful? Or are there more general reasons for both kinds of prevention policies?

On a maximalist view, life is presumptively better with more valuable capacities. It is simply better to have more senses, more intelligence, and a greater range of motion, even if they do not make one happier, have no practical value, and do not advance one's specific projects. This view regards standard disabilities as merely among the most salient limitations to which humanity is subject. Less is always worse, although how much worse depends on contingent circumstances. Most philosophers and disability scholars reject maximalism, in part because they balk at the implication that we should strive to acquire, and bear children who will possess, the greatest possible capacities.

Jeff McMahan offers a non-maximalist argument against neutrality, based on a view of how people with single disabilities flourish despite those disabilities:

> A single disability may seem neutral because it can be compensated for by other abilities that develop to fulfill its functions. Blindness,

potential lived amid ignorance and illusion is less successful than the reverse, even when happiness is held constant, but is the same true of a life (or many years) lived without running, walking, or playing basketball, or enjoying attendant goods like seeing the views from remote mountain trails?" (2011: 198). The goods absent in the latter case, unlike the former, "are just members of a broader class" (199), of which many others are available. But such "satisficing," as Moller describes it, may not be possible in the case of more comprehensive disabilities: "perhaps we really should say of someone unable to experience music (for some significant period, whether a whole life or many years, that their life went worse for them whether they realized it or not" (199). Even if this were so, however, it appears that Moller would still regard deafness as no more inimical to well-being than illiteracy.

for example, may be compensated for by the enhancement of other senses, particularly hearing. But if disabilities were individually entirely neutral, they ought also to be neutral in combination; but they are not. (2005a: 96)

McMahan argues that disabilities cannot be neutral in combination, because it is impossible to believe that a person who lacked *all* significant abilities could live as well as most people who had all or most of them. He takes this as self-evident, though some disability scholars would contend that the lives of people lacking many or most sensory and motor abilities can go as well as the lives of most people possessing those abilities. Our focus, however, is on McMahan's claim that neutrality for individual disabilities implies neutrality in combination. He supports this claim by arguing that the effects of disabilities on well-being "are largely additive," because with each additional disability, it becomes harder to compensate for other disabilities. This argument assumes that the possibility of living as well without as with any given ability depends on the possibility of compensating for its absence. We think this assumption is mistaken: the possibility of flourishing with a single disability depends less on compensation than on what we could call "saturation." As suggested earlier, a blind person can live as well as a sighted one not because she develops better hearing – she may not – but just because the senses and abilities she has are more than adequate to allow her to live as fully and richly as possible.

There may be a limited number of ways to realize important human goods like rich aesthetic experience, and those with disabilities may have fewer ways to do so. But the ways they have may be as good as the ways they lack, and employing the ones they have should not be seen as compensating for their inability to employ the ones they lack. Having more ways to realize a good does not mean that you can realize it more fully.

This response, however, suggests two final reasons for the asymmetry, both of which involve what we might call "welfare security." Even if people with a single major disability can live as well as people without one, 1) it requires more effort or luck for them to do so, and 2) they are at greater risk of lacking any means to do so. The first claim is that the fewer means there are to achieve a particular good like rich aesthetic experience, the more difficult it may be to achieve it. An individual who can meet his aesthetic quota, so to speak, with sunsets or symphonies, doesn't have to work as hard or need as aesthetically rich an environment as one who can meet his quota only with symphonies. The second claim is that people with single disabilities are at greater risk than people without them of lacking a means to achieve a specific good. This claim does not rely on the disputed assumption that people with disabilities are at greater risk of injury; it merely holds that the adverse consequences of injury, in terms of expected well-being, are greater for people with disabilities than without them. The plausibility of these claims depends on a myriad of unresolved issues: Is there an irreducible plurality of objective goods and if so, how they are individuated? Is there a limited number of means for attaining those goods? If it requires greater effort to attain a particular good with fewer functions, does that additional effort itself enhance or reduce well-being? We cannot address, let alone resolve, these issues here; we can only suggest that their resolution is difficult and uncertain.

A final argument for the presumptive undesirability of disabilities is suggested by the human variation model (Scotch and Shriner 1997), which treats a disability not as a discrete category, but as a range along a continuum of physical and mental difference. Although it is not intrinsically disadvantageous to be near the end of such a continuum, it may be disadvantageous in a society in which only a small proportion of people fall near that end. This is because many of the physical structures and social practices of that society will inevitably be designed for its average members. No matter how just a society, how committed to inclusion, there would still be some disadvantage in being toward the end of the spectrum. There may be some truth to this claim, but it is easy to exaggerate. Universal design advocates argue that it is, or will become, feasible to build structures and practices that fully or equally accommodate individuals across the ranges of human variation. Even if their claims are also overstated, they suggest a need for caution in concluding that minority status is intrinsically disadvantageous.

The arguments we have just considered question whether disabilities can be regarded as neutral even if pain, loss, disruption, and shorter life are factored out. We conclude by reviewing arguments that disabilities can be neutral, in the sense of not reducing overall well-being, even if those conditions are *not* excluded. We examine two grounds for claiming that disabilities, including painful, disruptive, and stigmatized ones, need not reduce overall well-being, although they may still be conditions worth preventing: (1) there is physiological or psychological compensation for living with a disability; and (2) there is a nonadditive relationship between parts or aspects of a life and life as a whole.

Elizabeth Barnes (2009) argues that that having a disability can make an individual's life more difficult and challenging at some points without making it go worse overall, or even making it more probable that it will. The challenges posed by disability are like those posed by other minority characteristics such as homosexuality; facing those challenges can give a life greater depth or direction. For example, some individuals who are disabled in adolescence or adulthood find that their previously shallow or aimless lives gained focus and purpose from the challenges they faced, and some individuals find that they acquired new skills or interests more rewarding than those precluded by their impairments. Because such enriching positive responses are so common, there is no basis for concluding that people with disabilities have lower quality of lives overall. But because disabilities "are, in general, the kinds of things that make life harder – they impose limitations, they cause pain, they subject their bearers to stigmas and discrimination" (339) – they can be regarded as harms and should be prevented in some circusmtances. They should not, however, be regarded as "negative difference-makers" – conditions that make lives worse in general and overall.

In blocking the inference from disability as a harm to disability as a negative difference-maker, Barnes adduces instances of the positive consequences that disabilities have had for specific individuals, despite, or sometimes because of the "local" hardships they cause. It may be, however, that no positive consequences are needed to "neutralize" the hardships associated with a disability. Those hardships may simply get absorbed in the immense complex of factors that make a life go better or worse. It is only on a simple additive or monotonic view of the relationship of parts to whole that a local harm would necessarily make a life go worse unless compensated for. It is difficult to be more precise about the impact of disability on whole lives, however, because it is not clear how the goodness or badness of parts of a life contribute to the goodness of the whole, on either objective or subjective accounts of well-being (Feldman, 2008).

It may also be, however, that no positive consequences are needed to neutralize the hardships associated with a disability. Those hardships may simply get absorbed in the immense complex of factors that make a life go better or worse. It is only on a simple additive or monotonic view of the relationship of parts to whole that a local harm would necessarily make a life go worse unless compensated for. It is difficult to be more precise about the impact of disability on whole lives, however, because it is not clear how the goodness or badness of parts of a life contribute to the goodness of the whole, on either objective or subjective accounts of well-being (Feldman 2008).

Another factor associated with disability – reduced lifespan – arguably has an adverse impact on well-being. Many disabilities, or their associated disease processes, result in lower than average life expectancy. On a simple additive or monotonic model, any life with a positive balance would be better if it was longer, and better the longer it was, as long as it continued to have a favorable balance. But the literature on life extension suggests that indefinite life extension should be regarded as a mixed blessing (Temkin 2008; Williams 1973; contra Overall 2008).

Still, there is a widely held belief that it is good to live out a "normal life span" a span that has not gotten much above "three score and seventy years" despite substantial increases in average life expectancy. Although some of the reasons why this life span seems natural reflect biological constraints, most appear to be socially constructed in an obvious sense. Within the biological limits set by male and female fertility, the stages of our lives are structured and ordered by society on the basis of an average life span. Even in a society with more flexible life stages, a life that lasted only half the average life span might reasonably be regarded as worse, or likely to be worse, than one of average length. To die at twenty-five rather than seventy-five is to miss out not only on fifty years, but on many types of valuable activity that are biologically or socially inaccessible to twenty- or thirty-year-olds: for example, raising children to adulthood, spoiling grandchildren, holding a range of public and private offices. A life can certainly go well without any of these individual activities, but the impact on well-being of a shorter life span is clearly qualitative as well as quantitative. Still, we lack a sufficiently clear understanding of well-being to conclude that, for example, the best thirty-year life could not go as well as the best eighty-year life. Perhaps death not need be imminent to concentrate one's mind and focus one's efforts on the realization of accessible goods.

THE IMPACT OF DISABILITY ON WELL-BEING: WHY DOES IT MATTER?

Several philosophers (e.g., Griffin 1993, 1986) have suggested that different conceptions of well-being are appropriate in different contexts; it may be appropriate to adopt a more comprehensive, value-laden conception in assessing how one's own life is going, or would go, than in allocating resources based on relative disadvantage. Scanlon has gone further, contending that well-being is not the "master value" some philosophers assume it to be, primarily but not exclusively consequentialists. He argues that from the first-person point of view – the things that contribute to well-being are obviously important, but the concept of well-being plays very little role in explaining why they are important (1998: 142); it is simply an inclusive concept encompassing many or most of the person's specific aims and concerns. From third-person points of view, some but not all aspects of well-being matter. A parent or guardian will be concerned about specific ways that things go well or badly for his charges, whereas a political society or cooperative scheme may be obliged to promote, or to equalize, some but not all aspects of well-being.

Well-being will not only be understood differently from different perspectives, but will have differing relevance for different roles. For example, the extent to which the hardships associated with a given disability are due to stigmatization and exclusion will have different relevance for prospective parents than for policy makers. A prospective parent may want to have children with reasonable prospects for a good life and may wonder if the stigmatization and exclusion of children with disabilities will dramatically reduce those prospects. She may well lack the means to change her environment or to move to a better one. For her, then, the social construction of disability may well have limited relevance. If she believes that a child with a major disability will experience sustained persecution and isolation, and she doubts that she can protect him from the impact of such treatment, the fact that these environmental features are in fact mutable may matter very little. She faces much the same predicament as a prospective parent deciding whether to have a girl, or a third girl, in a society that devalues and oppresses women. For the policy maker, in contrast, the source of the disadvantage may be highly relevant. It is her job to mitigate toxic social environments by systematic reform. She must regard the disabling features of her society as mutable – much the way she would have to regard its pervasive sexism.

At the same time, policy makers may have legitimate interests in cost saving that help justify disability prevention regardless of the impact of disabilities on those living with them. For example, the executive summary of the quasi-governmental Institute of Medicine report on Disability in America: Toward a National Agenda for Prevention states on its first page that "annual disability-related costs to the nation total more than $170 billion." This cost appears to be a legitimate consideration for policy makers dealing with record deficits.

Some of this cost, however, reflects an unjust lack of accommodation in the physical and social environment – a point the report's authors should endorse because they adopt a social model of disability. Moreover, even social model adherents may underestimate the extent to which the actual and estimated costs of disability reflect a lack of imagination. Universal design advocates maintain that it need be no more costly to create environments that enable all people to flourish than to maintain the status quo. Until policy makers take this claim seriously and give it the fair hearing it has yet to receive, estimates of the cost of disability must be taken with a grain of salt. It is not necessary to resolve this issue, however, to see that much of the support for preventive measures rests on assumptions about the social cost of disabilities rather than about their intrinsic disvalue.

CONCLUSION

We have not attempted to definitely answer the questions we raised at the outset, about whether disabilities are intrinsically disadvantageous or undesirable, and what it would mean to say they were. What we have done is to (1) argue that the impact of disability on well-being is complex and contingent on any plausible account of well-being; (2) considered the implications of treating disabilities as neutral characteristics, like race and sex, that are not intrinsically disadvantageous. We have examined the difficulty of explaining why disabilities should be prevented, once we have factored out pain, loss, disruption, and reduced life expectancy, as well as exclusionary social attitudes and practices. We examined two arguments for the residual disadvantage of disability. The first concerned what we called "welfare security" – that the well-being of people with major disabilities is more precarious than that of people without them. The second argument concerned the disadvantages of being in a statistical minority with respect to significant physical or mental attributes, even in a just society. These arguments may have some plausibility, but both rest on debatable empirical and normative assumptions.

It may well be that we have factored out too much. We have good reason to expect that many disabilities will be accompanied by pain, loss, disruption, or reduced life expectancy and met with exclusionary attitudes and practices. It is reasonable to treat these adversities as presumptive harms, despite the positive consequences that often result from facing them, and the doubtful value of entirely eliminating them from our lives. We should work to disassociate disabilities from both sets of harms by civil rights enforcement, social reconstruction, and biomedical advances. But unless and until we complete that work, we should continue to undertake some preventative measures against disabilities.

References

Albrecht, G. L. and Devlieger, G. (1999). "The Disability Paradox: High Quality of Life against the Odds," *Social Science and Medicine*, **48**(8): 977–88.

Amundson, R. (1992). "Disability, Handicap, and the Environment," *Journal of Social Philosophy*, **23**(1): 105–19.

Asch, A. (2003). "Disability, Equality and Prenatal Testing: Contradictory or Compatible?" *Florida State University Law Review*, **30**(2): 315–42.

Asch, A. & Wasserman, D. (2010). Making embryos healthy or making healthy embryos: How much of a difference between prenatal treatment and selection?" In J. Nisker, F. Baylis, I. Karpin, C. McLeod, & R. Mykitiuk (Ed.), *The Healthy Embryo*. New York, NY: Cambridge University Press, 201-219.

Barnes, E. (2009). "Disability, Minority, and Difference," *Journal of Applied Philosophy*, 26(4): 337–55.

Bickenbach, J. (1993). *Physical Disability and Social Policy*. Toronto and London: University of Toronto Press.

Crisp, R. (2008). "Well-Being," *Stanford Encyclopedia of Philosophy* http://plato. stanford.edu/entries/well-being/.

Crocker, D. (1995). "Functioning and Capability: The Foundations of Sen's and Nussbaum's *Development Ethics: Part II*." In *Women, Culture, and Development*, eds. M. Nussbaum and J. Glover. New York: Oxford University Press, 153–98.

Emens, E. (2012). "Framing Disability," *University of Illinois Law Review*, **2012**(5): 1383–441.

Feldman, F. (2008). "Whole Life Satisfaction Concepts of Happiness," *Theoria*, **74**(3): 219–38.

Glover, J. (2006). *Choosing Children: The Ethical Dilemmas of Genetic Intervention*. Oxford: Clarendon Press.

Griffin, J. (1993). "Commentary on Dan Brock: Quality of Life Measures in Health Care and Medical Ethics." In *The Quality of Life*, eds. M. Nussbaum and A. Sen. Oxford: Clarendon Press, 133–139

Griffin, J. (1968). *Well-Being: Its Meaning, Measure, and Moral Importance*. Oxford: Oxford University Press.

Harman, E. (2004). "Can We Harm and Benefit in Creating?" *Philosophical Perspectives*, 18: 89–113.

Hurka, T. (1987). "The Well-Rounded Life," *The Journal of Philosophy*, **84**(12): 727–46.

Kahane, G. and Savulescu, J. (2009). "The Welfarist Account of Disability." In *Disability and Disadvantage*, eds. K. Brownlee and A. Cureton. Oxford: Oxford University Press.

Kahneman, D., Diener, E., and Schwarz, N. (1999). *Well-Being: The Foundations of Hedonic Psychology*. New York: Russell Sage Publications.

McClimans, Leah, Bickenbach, Jerome, Westerman, Marjan, Carlson, Licia, Wasserman, David and Schwartz., Carolyn. 2012. Philosophical perspectives on response shift. Quality of Life Research. DOI 10.1007/s11136-012-0300-x

McMahan, J. (2005). "Causing Disabled People to Exist and Causing People to be Disabled," *Ethics*, 116: 77–99.

McBryde-Johnson, H. (2003). "Unspeakable Conversations," *The New York Times Magazine*, Feb. 11.

Menzel, P., Dolan, P., Richardson, J., and Olsen, J. A. (2002). "The Role of Adaptation to Disability and Disease in Health State Valuation: A Preliminary Normative Analysis," *Social Science and Medicine*, 55: 2149–58.

Moller, D. (2011). "Wealth, Disability, and Happiness," *Philosophy & Public Affairs*, 39(2): 177–206.

Murray, C. (1996). "Rethinking DALYs." In *The Global Burden of Disease: A Comprehensive Assessment of Mortality and Disability from Diseases, Injuries, and Risk Factors in 1990 and Projected to 2020*, eds. C. Murray and A. Lopez. Geneva: World Health Organization.

Nozick, R. (1974). *Anarchy, State and Utopia*. New York: Basic Books, 42–3.

Nussbaum, M. (1990). "Aristotelian Social Democracy." In *Liberalism and the Human Good*, eds. R. B. Douglass, G. Mara, and H. Richardson. London: Routledge, Kegan Paul.

Nussbaum, M. (1998). "Aristotelian Social Democracy." In *Necessary Goods: Our Responsibilities to Meet Others' Needs*, ed. G. Brock. Lanham, MD: Rowman and Littlefield, 135–56.

Nussbaum, M. (2006). *Frontiers of Justice: Disability, Nationality, Species Membership*. Cambridge, MA: Harvard University Press.

Overall, C. (2003). *Aging, Death, and Human Longevity: A Philosophical Inquiry*. Berkeley: University of California Press.

Panzarino, C. (1990). "What is Choice, and Who is Choosing?" *Roll Call*, (October/November): 7.

Parfit, D. (1984). *Reasons and Persons*. Oxford: Clarendon Press, 493ff.

Raz, J. (1986). *The Morality of Freedom*. Oxford: Oxford University Press.

Scanlon, T. M. (1998). *What We Owe to Each Other*. Cambridge, MA: Harvard University Press, 109ff.

Scotch, R. K. and Schriner, K. (1997). "Disability as Human Variation: Implications for Policy," *The Annals of the American Academy of Political and Social Science*, 549(1): 148–59.

Segal, J. (1998). "Living at a High Economics Standard: A Functionings Analysis." In *Ethics of Consumption: The Good Life, Justice, and Global Stewardship*, eds. D. Crocker and T. Linden. Lanham, MD: Rowman and Littlefield, 342–65.

Sen, A. (1980). "Equality of What?" In *Tanner Lectures on Human Values*, ed. S. MacMurrin. Cambridge: Cambridge University Press.

Sen, A. (1993). "Capability and Well-Being." In *The Quality of Life*, eds. M. Nussbaum and A. Sen. Oxford: Clarendon Press, 30–61.

Shiffrin, S. (1999). "Wrongful Life, Procreative Responsibility, and the Significance of Harm," *Legal Theory*, 5: 117–48.

(2012). "Harm and Its Moral Significance," *Legal Theory*, 18: 357–98.

Silvers, A., Wasserman, D., and Mahowald, M. B. (1998). *Disability, Difference, Discrimination*. Lanham, MD: Rowman and Littlefield, 256–7.

Temkin, L. (2008). "Is Living Longer Better?" *Journal of Applied Philosophy*, (25): 193–210.

Wasserman, D. (1998). "Distributive Justice." In *Disability, Difference, Discrimination: Perspectives on Justice in Bioethics and Public Policy*, eds. A. Silvers, D. Wasserman, and M. B. Mahowald. Lanham, MD: Rowman & Littlefield, 147–207.

Wasserman, D. (2001). "Philosophical Issues in the Definition and Social Response to Disability." In *Handbook of Disability Studies*, ed. G. L. Albrecht, Katherine D. Seelman, and Michael Bury. London: SAGE, 219, 222, 229.

Wasserman, D. (2005). "Disability, Capability, and Distributive Justice." In *Capability Equality*, ed. A. Kaufmann. New York: Routledge.

Wasserman, D, Asch., A., Blustein, J., and Putnam, D. (2011). "Disability: Definitions, Models, Experience," *Stanford Encyclopedia of Philosophy* http://plato.stanford.edu/entries/disability/.

Williams, Bernard. (1973). "The Makropulos case: reflections on the tedium of immortality." *Problems of the Self* : 82–100.

7

Disability and the Well-Being Agenda

JEROME E. BICKENBACH

BACKGROUND

In November 2010, UK Prime Minister David Cameron announced that his government, with the Office of National Statistics (ONS) in the lead, planned to initiate a program of measuring "our progress as a country not just by how our economy is growing, but by how our lives are improving, not just by our standard of living, but by our quality of life" (Bentley and Churcher 2010). The impetus for this announcement came years before in a program to introduce "well-being power" into local governments by the Labour government and by a consortium of politicians, bureaucrats, and academics called the New Economics Foundation (NEF). NEF's "A Well-being Manifesto for a Flourishing Society" proclaimed that the key focus for government should be to promote the well-being of citizens so that they are "happy, healthy, capable and engaged" (NEF 2004: 338). These calls to supplement basic economic indicators like Gross National Product (GNP) for measuring the success of governmental policy can be traced to work done in the early 1970s by the Organization for Economic Co-operation and Development (OECD) on measuring social well-being (OECD 1976). Cameron's rhetoric might be traced to an often-cited speech by Robert F. Kennedy in 1968 in which he asserted that GDP "measures neither courage, nor our wisdom, nor our devotion to our country. It measures everything, in short, except that which makes life worthwhile" (1968).

In its most recent manifestation, the key international milestones in the well-being agenda were the 2007 OECD World Forum and joint Istanbul Declaration with the United Nations, which expressed the commitment to develop indicators to measure "the progress of societies in all their dimensions" (OECD 2007), followed closely by the European Union's "Beyond GDP Conference" and Communication (EC 2009). In response, French President Sarkozy created the Commission on the Measurement of Economic Performance and Social Progress under the leadership of U.S. economist Joseph Stiglitz, who with two other Nobel Prize–winning economists, Amartya Sen and Daniel Kahneman, authored a report released in 2009 (Stiglitz, Sen, and Fitoussi 2009). The Stiglitz Report sets out the state of the art argument for the feasibility and importance of collecting meaningful and reliable data on subjective well-being (SWB), data that would enable countries to "shift emphasis from measuring economic production to measuring people's well-being" (2009: 17, 12). The tiny Himalayan kingdom of Bhutan had, by this time, developed and piloted a national survey to gather data for its Gross National Happiness Index. Buoyed by its successes, the kingdom funded the World Happiness Report (Helliwell, Layard, and Sachs 2012) that further underscored the importance of the well-being agenda for international development.

From 2008 on, HM Treasury and ONS in the United Kingdom produced a series of reports written by academic leaders in happiness research (HM Treasury 2008, 2011; see, for example, ONS 2011a–i, 2012a–d). After public consultations about which domains of well-being the proposed national survey and other technical measurement issues should include, a decision was made to begin an experiment to see if information about SWB could in fact be gathered from population-wide surveys. After much debate, four SWB questions were developed:

Overall, how satisfied are you with your life nowadays?
Overall, to what extent do you feel the things you do in your life are worthwhile?

Overall, how happy did you feel yesterday?
Overall, how anxious did you feel yesterday?

Between April 2011 and March 2012, these questions were included in the Integrated Household Survey and responses from one hundred sixty-five thousand adults across the United Kingdom were collected, using a 0 ("not at all") to 10 ("completely") scale. In late July 2012, results from the first Subjective Well-being Annual Population Survey (APS) were released to the public (ONS 2012e). The preliminary results showed that 75.9 percent of people reported their overall life satisfaction to be 7 or higher; the average rating for the "worthwhile" question was somewhat higher, and for both questions the familiar U-shaped curve for age was seen (with highest happiness among the youngest and oldest respondents and lowest happiness among the middle-aged group). Women were slightly more likely to report higher levels of SWB, and blacks and Arabs reported the lowest average SWB. The government expressed satisfaction with the results and began planning to continue the annual survey, refining questions and dealing with measurement issues.

On the surface, this recent history of the well-being agenda seems like a straightforward attempt, whether in good or bad faith, for the UK government to meet its obligation to pursue social and economic policies that are demonstrably beneficial to the citizenry. If, arguably, a population-level, aggregate, or averaging economic indicator such as GDP does not sufficiently capture the outcomes we desire from policies, then surely we should augment our policy monitoring with more relevant indicators. And what could be more relevant to policy and good governance than the happiness of the population? Admittedly, to be useful any indicator must be measureable in the strict sense of having at least an ordinal, if not scalar metric, so that it is possible to say: (1) that one person or subpopulation has higher SWB than another; and (2) optimally, that policy option A is capable of producing roughly twice as much average SWB for the population than option B. Measuring happiness is certainly a challenge, but not insurmountable.

In fact, however, the well-being agenda is at the apex of a bewildering, complex confluence of disciplinary controversies and theoretical stances on what makes a human life go well. There is, first of all, the hedonic utilitarian tradition that begins with eighteenth-century utilitarian Jeremy Bentham (1789) in which some salient experience or mental state – pain and pleasure or happiness and unhappiness – is at the core of economic cost-benefit analysis. In this tradition, happiness serves as a recurring solution to the challenge of operationalizing "utility" in which to ground a valuation methodology for cost-benefit analysis. In light of theoretical and practical concerns with stated and revealed preference valuation methodologies, some economists have urged a move "back to Bentham" for a more robust measure of utility (Dolan, Layard, and Metcalfe 2012; HM Treasury 2011).

Several other intellectual traditions have also left their mark on the well-being agenda. Social scientists from the social indicators tradition have contributed from the outset to the development of workable indicators for measuring aspects or domains of objective and subjective well-being (see, for example, Michalos 1980). Since the early 1970s, the new science of happiness – or hedonic psychology – has reshaped the traditional notion of well-being in light of theoretical foundations that have, for the first time, yielded testable hypotheses about the determinants and characteristics of the experience of SWB (Diener 1984; Diener and Biswas-Diener 2008; Diener and Suh 1997; Diener et al. 1999; and see Kahneman, Diener, and Schwarz 1999). Because of the seminal work of Daniel Kahneman and Amos Tversky (Kahneman and Tversky 1979; and see Kahneman and Tversky 2010; Hastie and Dawes 2010), researchers calling themselves behavioral economists looked critically at our capacity to accurately predict future preferences (Kahneman and Snell 1992) or to avoid framing biases (see HM Treasury 2011), thereby reinforcing the "back to Bentham" call in economics: If eliciting consumer preferences was fraught with cognitive and measurement problems, why not turn to the simple and pure mental state of happiness? As Richard Layard, one of the most influential figures in creating the well-being agenda, has argued, the only human phenomena that is self-evidently what makes life go well, is measurable, and is relevant to assessing policy is "feeling good – enjoying life and feeling it is wonderful" (2003, 2005). Finally, philosophical utilitarians contributed to the conceptual clarification of happiness or well-being (Griffin 1986; Sumner 1996), although this work tends to avoid the measurement issues that, for economists and policy analysts, are often the primary concern.

Although the relationship between happiness and income or wealth has been the central problematic for the well-being agenda, the link between health and happiness has also attracted attention. Indeed, both relationships have been the object of purported paradoxes: some early findings suggested that average levels of happiness in a population do not rise with growth in per capita income (Easterlin 1973, 1974, 1995). Although the rich tend to be happier than the poor, and average levels of SWB are higher in wealthy nations than in poor countries, within a country happiness does not increase with wealth (Alesina, Di Tella, and MacCulloch 2004). This Easterlin Paradox seemed to question the very premise of international economic development: If average income has little impact on happiness, why should we try to raise the overall absolute wealth of a low- or medium-resource country?

Although scholars have since roundly rejected the Easterlin Paradox (Clark, Frijters, and Shields 2008; Stevenson and Wolfers 2008; Veenhoven and Hagerty 2006), its influence continues unabated. Indeed, it has given credence to another apparent anomaly about happiness, called the *disability paradox*, in which people with objectively bad health experience levels of happiness higher than would be expected (Albrecht and Devlieger 1999). Although disability advocates cite the paradox as evidence that the disabled life is not, as is often mistakenly assumed, a life of misery and unhappiness, in general disability researchers are wary of asserting any correlations between disability and the quality of the disabled life, however assessed. And they have good reason to be wary: the view that the disabled life is not worth as much as the nondisabled life has influenced debates over allocation of scarce health resources (Kuhse and Singer 1985; Singer 1996; Walter 1995).

But, conceding this, should the disability community be suspicious of, or reject out of hand, the well-being agenda on the grounds that it will turn against them, as some have intimated (Edwards and Imrie 2008)? I argue that Claire Edwards and Rob Imrie are right to be concerned because addressing social and policy equality for people with disabilities in terms of SWB is indeed fraught with pitfalls. But I want to argue that, primarily because of an assumption that they and other disability advocates and researchers succumb to – which I term "disability exceptionalism" – they miss what is truly responsible for the legitimate concerns the disability community should have about the well-being agenda.

THE DISABILITY CRITIQUE OF THE WELL-BEING AGENDA

The definition of SWB or happiness most often cited is that of the founder of the science of happiness, Ed Diener:

> Subjective well-being refers to all of the various types of evaluations, both positive and negative, that people make of their lives. It includes reflective cognitive evaluations, such as life satisfaction and work satisfaction, interest and engagement, and affective reactions to life events, such as joy and sadness. Thus, subjective well-being is an umbrella term for the different valuations people make regarding their lives, the events happening to them, their bodies and minds, and the circumstances in which they live. (Diener, Lucas, and Scollon 2006: 399–400)

This definition is complex because it embodies a consensus about the multidimensional nature of happiness. Technical problems of measuring positive emotion led researchers to an array of survey methodological techniques called experience sampling that attempted to avoid the framing biases caused by the artificiality of asking people how happy they were. Daniel Kahneman and others in the 1990s proposed sophisticated methods such as the Daily Reconstructive Method in which respondents were asked, at random points over the course of a day, what, at that precise moment, they were feeling. These results were then averaged to construct what was somewhat misleadingly called a measure of "objective happiness" (Kahneman and Krueger 2006; Kahneman and Sugden 2005; Kahneman et al. 2004).

Sensing that even this was inadequate, researchers took up the suggestion of philosophers (in particular, Sumner 1996) and argued that human happiness was more than a collection of momentary positive feelings, but involved what Diener in his definition terms "reflective cognitive evaluations" about "how life was going." Assessments of life satisfaction were thus added to the mix. Still other researchers, drawing on other philosophical traditions going back to Aristotle, suggested that the ineffable recognition of personal meaningfulness or overall purpose and worthwhileness of life – usually called *eudemonic happiness* – was also missing. Thus when the Office of National Statistics began its investigation into the state of the art of measuring SWB, it relied on the Diener definition (Dolan et al. 2012) and proposed a complex measurement framework combining the three dimensions of experiential emotion or affect, evaluative or life satisfaction, and eudemonia. The four survey questions that resulted hone on all three dimensions of SWB (see earlier in this chapter).

But, even assuming the data collected from these questions are valid, it is surely appropriate to ask whether governments should be in the business of collecting and using SWB data for policy development and monitoring. U.S. political scientist Derek Bok, a cautious proponent of the well-being agenda, offers a quote from early libertarian political theorist Benjamin Constant that sums up this concern: "Let [government officials] confine themselves to being just. We shall assume the

responsibility of being happy for ourselves" (Bok 2010: 46). The debate
here goes far beyond doubts about the efficacy of government action to
increase population happiness to the deeper issue of the moral acceptability of doing so. Much of this latter debate reflects larger questions
in political theory about the proper role of the state, its obligations, and
its limitations. Even researchers sympathetic to the well-being agenda
strongly reject the notion that government should strive to maximize
aggregate happiness: such a policy goal would require a technocracy
that would push aside existing institutions and processes, as well as
individual rights of self-determination (Frey, Benz, and Stutzer 2003;
Frey and Stutzer 2002).

The recent disability critique of the well-being agenda offers an
interesting and more powerful variant of this essentially libertarian
objection to an SWB-maximizing social policy. Addressing the United
Kingdom's well-being agenda, Edwards and Imrie argue that as pres-
ently formulated the agenda will not contribute to a more politically
progressive understanding of disability or further policies that are in
the interests of persons with disabilities (2008). Theirs is essentially a
two-pronged critique: first, the agenda internalizes social problems,
thereby ignoring the impact of external forces such as discrimination
and oppression; and second, it institutes a kind of passivity that legiti-
mates paternalism of a sort that has prominently figured in the history
of disability policy.

Internalizing Oppression

At the heart of the well-being agenda is the belief that SWB is not
wholly determined by objective social conditions or, for that matter,
those objective goods we tend to think of as components of what a
"makes a life go well" (Parfit 1984) – for example, health, income,
education, employment, interpersonal relationships, community inclusion, and participation. Taken together, these good things in life are

variously called *welfare* or *objective well-being* (OWB). Capability theorists like Amartya Sen and Martha Nussbaum argue that the good human life consists, not of these resources precisely, but of the capability or opportunity to secure them if one wishes to (see, for example, Sen 1993; Nussbaum 2006). Candidates for the good human life are therefore, roughly, SWB, OWB, or capability.

These are not necessarily mutually exclusive accounts, because one might argue that the state of happiness is a component of OWB and an essential capability. The motivation for the well-being agenda, of course, is that OWB is not sufficient for the good life, because, the evidence suggests, SWB is not wholly determined by OWB. Rather, SWB seems to require internal psychological traits that are causally responsible for the degree or extent of SWB that an individual experiences. This theoretical consequence of the well-being agenda is the basis for the first prong of the Edwards and Imrie critique: the well-being agenda, they argue, is grounded in purported evidence that there is no guarantee that increasing wealth, providing education, or eliminating discrimination (i.e., increasing OWB) will make people happier; therefore the agenda advises governments to be more concerned about removing psychological or internal obstacles to SWB than making provision to provide, or removing the social obstacles to enjoying, the resources of OWB.

It is important not to overstate this objection: the well-being agenda does not assert that making external social changes – raising income levels; reducing inequality of income; providing jobs, education, and housing – is causally irrelevant to SWB; the claim is rather that these things are only indirectly relevant to SWB. Internal psychological traits mediate the effects of external social changes. Thus Edwards and Imrie see the well-being agenda as consistent with a "growing tendency to redefine public issues as the private problem of the individual" (Furedi 2004: 25). In effect, the well-being agenda encourages individuals to take more responsibility for their own happiness rather than rely on the state to increase access to external goods or to reduce the external obstacles to these goods: "Much of the discussion about wellbeing is based on the assumption that happiness is a subjective sense of self that is primarily related to, or conditioned by, genetics and personality, with social or structural circumstances of lesser importance" (Edwards and Imrie 2008: 344).

The implicit message of individual responsibility for unhappiness, Edwards and Imrie argue, is especially invidious for persons with disabilities because if the focus shifts from stigma, discrimination, and other social determinants of disability to inadequate coping strategies or other internal obstacles to happiness (cf. Delle Fave and Massimini 2005), or worse, if the obstacles are conceptualized as mental illness (cf. Layard 2006), then attention will turn away from discrimination, stigma, and other social barriers that are also (and often more) responsible for living a life of less value. Rather than addressing these social ills and injustices, Edwards and Imrie conclude, the well-being agenda implies that the plight of persons with disabilities is "best addressed by policies that promote, first and foremost, character and personality development" (2008: 347).

Legitimating Paternalism

The concern that the well-being agenda will encourage governments to shape social interventions to increase average population SWB points to a general worry about state paternalism. Unlike libertarians, most liberals acknowledge the considerable social benefits that can accrue from limited state paternalism: food and drug regulations, seat belt legislation, occupational health and safety regulations, and all forms of criminal prohibition or noncriminal regulation of self-harming behavior. But taking steps to increase happiness is a different matter. Should the state encourage or mandate participation in employment, marriage, community, or religious activity on the grounds that evidence shows that it is conducive to increased SWB?

Although, again, this is a concern that anyone might have with the well-being agenda, Edwards and Imrie insist that it is a particularly alarming concern for persons with disabilities. The disability rights movement in part grew out of a rejection of the paternalistic and charity approach to disability that undermined self-determination (Scotch 1984). Social and interactional models of disability were conceptually grounded, not only in the realization that external social forces shaped the disability experience, but that these forces tended to strip away social standing and full participatory citizenship for paternalistic reasons. The well-being agenda puts the onus on the state to enforce standard, normal social relationships conducive to happiness, thereby paternalistically managing personal dispositions toward responsibility and normalization.

In the end, because of these two concerns, Edwards and Imrie argue that the well-being agenda may do no more than reproduce and entrench existing social and economic inequalities – that is, inequalities of OWB or welfare – in its quest to secure equality of SWB. In this sense, given positive developments in policy and legislation in the United Kingdom and elsewhere to promote the independence and equality of persons with disabilities, the "politics of happiness," they believe, is a retrograde step (2008: 251). Edwards and Imrie do not argue that the UK government in particular, or political theory in general, should ignore individual or collective subjective well-being. They rather argue that social justice presumes a plurality of social goods, some subjective, others objective.

SECOND THOUGHTS

Edwards and Imrie tie their concerns about the well-being agenda to the assumption that disability is primarily a health problem and this "emphasis on biologism" inevitably means that the agenda will focus on personality and character traits, a focus that "revolves around

self-help and therapy, or individuated actions and (self) responsibilities" (2008: 339). Disability policy since the 1960s, with its emphasis on economic and social inclusion, human rights, and equality,
has pursued a political agenda – in large part dictated by the social
model analysis of disability (Bickenbach 2012) – defined by equal
access to resources and opportunities, that is, the good life as captured by objective well-being. One can search in vain in the United
Nations' Convention on the Rights of Persons with Disabilities (UN
2006) for rights to happiness or subjective well-being. There are
none; all are rights to resources and opportunities. The Edwards
and Imrie critique reflects this political focus: although they admit
that "it is hard to argue against the notion that most people want
to be happy," in the end they reassert their belief that the road to
happiness for persons with disabilities lies in securing OWB: "For
disabled people, claims to justice and rights expressed in changes
in the social and structural relations of society are where progress
towards disabled people's equal status and participation are likely to
be made" (2008: 351).

I want to argue that addressing issues of disability and social and
political equality in terms of – to use G. A. Cohen's famous phrase
(1989) – the "currency" of happiness or SWB is indeed fraught with
pitfalls, as Edwards and Imrie argue, but that there may be a way to
redeem this approach, and perhaps even the well-being agenda as well,
but only if disability advocates abandon what I describe as "disability
exceptionalism."

The best way to make this argument is to look more closely at
the disability paradox and what it signifies. The paradox, to recall, is
"[W]hy do many people with serious and persistent disabilities report
that they experience a good or excellent quality of life when to most
external observers these individuals seem to live an undesirable daily
existence?" (Albrecht and Devlieger 1999: 977). Assuming that quality of life is more or less equivalent to SWB (an assumption I return
to), we need first to distinguish two interpretations of the paradox.

Either the paradox arises from a conflict between the *reported happiness* of persons with disabilities and the *expected or anticipated levels of happiness* assessed by others, or it arises from a conflict between reported happiness and an *external assessment of objective well-being*. (There is, of course, a third possibility – a conflict between self-assessment of objective well-being by the person with disabilities and the assessment by others of that person's objective well-being – but I ignore this interpretation in what follows.)

Ron Amundson has thoughtfully explored the first interpretation. He calls upon the resources of Kahnemanian hedonic psychology to make the case that we have good reasons for thinking that the quality of life assessments made by others – especially if they themselves are not disabled – are simply mistaken, while self-assessments, although also prone to framing and other bias, are much more likely to be valid (Amundson 2010). Other than those who insist, a priori, that the subjective reports of persons with disabilities are inaccurate because of measurement bias or "response shift" (Schwartz and Sprangers 1999; Wilson 1999), the bulk of the empirical work on this issue confirms Amundson's observations (see Lacey et al. 2008; Smith et al. 2009; Ubel, Loewenstein, and Jepson 2003; Ubel et al. 2005). On this first interpretation, there is no paradox: experienced SWB is simply more valid than expected SWB.

The other interpretation of the disability paradox is more challenging. Suppose we have strong evidence that it is common for the level of a person's reported quality of life – using some generally acceptable measure – to be higher than we would expect it to be given the *objective seriousness* of the person's disability. For concreteness, suppose individuals with spinal cord injury, resulting in paraplegia or tetraplegia, commonly report levels of quality of life that are more or less equivalent to those reported by people without serious impairments, as some evidence suggests (Krause and Sternberg 1997). If this is paradoxical, it is paradoxical in the same way as the Easterlin Paradox in which levels of wealth – the objective state of affairs – are not matched to levels of experienced happiness. So interpreted and assuming for the moment that it is factually supported, what does the disability paradox tell us about disability?

Many disability researchers respond to this version of the paradox in the same way they do to the other interpretation, namely that it shows the impact of stigma and misperception on people's expectations (Albrecht and Devlieger 1999; Asch 2001; Asch and Wasserman 2005). As mentioned, challenging this misperception has been an important political strategic response to practices such as the termination of pregnancies when there is evidence of severe impairment (Parens and Asch 2000), withholding treatment for newborns with impairments (Kuhse and Singer 1985), and involuntary euthanasia and assisted suicide of people with impairments (see discussion in Battin, Rhodes, and Silvers 1998). Assumptions about the low value of the disabled life have also played a role in policy concerning allocation of scarce or expensive health resources, in which it is argued that the cost of treating a person with a severe impairment does not warrant the health benefit achieved (see discussion in Brock 1993). The claim that disability is not automatically associated with low SWB has also figured in the persistent debate about the application of summary measures of health, such as quality-adjusted life years, or QALYs, that discount the value of a year of life lived with an impairment – measures health economists standardly use when doing cost-benefit studies on health resource allocations (e.g., Harris 1987; Kamm 2009; Nord, Daniels, and Hamlet 2009; Singer et al. 1995).

In the domain of public opinion, to argue that the disabled life can be as subjectively positive and fulfilling may be an effective tool for changing people's minds about disability. In the context of policy, however, especially economic policy, the response falls flat because the point of the paradox is that SWB does not match OBW, and it is objective well-being that is at issue in resource allocation decisions. At the end of the day, it is a contingent question whether a person with spinal cord injury is happy or not; but if, as Martha Nussbaum and others have argued, physical health is an essential objective feature of human flourishing and the good human life, then it is not at all a contingent matter that a person with paraplegia is living an objectively suboptimal human life (Nussbaum 2001). Thus the explanation of the paradox favored by the disability rights community, even if plausible, has little policy impact.

The explanation of the paradox that does profoundly affect policy is very different. The favored explanation of the paradox in the scientific literature has centered around a theorized, psychological phenomenon known as *hedonic adaptation* or, more figuratively, the "hedonic treadmill" (Diener et al. 2006). The impact of the theory of hedonic adaptation on the well-being agenda is potentially far more damaging to the interests of people with disabilities than the adverse effects that Edwards and Imrie identify of internalizing oppression and legitimating paternalism, in part because the hedonic adaptation provides theoretical support for both internalization and paternalism.

In 1978, Philip Brickman, Dan Coates, and Ronnie Janoff-Bulman gave credence to the suspicion that people get used to adversity by offering evidence that the happiness of people who had developed paraplegia following a motor vehicle accident, if assessed after a year or two later, did not differ substantially from that of recent lottery winners (Brickman et al. 1978). Happiness adaptation, they argued, is another version of "automatic habituation," the deeply engrained biological and psychological process by which people who experience any sort of traumatic life change, good or bad, become emotionally accustomed to it in time (Frederick and Loewenstein 1999). The original treadmill theory (Brickman and Campbell 1971) suggested that happiness and unhappiness are merely short-lived reactions to events that quickly fade back to some set point level – perhaps genetically determined for each individual (as argued by Lykken and Tellegen 1996). Economists had similarly noticed natural adaptation processes at work in the effect of gradual income changes on SWB (Arthaud-Day and Near 2005; DiTella, MacCulloch, and Haisken-DeNew 2005). And

adaptation process has been argued to fully explain the disability paradox (Dolan, Peasgood, and White 2008; Menzel et al. 2002).

From the outset, hedonic adaptation was thought to send us an
important life message, captured by the image of the treadmill: there
is no point in striving to be happy or happier because there is nothing that can be done about one's set point in the long run (although
the good news is that we need not be worried about the long-term
consequences of catastrophes either: Myers 1992). Perceptive policy
scholars, however, have not failed to notice that, this bromide aside,
the theory of hedonic adaptation is particularly prejudicial to people
with disabilities. Though adaptation to severe impairment is arguably
a good thing, it should not be thought to ameliorate the inherent disadvantages of having the impairment: one might get used to living in a
wheelchair and experience a rebounding level of SWB over time, but
the threat of pressure sores, uncontrollable spasticity, and other health
miseries remains. Two leaders in this area of empirical research have
gone further and insisted that hedonic adaption raises serious doubts
about basing health and social policy on SWB or "experience utility":

> Most people agree that kidney failure and paraplegia are highly
> undesirable outcomes, and that life with the use of one's kidneys or
> limbs is superior to life without their use, yet measures of welfare
> based on experience utility would give very little negative value to
> these patently undesirable conditions. If we based public policy on
> experience utility, we might avoid spending scarce public resources
> on measures to prevent adversities like leg amputations, spinal cord
> injuries, and kidney failure which most people would be very averse
> to experiencing but which lead, for most people, to significant emo-
> tional adaptation ... although people may be able to emotionally
> adapt to a wide range of positive and negative circumstances, that
> does not mean they do not care about what circumstances they are
> going to experience. The existence of emotional adaptation, there-
> fore, raises serious questions about whether the goal of policies
> should be to maximize experience utility. (Loewenstein and Ubel
> 2008: 1799)

Unfortunately, a persistent strain in disability studies ideology under-cuts the impact of this crucially important observation. To counter the prejudicial misperception that the disabled life is one of inevita-ble and near total misery, disability advocates have resorted to *disabil-ity exceptionalism* – the view that living with a severe impairment may well be preferable to living without it because the disability experience provides one with special talents, strengths, and insights denied those without impairments. There are two concerns with what the disabil-ity studies community has itself parodied as this "supercrip" tactic: first, as the quote cited previously intimates, if disability neither lowers SWB nor is an objective problem, then why bother with social policy that addresses the health requirements created by impairments, or why have social policy that puts into place accessible environments or other accommodations made necessary by the functional limitations created by the impairments? This is a serious political worry. The other, less practically serious, problem is conceptual incoherence.

Consider two recent attempts to find a middle ground in order to reconcile: (1) the recognition that impairments are intrinsically bad (so as to justify, inter alia, vaccination to prevent diseases and seat belt legislation to prevent spinal cord injury); (2) apparent high lev-els of SWB among the seriously disabled; and (3) claims of disability exceptionalism, to the effect that the OWB of people who acquire seri-ous impairments can be as high as or higher than it was before their impairment.

Dan Mollar asks how we might acknowledge that a person with a serious impairment can be quite content with his or her life, while insisting that, from both a moral and policy perspective, we should do everything we can to avoid others acquiring the impairment (2011). His answer is that there is nothing inconsistent about finding one's current, post-adaptation life just as worthwhile as the past, pre-adap-tation life, while at the same time being averse to the impairment that one has acquired. Assuming that by "being averse to" Mollar means judging the impairment to be an objective decrement in the value of one's life, something it would have been better to avoid (Mollar is not clear what he means by "averse"), then in effect Mollar is arguing that one's current life can be objectively valuable even though something bad happened to one's life and that bad thing has persisted unabated.

But is this coherent? It is certainly plausible to argue, as Mollar does, that when assessing one's overall OWB, the decrement in one component of OWB, in this case health, can be compensated for by increases in another component: more friends, more meaningful activities, a better and more fulfilling job, and so on. But that does not mean that, post-adaptation, the decrement in one's health *no longer lowers* one's overall objective well-being. However high the objective value of the person's life after the impairment, it would be *still higher* without the impairment. Even if the new enriching relationships that a person with spinal cord injury now enjoys, even if the fulfilling career and meaning in her life came as an indirect result of her injury, still her life would be objectively better if she had these relationships, career, and meaningfulness, *but no spinal cord injury*. In short, it makes no sense to say that life with a serious impairment is more valuable, overall, than life without the impairment, if one also acknowledges that the impairment is objectively bad.

A more contentious way of expressing this conclusion is this: if a person with a serious impairment asserts, not merely that she is as happy as before the injury or that, because of compensation, her overall OWB is the same as, or higher, than before, but rather that post-adaptation her impairment *no longer decreases her overall OWB*, then we can justifiably say she is mistaken. This is a contentious way of putting the issue because it focuses directly on what I am calling disability exceptionalism, namely that, because of the disability experience, a person with a disability is an unimpeachable, incorrigible authority of their own level of well-being, both subjective *and* objective.

Elizabeth Barnes rejects the view that one person can justifiably warrant the claim that he knows more about another's objective well-being than he or she does (2009a, b). Her argument is straightforward:

granting that an impairment can have a negative impact on some aspects of quality of life (the paraplegic may not be able to jog on forest paths as she once did), still disability itself is not a negative difference maker, that is, a difference detrimental to one's overall objective quality of life. This is essentially Mollar's argument as well, but Barnes strengthens it by claiming that the impairment may have a positive effect on another component of well-being (say making new friends among people with paraplegia, or gaining meaning in life as a disability rights advocate) and that this effect is intrinsically related to the impairment:

> The experience of disability, for many disabled people, is not just one of absence (of a sense of modality, a function, physical health, etc). It is, rather, one of absence in particular areas that creates (*in virtue of that very absence*) opportunities in other areas – opportunities not open to the non-disabled. And some disabled people report that the resulting experiences disability creates mean that, on the whole, disability is of great benefit to them. (2009a: 15)

The assertion that disability creates "opportunities not open to the non-disabled" is a version of what I am calling disability exceptionalism, as is Barnes's argument that persons without a disability cannot legitimately challenge claims made by persons with a disability about their perception of their own objective well-being. If this were true, then it would be impossible to argue, as I just did in Mollar's case, that however high the well-being of a person with a serious impairment is, if everything remained the same, not having the impairment would make that life objectively better. But, short of denying the possibility of objective well-being (which Barnes comes very close to doing, but which is an option far too absurd to take seriously), the only support for Barnes's claims is disability exceptionalism – that somehow having a disability gives one special skills and insight into one's own objective well-being. (Inconsistently, it should be noted, she is careful to restrict the scope of her exceptionalism, arguing that the preference for a submissive gender role by a woman in a deeply patriarchal society, or the sympathies of someone experiencing Stockholm syndrome, can simply be dismissed out of hand.)

For both Mollar and Barnes, some version of disability exceptionalism serves as an ad hoc assumption used to buttressed an implausible argument. Exceptionalism might be the result of confusion between subjective and objective well-being, or an unwarranted inference from the fact that people with serious impairments can still be very happy with their lives, or perhaps an emotional reaction to the suggestion that, at the end of the day, impairments are health problems that, if serious, are challenges to the good human life. Whatever the explanation, the assumption is both incoherent and politically self-defeating.

DISABILITY AND THE WELL-BEING AGENDA

Both Mollar and Barnes make a point of rejecting hedonic adaptation in the case of disability, and in this they are in good company. An ever-growing body of evidence suggests that the adaptation theory needs serious revision (Diener et al. 2006; Headey 2010; Lucas 2007). Adaptation occurs, but it is neither inevitable nor permanent; people may have genetically determined hedonic set points, but the evidence suggests that for most people these change over time and under different external conditions. In Diener and colleagues' secondary analysis of the data from disability adaptation studies, the estimated degree of hedonic adaptation ranges from 30 percent to 50 percent (depending on the severity of disability). Even if true, it is far more significant that the cause of the remaining 70 percent to 50 percent variation is not a psychological but an environmental determinant.

It is somewhat inexplicable why the mountain of literature on hedonic adaption gives so little recognition to evidence reported in the health and rehabilitation literature about the relationship between quality of life and disabilities, such as spinal cord injury. Unfortunately, the notion of quality of life used in the health literature is hopelessly vague, primarily because quality of life is operationalized differently in the different instruments and questionnaires used to measure it, and dozens of these instruments are in common use. Just in the spinal cord literature, the quality of life instrument defines the notion sometimes in terms of aspects of physical functioning; sometimes perceived health or symptoms; and sometimes need satisfaction, levels of psychiatric disturbance, happiness, or combinations of these and other phenomena (Post and Van Loeuwen 2012).

Since the term *quality of life* is used in the literature, it is difficult to avoid it. For the purposes of this discussion, I am equating *quality of life* with SWB, but this is dangerous because many, if not most, quality of life instruments ask questions that are ambiguous about the information the respondent is reporting: Is it information about the respondent's report of what is objectively problematic about his or her health ("Do you have difficulties walking 100 meters?") or about whether, or the extent to which, the respondent is satisfied with this aspect of his or her health status?

For this reason, generalizations from this literature are dangerous, though a couple of results are well documented and relatively unambiguous: (a) people with spinal cord injury experience on average lower levels of life satisfaction compared to the general population (Post and Van Loeuwen 2012); (b) there is no consistent evidence of hedonic adaptation, although there are discernible trajectories, some moving from low life satisfaction to higher levels over time, others moving from high to low, others remaining stable (Van Leeuwen et al. 2011); (c) although some psychological factors are consistently related to quality of life, the evidence is unreliable given the vagueness of the factors cited ("locus of control," "emotion-focused coping") and the inconsistency in questions used to capture this correlation (Van Leeuwen et al. 2012); and (d) finally, there is evidence that external circumstances, especially the presence or absence of social support, is a more consistent determinant of quality of life than the various psychological factors researched (Van Leeuwen et al. 2010).

The lesson to learn from this, I believe, is that people with disabilities are no different from anyone else living a life of circumstantial highs and lows – tragedies and triumphs, losses and achievements, frustration and satisfaction. People with disability are no better or worse in being able to make reliable judgments about their own happiness or predictions about their future happiness. Although acquiring a severe impairment from an accident or adverse health condition may have a huge impact on a person's life, other disruptive life events – divorce, illness or death of a spouse or child, war, famine, or natural disaster – will also impact one's happiness. Like everyone else, persons with disabilities are vulnerable to changes in their world or their psychological states and experience less than optimal well-being, both objective and subjective. Finally, like everyone else, people with disabilities do not have special insight into what makes their lives objectively better; although we may disagree whether, and to what extent, ill health or functional loss, poverty, environmental degradation, violence and war, or breakdown of the family and community present the most important challenges to the good human life, this is a matter for debate and consensus, not the decree of those who insist they have privileged access to what makes their life objectively good.

With respect to the United Kingdom's well-being agenda, people with disabilities have no more reason to worry about it than do people without disabilities. But also, no less. The tendencies that Edwards and Imrie discern of internalization of oppression and legitimating paternalism are real enough. The quality of life literature, and less so the SWB literature, has focused on the psychological determinants of unhappiness: lack of coping strategies, locus of control, self-blame, low self-esteem, and depression (see the complete list in Van Leeuwen et al. 2012). Yet surely lack of social support, poverty, lack of assistive technology, unemployment, stigma, and other external determinants also have a profound impact on the SWB of a person, for example, with a spinal cord lesion. Unfortunately, we do not know for sure because there are very few empirical studies of the impact of these external factors on SWB for persons with severe impairments.

Even if it is true, as the Easterlin Paradox suggests, that people think only of relative income levels when assessing the impact of their income on their happiness, that is no reason not to improve standards of living or expand opportunities. For precisely the same reason, even if people with severe impairments are not uniformly and persistently miserable because they adapt to their condition, that should not mean that society should ignore their education, employment, and community participation or ignore discrimination, exclusion, and accommodation. Social policy does not have to choose between using SWB or OWB as outcome measures; a civilized society will probably need to take both into account (see Taylor 2011).

Although the specter of state paternalism is not at all attractive, and the kind of paternalism that has historically defined the state's response to disability in general and to intellectual impairment and mental ill health in particular is inconsistent with respect for human dignity, there is less to fear when state agencies assist people in avoiding common decision errors – involving the high risk of injury, deprivation, or alienation – without unduly curtailing autonomy. Soft paternalism, or "nudging" (Thaler and Sunstein 2008) is a common enough practice already (witness seatbelt legislation and mandatory car insurance), but it too requires a recognition of the value of OWB outcomes that depend on whether or the degree to which they are linked to average increased happiness levels.

Several years ago, renowned disability sociologist Irving Zola argued for "universalizing" disability policy (Zola 1989). He argued that, although politically expedient, characterizing people with disabilities as a "discrete and insular minority" who possess a "disability consciousness" that secures solidarity and common cause is not a viable long-term policy solution. What is required is to proactively and systematically change the basic contours of society in employment, education, transportation, and the human-built environment so that the world is maximally useable by all. Although Zola, like most disability human rights advocates, was addressing equality with respect to the good human life understood in terms of objective well-being, he could just as easily have been addressing equality of subjective well-being. Undoubtedly Zola would have been concerned about the current well-being agenda, but I imagine he would be cautiously optimistic that this new policy direction might well be of universal benefit.

References

Albrecht, G. L. and Devlieger, P. J. 1999. The disability paradox: High quality of life against all odds. *Social Science and Medicine*. 48: 977–88.

Alesina, A., Di Tella, R., and MacCulloch, R. 2004. Inequality and happiness: Are Europeans and Americans different? *Journal of Public Economics*. 88: 2009–42.

Amundson, R. 2010. Quality of life, disability, and hedonic psychology. *Journal for the Theory of Social Behaviour*. 40(4): 374–92.

Arthaud-Day, J. and Near, P. 2005. The wealth of nations and the happiness of nations: Why 'accounting' matters. *Social Indicators Research*. 74(3): 511–48.

Asch, A. 2001. Disability, bioethics, and human rights. In G. Albrecht, K. D. Seelman, and M. Bury (eds.), *Handbook of Disability Studies*. Thousand Oaks, CA: Sage Publications. Pp. 297–326.

Asch, A. and Wasserman, D. 2005. Bioethics. In G. Albrecht (ed.), *Encyclopedia of Disability*, Vol. I. Thousand Oaks, CA: Sage Publications. Pp. 165–71.

Barnes, E. 2009a. Disability and adaptive preference. *Philosophical Perspectives*. 23: 1–21.

2009b. Disability, minority, and difference. *Journal of Applied Philosophy*. 26(4): 337–55.

Battin, M. P., Rhodes, R., and Silvers, A. (eds.) 1998. *Physician Assisted Suicide: Expanding the Debate*. New York: Routledge.

Bentham, J. 1789. *Introduction to the Principles of Morals and Legislation*. J. H. Burns and H. L. A. Hart (eds.) 1996. New York: Oxford University Press.

Bentley, D. and Churcher, J. Cameron defends wellbeing measure. *The Independent* (25.11.2010). Available at http://www.independent.co.uk/news/uk/politics/cameron-defends-wellbeing-measure-2143595.html.

Bickenbach, J. 2012. *Ethics, Law, and Policy. The Sage Reference Series on Disability: Key Issues and Future Directions*, Vol. 4. Thousand Oaks, CA: Sage Publications.

Bok, D. C. 2010. *The Politics of Happiness*. Princeton, NJ: Princeton University Press.

Brickman, P., and Campbell, D. T. 1971. Hedonic relativism and planning the good society. In M. H. Appley (ed.), *Adaptation Level Theory: A Symposium*. New York: Academic Press. Pp. 287–302.

Brickman, P., Coates, D., and Janoff-Bulman, R. 1978. Lottery winners and accident victims: Is happiness relative? *Journal of Personality and Social Psychology*. 36: 917–27.

Brock, D. 1993. Quality of life measures in health care and medical ethics. In A. Sen and M. C. Nussbaum (eds.), *Quality of Life*. New York: Oxford University Press. Pp. 95–132.

Bruckner, D. W. 2009. In defense of adaptive preferences. *Philosophical Studies*. 142: 307–24.

Clark, A. E., Frijters, P., and Shields, M. A. 2008. Relative income, happiness and utility: An explanation for the Easterlin Paradox and other puzzles. *Journal of Economic Literature*. 46(1): 95–144.

Cohen, G. A. 1989. On the currency of egalitarian justice. *Ethics*. 99(4): 906–44.

Delle Fave, A. and Massimini, F. 2005. The relevance of subjective well-being to social policies: Optimal experience and tailored intervention. In F. A. Huppert, N. Baylis, and B. Keverne (eds.), *The Science of Well-Being*. Oxford: Oxford University Press. Pp. 379–404.

Diener, E. 1984. Subjective well-being. *Psychological Bulletin*. 95(3): 542–75.

Diener, E. and Biswas-Diener, R. 2008. *Happiness*. Oxford: Blackwell.

Diener, E., Lucas, R. E., and Scollon, C. N. 2006. Beyond the hedonic treadmill: Revising the adaptation theory of well-being. *American Psychologist*. 61(4): 305–14.

Diener, E., and Suh, E. 1997. Measuring quality of life: Economic, social, and subjective indicators. *Social Indicators Research*. 40: 189–216.

Diener, E., Suh, E., Lucas, R., and Smith, H. 1999. Subjective well-being: Three decades of progress. *Psychological Bulletin*. 125(2): 276–302.

Di Tella, R., MacCulloch, R., and Haisken-DeNew, J. P. 2005. Happiness adaptation to income and to status in an individual panel. Harvard Business School Working Paper.

Dolan, P., Layard, R., and Metcalfe, R. 2012. Measuring subjective wellbeing for public policy: Recommendations on measures. *Journal of Social Policy*. 41(2): 409–27.

Dolan, P., Peasgood, T., and White, M. P. 2008. Do we really know what makes us happy? A review of the economic literature on the factors associated with subjective wellbeing. *Journal of Economic Psychology*. 29: 94–122.

Easterlin, R. A. 1973. Does money buy happiness? *The Public Interest*. 30: 3–10.

1974. Does economic growth improve the human lot? Some empirical evidence. In P. A. David and M. W. Reder (eds.), *Nations and Households in Economic Growth: Essays in Honor of Moses Abramowitz*. New York: Academic Press.

1995. Will raising the incomes of all increase the happiness of all? *Journal of Economic Behavior and Organization*. 27(1): 35–48.

EC. 2009. GDP and beyond measuring progress in a changing world. Brussels, 20.8.2009 COM(2009) 433 final. Available at: http://eur-lex.europa.eu/LexUriServ/LexUriServ.do?uri=COM:2009:0433:FIN:EN:PDF.

Edwards, C. and Imrie, R. 2008. Disability and the implications of the wellbeing agenda: Some reflections from the United Kingdom. *Journal of Social Policy*. 37(3): 337–55.

Frederick, S. and Loewenstein, G. 1999. Hedonic adaptation. In D. Kahneman, E. Diener, and N. Schwartz (eds.), *Well-Being: The Foundations of Hedonic Psychology*. New York: Russell Sage Foundation. Pp. 289–301.

Frey, B. and Stutzer, A. 2002. *Happiness and Economics: How the Economy and Institutions Affect Human Well-Being*. Princeton, NJ: Princeton University Press.

Frey, B., Benz, M., and Stutzer, A. 2003. Introducing procedural utility: Not only what, but also how matters. Working Paper, Centre for Research in Economics, Management and the Arts, No. 2003–2.

Furedi, F. 2004. *Therapy Culture: Cultivating Vulnerability in an Uncertain Age*. London: Routledge.

Griffin, J. 1986. *Well-Being: Its Meaning, Measurement and Moral Importance*. New York: Oxford University Press.

Harris, J. 1987. QALYfying the value of human life. *Journal of Medical Ethics*. 12: 117–23.

Hastie, R. and Dawes, R. 2010. *Rational Choice in an Uncertain World*. 2nd edition. London: Sage Publications.

Headey, B. 2010. The set point theory of well-being has serious flaws: On the eve of a scientific revolution. *Social Indicators Research*. 97(1): 7–21.

Helliwell, J., Layard, R., and Sachs, J. 2012. *The World Happiness Report*. New York: Earth Institute.

HM Treasury. 2008. Developments in the economics of well-being. Treasury Economic Working Paper 4, J. Lepper and S. McAndrew, London: HM Treasury. Available at: http://www.hm-treasury.gov.uk/d/working-pager4_031108.pdf.

2011. *Valuation Techniques for Social Cost-Benefit Analysis: Stated Preference, Revealed Preference and Subjective Well-Being Approaches, A Discussion of the Current Issues.* D. Fujiwara and R. Campbell. Available at: http://www.hm-treasury.gov.uk/d/green_book_valuationtechniques_250711.pdf.

Kahneman, D., Diener, E., and Schwarz, N. (eds.). 1999. *Well-Being: The Foundations of Hedonic Psychology.* New York: Russell Sage Foundation.

Kahneman, D. and Krueger, A. B. 2006. Developments in the measurement of subjective well-being. *Journal of Economic Perspectives.* 20(1): 3–24.

Kahneman, D., Krueger, A. B., Schkade, D. A., Schwarz, N., and Stone, A. A. 2004. A survey method for characterizing daily life experience: the Day Reconstruction Method. *Science.* 306: 1776–80.

Kahneman, D. and Snell, J. 1992. Predicting a changing taste: Do people know what they will like? *Journal of Behavioral Decision Making.* 5: 187–200.

Kahneman, D. and Sugden, R. 2005. Experienced utility as a standard of policy evaluation. *Environmental and Resource Economics.* 32: 161–81.

Kahneman, D. and Tversky, A. 1979. Prospect theory: An analysis of decision under risk. *Econometrica.* 47: 263–91.

  (eds.). 2010. *Choices, Values and Frames.* Cambridge: Cambridge University Press.

Kamm, F. 2009. Aggregation, allocating scarce resources, and the disabled. *Social Philosophy and Policy.* 26: 148–97.

Kennedy, R. F. 1968. Speech given at the University of Kansas, 18 March 1968. Available at: http://www.jfklibrary.org/ Historical+Resources/Archives/Reference+Desk/Speeches/RFK/RFKSpeech68.

Krause, J. and Sternberg, M. 1997. Aging and adjustment after spinal cord injury: The roles of chronological age, time since injury, and environmental change. *Rehabilitation Psychology.* 42: 287–302.

Kuhse, H. and Singer, P. 1985. *Should the Baby Live? The Problem of Handicapped Infants.* New York: Oxford University Press.

Lacey, H. P., Fagerlin, A., Loewenstein, G., Smith, D. M., Riis, J., and Ubel, P. A. 2008. Are they really that happy? Exploring scale recalibration in estimates of well-being. *Health Psychology.* 27(6): 669–75.

Layard, R. 2003. Lionel Robbins Memorial Lectures 2002/3. Happiness: Has social science a clue? Delivered on 3, 4, 5 March 2003 at the London School of Economics. Available at: http://stoa.org.uk/topics/happiness/Happiness%20-%20Has%20Social%20Science%20A%20Clue.pdf.

  2005. *Happiness: Lessons from a New Science.* London: Penguin Books.

  2006. *The depression report: A new deal for depression and anxiety disorders.* London: Mental Health Policy Group, Centre for Economic Performance, London School of Economics.

Loewenstein, G. and Ubel, P. A. 2008. Hedonic adaptation and the role of decision and experience utility in public policy. *Journal of Public Economics*. 92: 1795–810.

Lucas, R. E. 2007. Adaptation and the set-point model of subjective well-being. *Current Directions in Psychological Science*. 16(2): 75–9.

Lykken, D. and Tellegen, A. 1996. Happiness is a stochastic phenomenon. *Psychological Science*. 7(3): 186–9.

Menzel, P., Dolan, P., Richardson., J., and Olsen, J. A. 2002. The role of adaptation to disability and disease in health state valuation: A preliminary normative analysis. *Social Science and Medicine*. 55: 2149–58.

Michalos, A. C. 1980. Satisfaction and happiness. *Social Indicators Research*. 8: 358–422.

Mollar, D. 2011. Wealth, disability, and happiness. *Philosophy and Public Affairs*. 39(2): 177–206.

Myers, D. 1992. *The Pursuit of Happiness*. New York: Morrow.

NEF (New Economics Foundation) 2004. A well-being manifesto for a flourishing society. Available at: http://www.neweconomics.org/publications/well-being-manifesto-flourishing-society.

Nord, E., Daniels, N., and Hamlet, M. 2009. QALYs: Some Challenges. *Value in Health*. 12(supplement 1): S10–S15.

Nussbaum, M. C. 2001. Symposium on Amartya Sen's philosophy: Five adaptive preferences and women's options. *Economics and Philosophy*. 17: 67–88.

2006. *Frontiers of Justice: Disability, Nationality and Species Membership*. Cambridge, MA: The Belknap Press of Harvard University Press.

OECD. 1976. *Measuring Social Well-Being: A progress report on the development of social indicators*. Paris: OECD.

2007. Istanbul Declaration. Measuring the progress of societies, world forum on statistics, knowledge and policy. Available at http://www.oecd.org/dataoecd/14/46/38883774.pdf.

ONS. 2011a. Measuring National Well-being – Summary of proposed domains and measures (24.7.2011). Office for National Statistics. Available at: http://www.ons.gov.uk/ons/guide-method/user-guidance/well-being/publications/index.html.

2011b. Measuring what Matters: National statistician's reflections on the national debate on measuring national well-being (25.7.2011). Office for National Statistics. Available at: http://www.ons.gov.uk/ons/guide-method/user-guidance/well-being/publications/index.html.

2011c. Findings from the National Well-Being Debate (25.7.2011). Office for National Statistics. Available at: http://www.ons.gov.uk/ons/guide-method/user-guidance/well-being/publications/index.html.

2011d. Measuring Subjective Well-Being (25.7.2011). Office for National Statistics. Available at: http://www.ons.gov.uk/ons/guide-method/user-guidance/well-being/publications/index.html.

2011e. Developing a Framework for Understanding and Measuring National Well-Being (25.7. 2011). Office for National Statistics. Available at: http://www.ons.gov.uk/ons/guide-method/user-guidance/well-being/publications/index.html.

2011f. Measuring Subjective Well-Being for Public Policy, Dolan, P., Layard, R., and Metcalfe, R., Office for National Statistics. Available at: http://www.statistics.gov.uk/articles/social_trends/measuring-subjective-wellbeing-for-public-policy.pdf.

2011g. Measuring National Well-Being – Discussion paper on domains and measures – (31.10. 2011). Office for National Statistics. Available at: http://www.ons.gov.uk/ons/guide-method/user-guidance/well-being/publications/index.html.

ONS 2011h. Initial Investigation into Subjective Well-Being Data from the ONS Opinions Survey (1.12. 2011). Office for National Statistics. Available at: http://www.ons.gov.uk/ons/guide-method/user-guidance/well-being/publications/index.html.

ONS 2011i. Initial Investigation into Subjective Well-Being data from the ONS Opinions Survey (1.12.2011). Office for National Statistics. Available at: http://www.ons.gov.uk/ons/guide-method/user-guidance/well-being/publications/index.html.

ONS 2012a. Initial Findings from the Consultation on Proposed Domains and Measures of National Well-Being, Office for National Statistics. Measuring National Well-being – Health. (28.2.2012). Office for National Statistics. Available at: http://www.ons.gov.uk/ons/guide-method/user-guidance/well-being/publications/index.html.

ONS 2012b. Analysis of Experimental Subjective Well-Being Data from the Annual Population Survey, April–September 2011 (28.2.2912). Office for National Statistics. Available at: http://www.ons.gov.uk/ons/guide-method/user-guidance/well-being/publications/index.html.

ONS 2012c. Measuring National Well-Being – Health (24.07.2012). Office for National Statistics. Available at: http://www.ons.gov.uk/ons/guide-method/user-guidance/well-being/publications/index.html.

ONS 2012d. Report on the Consultation on Proposed Domains and Measures Measuring National Well-Being – Health (24.07.2012). Office for National Statistics. Available at: http://www.ons.gov.uk/ons/guide-method/user-guidance/well-being/publications/index.html.

ONS 2012e. First Annual ONS Experimental Subjective Well-Being Results (25.07.2012). Office for National Statistics. Available at: http://www.ons.gov.uk/ons/guide-method/user-guidance/well-being/publications/index.html.

Parens, E. and Asch, A. (eds.) 2000. *Prenatal Testing and Disability Rights.* Washington, DC: Georgetown University Press.

Parfit, D. 1984. *Reasons and Persons.* Oxford: Oxford University Press.

Post, M. W. M. and van Leeuwen, C. M. C. 2012. Psychosocial issues in spinal cord injury: A review. *Spinal Cord.* 50: 382–9.

Schwartz, C. E. and Sprangers, M. A. 1999. Methodological approaches for assessing response shift in longitudinal health-related quality-of-life research. *Social Science and Medicine.* 48: 1531–48.

Scotch, R. K. 1984. *From Good Will to Civil Rights: Transforming Federal Disability Policy* (2nd ed. 2001). Philadelphia, PA: Temple University Press.

Sen, A. 1993. Capability and well-being. In M. C. Nussbaum and A. Sen (eds.), *The Quality of Life.* Oxford: Oxford University Press. Pp. 30–53.

Singer, P. 1996. *Rethinking Life and Death.* New York: St. Martin's Griffin.

Singer, P., McKie, J., Kuhse, H., and Richardson, J. 1995. Double jeopardy and the use of QALYs in health care allocation. *Journal of Medical Ethics.* 21: 144–50.

Smith, D. M., Loewenstein, G., Jankovic, A., and Ubel, P. A. 2009. Happily hopeless: Adaptation to a permanent, but not to a temporary, disability. *Health Psychology.* 28(6): 787–91.

Stevenson, B. and Wolfers, J. 2008. Economic Growth and Subjective Well-Being: Reassessing the Easterlin Paradox. Brookings Papers on Economic Activity.

Stiglitz, J. E., Sen, A., and Fitoussi, J. P. 2009. *Report by the Commission on the Measurement of Economic Performance and Social Progress.* OECD.

Sumner, L. W. 1996. *Welfare, Happiness and Ethics.* New York: Oxford University Press.

Taylor, D. 2011. Wellbeing and welfare: A psychosocial analysis of being well and doing well enough. *Journal of Social Policy.* 40(4): 777–94.

Thaler, R. and Sunstein, C. 2008. *Nudge: Improving Decisions about Health, Wealth, and Happiness.* New Haven, CT: Yale University Press.

Ubel, P. A., Loewenstein, G., and Jepson, C. 2003. Whose quality of life? A commentary exploring discrepancies between health state evaluations of patients and the general public. *Quality of Life Research.* 12: 599–607.

Ubel, P. A., Loewenstein, G., Schwarz, N., and Smith. D. 2005. Misimagining the unimaginable: The disability paradox and health care decision making health. *Psychology.* 24(4) (Suppl.): S57–S62.

United Nations. 2006. Convention on the Rights of Persons with Disabilities, G. A. Res. 61/106 (2007). Available at: http://www.un.org/esa/socdev/enable/rights/convtexte.htm.

van Leeuwen, C. M. C., Post, M. W. M., van Asbeck, F. W. A., van der Woude, L. H. V., de Groot, S., and Lindeman, E. 2010. Social support and life satisfaction in spinal cord injury during and up to one year after inpatient rehabilitation. *Journal of Rehabilitative Medicine*. 42: 265–71.

van Leeuwen, C. M. C., Post, M. W. M., Hoekstra, T., van der Woude, L. H. V., de Groot, S., Snoek, G. J., Mulder, D. G., and Lindeman, E. 2011. Trajectories in the course of life satisfaction after spinal cord injury: Identification and predictors. *Archives of Physical Medicine and Rehabilitation*. 92: 207–13.

van Leeuwen, C. M. C, Kraaijeveld, S., Lindeman, E., and Post, M. W. M. 2012. Associations between psychological factors and quality of life ratings in persons with spinal cord injury: A systematic review. *Spinal Cord*. 50: 174–87.

Veenhoven, R. and Hagerty, M. 2006. Rising happiness in nations 1946–2004: A reply to Easterlin. *Social Indicators Research*. 79(3): 421–36.

Walter, J. J. 1995. Life, quality of life, quality of life in clinical decisions. In W. T. Reich (ed.), *The Encyclopedia of Bioethics*. New York: Simon and Schuster. Pp. 1352–8.

Wilson, I. B. 1999. Clinical understanding and clinical implications of response shift. *Social Science and Medicine*. 48: 1577–88.

Zola, I. 1989. Toward the necessary universalizing of a disability policy. *Milbank Quarterly*. 67: 401–28.

8

Disability and Quality of Life: An Aristotelian Discussion

HANS S. REINDERS

In Memory of Sam Galesloot

SETTING THE STAGE

The concept of quality of life (QoL) has gained considerable importance in health care policy in recent times. Not only has it been introduced as a standard in medical ethics, but it is also used in instruments
for assessing the quality of human services. I have the latter context
particularly in mind in this chapter. Without exaggeration, one can say
that a QoL industry has emerged accompanied by an explosion of
QoL research, especially in the social sciences. With the introduction
of consumer models in the area of human services the question of how
to make sure that consumers receive the services they want has been
answered by means of quality assurance systems. In the field of disability services these systems typically operate with the notion of QoL
at their core. As a general rule, one can say that in many Western countries the quality of disability services is defined in terms of the contribution they make to the QoL of their users. In other words, quality in
this context is what David A. Garvin has called *user quality*.[1] Quality
assessment asks whether consumers are satisfied with what they get
out of their service system. One can ask people about their experiences
with the services they receive and measure their level of satisfaction.

---

[1] D. A. Garvin. *Managing Quality*. New York: Freedom Press, 1988.

The instruments used in this connection are commonly labeled the *consumer quality index.*[2]

In this chapter, I discuss a theory of QoL that is prominent in the area of disability services, particularly in service systems for people with intellectual disabilities. Embarking on the same course as the general quality assessment research, scientists soon discovered that satisfaction as the prime indicator of quality produced unreliable results. Quite often, service users in this area were satisfied with outcomes significantly lower than similar outcomes for the general population. Consequently, researchers turned to the concept of QoL for a more comprehensive approach to assess human service systems. The resulting theories of QoL that came out of this development are what philosophers call *objective list theories.*[3] These are theories that conceptualize QoL as a composite notion of the kinds of things that people consider to contribute to the goodness of their lives.

In discussing a prominent example of this type of theory, my aim is to show a limitation of its approach to QoL, and to argue for a different approach that proceeds from the notion of human flourishing as its key concept. I explore the notion of human flourishing along Aristotelian lines, and turn to friendship as its most significant component.

AN OBJECTIVE LIST THEORY OF QUALITY OF LIFE

The theory explored in this connection is generally known in the disability field by the names of two of the most important contributors, Robert L. Schalock and Miguel A. Verdugo Alonso.[4] Looking at the

[2] A simple search on Google of the term *consumer quality index* produces more than 75 million hits.
[3] R. Crisp. Well-Being. *Stanford Encyclopedia of Philosophy.* 2001. http://plato.stanford.edu/-entries/well-being/ (visited 19–05–2010).
[4] R. L. Schalock and M. A. Verdugo Alonso. *Handbook of Quality of Life for Human Service Practitioners.* Washington: American Association on Mental Retardation, 2002.

literature on what people in various parts of the world consider as contributing to the goodness of their lives they found a remarkable similarity. It turned out that the things people mentioned can be divided into eight domains that, taken together, comprise the most important aspects of human lives. From these findings they concluded that, empirically, QoL apparently consists of a universal set of core values or "goods."[5] Even though other researchers proposed different lists,[6] the general consensus emerged that QoL is a comprehensive concept covering all important aspects of life.[7] To develop this theory into a tool for measuring QoL Schalock and others selected and tested a number of indicators for each of these domains.[8] The resulting instruments enabled quantitative assessments of the QoL of service users.

Characteristic of these instruments is that they enable one to look at the various goods contributing to QoL independently from one another. Theoretically, people with a below average level of material well-being (for example, their monthly income) can nonetheless enjoy a physical health that is above average.[9] They can enjoy a relatively

---

[5] These domains (in no particular order) are: physical well-being, mental well-being, personal development, social relations, participation, self-determination, material well-being, and rights. See R. L. Schalock, "The Concept of Quality of Life: What We Know and Do Not Know." *Journal of Intellectual Disability Research* 48(3) (2004): 203–16.

[6] For example, David Felce identified six dimensions of well-being: physical, emotional, social, productive, material, and civil (D. Felce. "Defining and Applying the Concept of Quality of Life." *Journal of Intellectual Disability Research* 41 (2) (1997): 126–35).

[7] R. L. Schalock. "Guest Editorial. Introduction and Overview." *Journal of Intellectual Disability Research* 49 (2005): 695–8.

[8] R. L. Schalock, I. Brown, R. Brown, R. A. Cummins, D. Felce, L. Matikka, K. D. Keith, and T. Parmenter. "Conceptualization, Measurement, and Application of Quality of Life for People with Intellectual Disabilities: Report of an International Panel of Experts." *Mental Retardation* 40 (6) (2002): 457–70; M. A. Verdugo, R. L. Schalock, K. D. Keith, and R. J. Stancliffe. "Quality of Life and Its Measurement: Important Principles and Guidelines." *Journal of Intellectual Disability Research* 49 (10) (2005): 707–17.

[9] Empirically the reverse is more probable, however. See, for example, E. Emerson, R. Madden, H. Graham, G. Llewellyn, C. Hatton, and J. Robertson. "The Health of Disabled People and the Social Determinants of Health." *Public Health* 125 (3) (2011): 145–7.

extended social network and yet suffer poor physical health, and so on. *List theories* organize various goods in clusters (domains) that can be independently measured such that the underlying notion of QoL is an aggregate, rather than a composite concept. That is to say, the theory built on this conceptualization does not provide any insight into people's *overall quality of life* other than accounting for their scores in separate clusters of goods.

How to assess whether people's scores in a given domain indicate (in)sufficient quality? There are various possibilities. One is to compare outcomes of different service systems for users with comparable support needs such that significant differences in outcomes indicate difference in quality. This approach is flawed, however, from the point of view of validity. Given the relative importance of varying environmental contexts, it is hard to say to what extent the measured outcomes actually reflect a difference in the performance of support systems.[10]

Another possibility is to compare the scores in the same domain between different populations. How do outcomes of service systems in the domain of participation, for example, compare with outcomes in that domain in the general population? Proceeding in this way one is in fact introducing *social indicators* to assess people's QoL.[11] Here there are problems too, however. To use social indicators in assessing the scores of a particular group of people implies the norm of what in their society is accepted as (in)sufficient level of goods within that domain. But what is the justification for introducing social acceptability as a norm?

---

[10] Schalock et al., "Conceptualization, Measurement, and Application of Quality of Life for People with Intellectual Disabilities."

[11] R. L. Schalock. "Attempts to Conceptualize and Measure Quality of Life," in *Quality of Life: Perspectives and Issues*, ed. R. L. Schalock and M. J. Begab. Washington, DC: American Association on Mental Retardation, 1990, 141–8; Schalock "The Concept of Quality of Life," 203–16.

The question is usually answered with the claim that QoL for people with disabilities is essentially the same as the QoL for other people.[12] In other words, QoL requires a universal standard. The underlying principle, according to this view, would be a principle of equality. A standard for QoL assessment for people with disabilities should not differ from the standard used for other people. While this is justifiable from an objective point of view, the difficulty with the social indicators approach lies elsewhere, namely on the subjective side. To explain why, let me introduce the reader to Sam.

SAM'S QUALITY OF LIFE

A few years ago, Sam was the leading character in a documentary film broadcast on Dutch television that received much attention because of his extraordinary story. After the film was shown, experts were asked to comment on it. That is how I got to know Sam. As a preschooler, Sam developed an unknown variety of dystrophy that ate his muscular tissue away. Within a few years, Sam lost most of his visual and auditive capabilities, and at the age of six he needed assistance from a ventilator because of his shortness of breath. To prevent the foreseeable loss of communication, a teacher developed a special tool for him, which was an alphabet consisting of signs made by her fingers on his cheek. The tool worked and after having become completely deaf and blind, Sam nonetheless retained his ability to speak and to receive messages from others on his cheek.

Soon afterward his condition got worse, and the decision had to be made whether to put Sam permanently on a ventilator, which raised a question about his quality of life. When the documentary film arrives

[12] Schalock et al., "Conceptualization, Measurement, and Application of Quality of Life for People with Intellectual Disabilities"; Schalock, "The Concept of Quality of Life"; R. A. Cummins. "Moving from the Quality of Life Concept to a Theory." *Journal of Intellectual Disability Research* 49 (10) (2005): 699–706.

at this point you see a very lively young kid, full of interest in the world and eager to learn and expand his experience of it. You see him with his mother in the library looking for books on subjects he wants to learn about. On another occasion, they are walking at the riverside, and Sam is asking her about the vessels passing by. He can't see nor hear them, but he wants to know everything about these vessels.

In the next scene, the film shows his parents in the office of Sam's doctor. The doctor informs them that Sam does not qualify for permanent ventilation treatment because of his poor communicative skills. To justify this verdict the doctor says: "Objectively speaking, the bottom of his quality of life has been reached." This is the reason a non-reanimation form sits on the table. Sam's parents are full of doubt, and in the end Sam's mother refuses to sign. Sam enjoys too many things in his life, she says.

The film continues with an emergency situation. One night Sam is taken to the hospital with asphyxia. In the emergency room he is immediately put on the ventilator and remains so for a few days, which in fact means that he has entered the treatment that his doctor did not want to give him. Had his mother's signature been on that form, Sam would probably not have survived that day.

The last part of the film shows how in the years since, Sam not only traveled the world, but finished high school. When I spoke to him on the occasion of the release of his documentary film, he told me that he wanted to study law. The final shot of the film shows Sam telling his viewers why he wants people to see this film. "I want them to understand that people with disabilities can have a very good life." When asked how he would rate his QoL he answered without hesitation: "A minus."

A story like Sam's does not stand alone, of course, as we all know. Many people with disabilities and their parents can tell you stories like his, indicating a serious disagreement on their quality of life. According to Sam's doctor, his QoL had objectively reached the bottom. With this judgment the doctor presumably meant to indicate that in view of normal functioning, Sam's condition was so severely impaired that his QoL was worse than below average.

OBJECTIVE AND SUBJECTIVE QUALITY

The use of objective standards for QoL assessment is problematic, not because there are no such standards, but because from a first-person perspective their application may appear arbitrary. On any account of standards like social indicators or normal functioning, Sam's life will fail to qualify as good, but he himself strongly disagrees, objective as such standards may be.[13] Some people – perhaps quite a large number of people – are content with their lives even though they appear to be lesser off than most other people. They do not enjoy the same goods that other people enjoy, or enjoy them to a lesser degree. So what is theoretically possible, turns out – at least in some cases – to be empirically true. Some people are content with their QoL even when others think they shouldn't be.

Who is to say that they are mistaken? Even if one can argue that they are objectively mistaken, that does not make their own judgment irrational. After all, QoL is always the QoL of somebody.[14] Why should this person accept a negative evaluation of her QoL when from her own perspective her life appears pretty good? By the same token, objective standards are also the standards of somebody, usually from a particular class of people, for example, a group of professionals, or the majority of people in a given society.

These questions point to the distinction that the literature usually addresses as the difference between "subjective" and "objective" aspects

[13] For the use of normal functioning as a medical standard, see N. Daniels. "Normal Functioning and the Treatment-Enhancement Distinction." *Cambridge Quarterly of Healthcare Ethics* 9 (3) (2000): 309–22.
[14] C. Hatton. "Whose Quality of Life Is It Anyway? Some Problems with the Emerging Quality of Life Consensus." *Mental Retardation* 36 (2) (1998): 104–15.

of QoL.[15] In Western society, mobility by means of one's own vehicle is an objective indicator for material well-being, but the extent to which someone values its possession from a first-person perspective is variable. The number of visits to a family physician per annum is an objective health indicator, but this may differ from the extent to which someone subjectively experiences good health. A person's opportunities for career changes may be an objective indicator of his or her capacity for personal development, but whether this person is content about his or her actual development is dependent of subjective factors, and so on.

These examples indicate a major problem for the theory of QoL as described. There is a possible discrepancy between QoL from an objective and from a subjective point of view. People can be satisfied with circumstances and conditions that others would find unacceptable. The reverse is also true. People can be dissatisfied with circumstances and conditions that others see as quite acceptable. Empirical research corroborates these discrepancies in the sense that there is generally no proof for strong links between objective and subjective QoL.[16]

---

[15] Schalock et al., "Conceptualization, Measurement, and Application of Quality of Life for People with Intellectual Disabilities"; Schalock, "Guest Editorial. Introduction and Overview"; Cummins, "Moving from the Quality of Life Concept to a Theory"; Verdugo et al., "Quality of Life and Its Measurement: Important Principles and Guidelines." For example K. G. J. Janssen, M. A. Geesink, C. G. C. Janssen, and A. Došen. Kwaliteit van het bestaan: visies van volwassenen met een licht verstandelijke handicap binnen een SGLVG-centrum. *Nederlands Tijdschrift voor Zwakzinnigenzorg* 21 (3) (1995): 147–63; G. J. Vreeke, C. G. C. Janssen, S. Resnick, and J. Stolk. De kwaliteit van het bestaan van mensen met een verstandelijke handicap. Zoektocht naar een adequate benadering. *Nederlands tijdschrift voor opvoeding, vorming en onderwijs* 12 (1) (1996): 2–16.

[16] E. Hensel. "Is Satisfaction a Valid Concept in the Assessment of Quality of Life of People with Intellectual Disabilities? A Review of Literature." *Journal of Applied Research in Intellectual Disability* 14 (4) (2001): 311–26; J. Perry and D. Felce. "Subjective and Objective Quality of Life Assessment: Responsiveness, Response Bias, and Resident: Proxy Concordance." *Mental Retardation* 40 (6) (2002): 445–56; J. Perry and D. Felce. "Correlation between Subjective and Objective Measures of Outcome in Staffed Community Housing." *Journal of Intellectual Disability Research*

Such findings led some theorists to argue that QoL should be considered as a subjective assessment.[17] A person's QoL corresponds with her first-person assessment, which comes down to the view that QoL is equivalent to life satisfaction.[18] Further research has shown, however, that satisfaction is a relatively constant factor in people, which suggests that it may not be strongly dependent on experiences with external agents such as service systems. Some researchers have suggested further that instead of being an independent variable, satisfaction seems to be more of a personality trait.[19] Some people are hard to please, others can be satisfied quite easily as long as there are no serious disruptions in their lives. Continuity and reliability are factors that may be better in predicting satisfaction than circumstances and conditions produced by care and support they have received.[20]

Especially with regard to people with intellectual disabilities, these findings are augmented by the earlier finding that their subjective QoL hardly stays behind that of general populations even though objectively their circumstances and conditions of life are significantly

49 (4) (2005): 278–87; R. L. Schalock and D. Felce. "Quality of Life and Subjective Well-Being: Conceptual and Measurement Issues." In *International Handbook of Methods for Research and Evaluation in Intellectual Disabilities*, ed. E. Emerson, T. Thompson, T. Parmenter, and C. Hatton. New York: Wiley, 2004, 267–8.

[17] R. A. Cummins, "On the Trail of the Gold Standard for Subjective Well-Being." *Social Indicators Research* 35 (1995): 179–200.

[18] This conclusion made some researchers in the area look at personal indicators for subjective well-being. Bob Cummins, for example, developed a "homeostasis" model. His research shows that, as long as there are no very serious life-changing events, people's level of subjective well-being remains relatively stable. See R. A. Cummins. "A Homeostatic Model for Subjective Quality of Life." *Proceedings, Second Conference on Quality of Life in Cities*. Singapore: National University of Singapore, 2000, 51–9.

[19] Schalock and Felce report results of a study showing that satisfaction hardly correlates with objective indicators; that environmental factors, such as size of support facility or client staff ratio, do not strongly influence client satisfaction; and that personal satisfaction scores again and again measured between 70 and 75 on a scale of 0 to 100. "Quality of Life and Subjective Well-Being."

[20] Ibid., 267.

worse.[21] As a result we find in the literature the repeated suggestion that QoL research must include subjective as well as objective indicators.[22] Accordingly, QoL is presented as a composite concept including different kinds of goods to be evaluated in terms of both their objective and subjective dimensions.

This proposal evidently cannot solve the problem. When eventual scores on both dimensions do not correlate, how is one to proceed to arrive at a comprehensive assessment of QoL? One can calculate scores on objective indicators as well as on subjective indicators, but one cannot meaningfully sum up both aggregates. Lacking is a method to determine a sufficient *goodness of fit* between both kinds of outcomes. Do the scores on the objective indicators qualify those on the subjective indicators, or should the order of priority be reversed?

In view of this question, scholars have argued that *personal preferences* should be taken as decisive. That is to say, realized goods ought to be assessed in terms of the relative weight the persons involved assign to their respective domains. This principle can be backed up by philosophical arguments in support of *internalism*: assessments of QoL should at least not contradict what the persons involved experience as the goodness of their lives.[23]

Even so, however, introducing the principle of *personal preferences* takes us back to where the discussion started, namely with the question of how to avoid the fact that lower QoL scores for people with

[21] R. L. Schalock and M. J. Begab, eds. *Quality of Life: Perspectives and Issues.* Washington DC: American Association on Mental Retardation, 1990.

[22] Cummins "Moving from the Quality of Life Concept to a Theory"; see also the earlier argument for a "combined approach" in C. G. C. Janssen, G. J. Vreeke, S. Resnick, and J. Stolk. "Quality of Life of People with Mental Retardation; Residential versus Community Living." *The British Journal of Developmental Disabilities* 45 (1) (1999): 1, 3–15.

[23] C. Rosati. "Internalism and the Good for a Person." *Ethics* 106 (2) (January 1996): 297–326. "An individual's good must not be something *alien* – it must be 'made for' or 'suited to' her. But something can be suited to an individual ... only if a concern for that thing lies within her motivational capacity."

disabilities are accepted simply because they score high on satisfaction.[24] It is very well possible that personal preferences are conditioned by internalized social disadvantage. When people with disabilities have been socialized in ways to make them expect that their current circumstances are all that life has in store for them while other opportunities remain unknown to them, there is very little reason to expect a below average subjective well-being.

This observation has in an early stage of the research on QoL been identified as *the paradox of disability*.[25] As indicated before, the behavior of a relatively stable level of satisfaction relatively independent from their environment is not specific to people with disabilities. It has been observed in the general population as well. What makes it problematic is that, in their case, subjective well-being goes with a significantly lower level of realized objective goods. People with disabilities quite frequently have less reason to be content with their lives than other people, but they are nonetheless.

A DYNAMIC THEORY

The unresolved problem of failing correlations between objective and subjective QoL is one of those cases where a problem cannot be solved unless we change the terms that define it. In the present case, unless we find a way to transcend the difference between the objective and subjective dimension, we cannot arrive at a convincing solution.

The approach taken in this chapter is not to ignore the fact that people with disabilities may be content with their lives because they are unfamiliar with other possibilities, but to integrate the element of

[24] R. L. Schalock, G. S. Bonham, and C. B. Marchand. "Consumer-based Quality of Life Assessment: A Path Model of Perceived Satisfaction." *Evaluation and Program Planning* 23 (2000): 77–87.

[25] G. L. Albrecht and P. J. Devlieger. "The Disability Paradox: High Quality of Life against all Odds." *Social Science & Medicine*, 48 (1999): 977–88.

the unknown in the theory. Life may have different things in store for us that we as yet are unaware of. Contrary to the received opinion that the theory of QoL is *comprehensive* – in the sense that its distinction of various domains and the social indicators attached to them provide an exhaustive description of a human life – I want to suggest a different conception. The concept of QoL is necessarily open ended. There is on any account of the matter a dimension of incompleteness in assessments of QoL in the sense that we may discover things about ourselves that in due time will change our judgments. Precisely as a comprehensive concept QoL must entail an element of the unknown future of our existence. People with disabilities may be currently satisfied with conditions that they would consider disappointing once they have experienced themselves as individuals with different abilities than they currently are aware of. What is lacking in theories of QoL of the kind that I have described is the anticipation of a different future. This suggestion presupposes a conception of QoL that Garvin has identified as *transcendental*.[26] It is necessarily an open-ended concept for the simple reason that our existence is not yet completed. In other words, the problem of a *goodness of fit* between objective and subjective QoL is not resolved in favor of one or the other, but it becomes part of a theory that projects QoL in a perspective of personal development. QoL is posited as a dynamic rather than a comprehensive concept.

According to a dynamic theory of QoL, people enjoy a good life when the limits of their expectations are transcended. A good QoL, in other words, is a matter of rising expectations. Put negatively, insufficient QoL is a matter of relative deprivation. People can be discontent because they do not enjoy the same level of objective goods that people in a similar position enjoy.[27] But they can also be discontent in view of

---

[26] Garvin. *Managing Quality* (1988).

[27] C. G. C. Janssen, C. Schuengel, and J. Stolk. "Perspectives on Quality of Life of People with Intellectual Disabilities: The Interpretation of Discrepancies between Clients and Caregivers." *Quality of Life Research* 14 (1) (2005): 57–69.

what they believe they can realize for themselves. A dynamic approach to QoL allows people with disabilities to be discontent with their level of objective goods, not necessarily in comparison to other people in society, but because they expect to do better if they are enabled to develop their own capabilities. On the other hand, when people are content with their present lives because they do not know any better, then their QoL will be improved by enabling them to find out. The exploration of one's own capabilities adds the dimension of a future to the theory. In a future-oriented approach, QoL is experienced as an expanding or shrinking horizon.

The dynamic theory of QoL proposed here, then, is oriented toward the goal of *human flourishing*. Human beings flourish to the extent that they are enabled to develop their own capabilities. Because developing one's capabilities depends on the interplay between one's talents and the opportunities that one's environment provides, a dynamic conception of QoL is primarily interested in the process of personal development. From a philosophical point of view, this approach is indebted to the Aristotelian tradition, according to which human beings flourish to the extent that they are capable of actualizing their own potential.[28] Human flourishing, in other words, is the result of an interplay between people's potential and their natural and social circumstances and conditions.

One further consideration in this connection regards a concern with people with severe intellectual disabilities, for whom the prospect of human flourishing does not appear to be very bright. This is particularly the case when personal development is directly linked to their intellectual disability.[29] To ascertain that a dynamic theory of

[28] J. Annas. *The Morality of Happiness.* New York: Oxford University Press, 1993. See also M. C. Nussbaum, "Social Justice and Universalism: In Defense of an Aristotelian Account of Human Functioning." *Modern Philology* 90, (1993): Supplement, 46–73.

[29] In the list theory of Schalock and Verdugo, for example, personal development as a separate domain has a few indicators that suggest that development is taken as intellectual or cognitive development (see Schalock and Verdugo, *Handbook of Quality of Life for Human Service Practitioners*).

QoL is applicable with regard to every person, the concept of human flourishing involved in the theory can be made operational through the concept of expanding people's world of experience. Human service systems, this is to say, enhance people's QoL when they are enabled to expand the range of their experiences. Smelling a lemon or dipping one's hand in the snow for the first time is such an expansion, no less than is writing one's own name, reading a novel, or driving a car for the first time. Like all living beings, human beings develop their potential in interaction with their environment. There is no need to limit the notion of flourishing to only part of their potential, for example the part that concerns intellectual and cognitive activities.[30]

Expanding their world occurs when people participate in experiences that they did not have before. This is crucial in each and every stage of their development. Enhancing human flourishing as expanding one's world means expanding opportunities to discover who they are and what they can do. Therefore it is important to posit human flourishing as an overarching concept in a dynamic theory of QoL.

THE CAPABILITIES APPROACH

The best-known example of a dynamic approach to QoL is the theory of *human capabilities* developed by economist Amartya Sen and philosopher Martha C. Nussbaum.[31] Human beings flourish when they

[30] The question of whether this is true for *all* human beings, or whether there are limits to the applicability of flourishing as developing one's potential falls outside the scope of this chapter. For an in-depth discussion of this question and how it can be answered, see H. S. Reinders, *Receiving the Gift of Friendship: Profound Disability, Theological Anthropology, and Ethics.* Grand Rapids, MI: Eermands Publishing, 2008.

[31] A. Sen. *Development as Freedom.* New York: Anchor Books, 1999; M. C. Nussbaum, *Frontiers of Justice: Disability, Nationality, and Species Membership.* Cambridge, MA: Harvard University Press, 2006; Nussbaum, *Creating Capabilities. The Human Development Approach.* Cambridge MA: The Belknap Press, 2011. At an earlier stage, the capabilities approach was presented by Sen with regard to the QoL of people

receive sufficient opportunities to develop their own gifts and talents. Accordingly, Sen and Nussbaum define *human capabilities* as human potentialities that people actualize when their environment enables them to do so. Examples include physical and mental functions like motor skills, speech, thought, and so on.[32]

Compared to the list theory of Schalock and Verdugo, the capabilities approach has the same dynamic aspect as the theory just outlined, which is apparent from Sen's statement that the notion of capabilities regards the functions that people develop when they are enabled to. Capability is an ingredient of human flourishing indicating "what a person can do or *become*."[33] In the same vein, Sen observes in his book *Development as Freedom* that assessing the level of development should not be limited to measuring outcomes but should also include assessing the process. Without taking the process of development into account, the motivations and strategies that people themselves employ remain invisible.[34] In other words, development is an activity involving the agency of the persons involved.

in so-called developing countries, but recently Nussbaum has presented her own version of this theory with regard to people with (severe) disabilities (*Frontiers of Justice*, 5–6).

[32] In *Frontiers of Justice*, Nussbaum provides a list of ten capabilities: "life," "bodily health," "bodily integrity," "senses/imagination/thought," "emotions," "practical reason," "affiliation," "other species," "play," and "control over one's environment" (77–8).

[33] "Equality of What?" Tanner Lecture on Human Value, 1979. In A. Sen (1982), *Choice, Welfare and Measurement*. Oxford: Oxford University Press, 1982, 365–7.

[34] Sen, *Development as Freedom*, 3. The fact that Sen discusses developing nations rather than individual people does not make a fundamental difference. On the contrary, his claim regarding the importance of development as a process in which the people themselves are involved is part of the argument that "developing nations" – so called in the 1970s and '80s – should not only be seen as delayed in development, but as nations actively engaged in the process of developing themselves. There is clearly a parallel here with the received criticism of "defect models" of disability that runs along similar lines: people with disabilities should be seen from the perspective of what they can do rather than what they cannot do. Recognizing their motivations and initiatives, therefore, is characteristic for a dynamic theory of QoL.

A clear indication of the difference between the two theories is the fact that Schalock and Verdugo's theory accounts for personal development as a separate domain among seven others. The *capability approach* regards all aspects of QoL.[35] Evaluating both kind of theories at this point, one could say that in a dynamic theory the irresolvable tension between the subjective and objective dimension is overcome by positing personal development as the unifying dimension rather than a separate domain of QoL. The main concern regarding the various domains of QoL, then, is to ask how people can be supported in developing their gifts and talents and how their own *capabilities* can be put to work for them in this respect. One way to look at this difference is to say that without further qualification objective list theories do not actually measure the quality of *life*, but only of separate domains of it. People do not typically experience their QoL as divided among separate domains, however, but rather evaluate how their experiences within these various domains interact with one another. Think of how problems at home may interfere with performance at work, how friendships may enhance self-esteem, and how physical health is impacted by material well-being, and so forth.

A capabilities approach to QoL reflects the Aristotelian conception in that it in fact conceives of QoL as an activity rather than a state of being. QoL is reflected by what people *can do or become*, as Sen had it. This claim can be rephrased by saying that QoL in a capabilities approach is *agent relative*, and that they are typically owned by agents.[36]

---

[35] See, for example, R. L. Schalock, "Reconsidering the Conceptualization and Measurement of Quality of Life," in: *Quality of Life Volume I: Conceptualization and Measurement*, ed. R. L. Schalock, 123–39. Washington, DC: American Association of Mental Retardation, 1996.

[36] According to G. Hincliffe; "The subjective dimension to capability cannot be underestimated simply because of the kind of things capabilities are: by their nature they are agent relative. If the agent herself feels that a capability has not developed then her functioning is diminished accordingly. Capabilities have to be owned by agents" (G. Hinchcliffe. "Capabilities, Learning and Value." http://www.philosophy-of-education.org/pdfs/Sunday/Hinchliffe.pdf).

In this sense, *agent relative* implies an individualized perspective on QoL. The question of what experience will enhance developing one's capabilities and therefore contribute to one's QoL depends on what experiencing oneself in the world has meant so far. Put differently: the question of what the next enhancing experience may be requires narrative display. It depends for its answer on the story of which experiences have enabled the person so far to develop his or her potential and to discover herself or himself in the world. *Life story* provides the hermeneutical context within which agent-relative capabilities are discovered and realized.

Sam's Life

It is appropriate to finish this chapter by returning briefly to Sam. I recall that when we last spoke he told me that he wanted to study law. I promised to try and find a law student from my university who could assist him in dealing with logistics such as getting heavy legal manuals from the library. In the meantime, Sam also had found a girlfriend, Lian, a wheelchair user herself, and also a student. With their physical limitations, the two of them enjoyed very much discussing the world as a way to find their own place in it. Many years before, when Sam needed to be permanently connected to a ventilator, his doctor argued that at that moment his QoL had objectively hit the bottom. Sam's life did prove him wrong, I would think. Not so much because Sam himself rated his QoL to be "A minus," but because he had only just begun expanding his world of experience, and was thrilled by discovering his many gifts and talents. Those who knew him, or knew his story, were therefore quite shocked when Sam died unexpectedly on New Year's Eve 2011. Had they shared his doctor's view expressed many years ago, they would have mourned his death but not without thinking, perhaps, that it might be better this way. I am pretty certain, however, that not many who knew him actually thought so.

References

Albrecht, G. L., and P. J. Devlieger (1999). The Disability Paradox: High Quality of Life against all Odds. *Social Science & Medicine*, 48: 977–88.

Annas, J. (1993). *The Morality of Happiness*. New York: Oxford University Press.

Crisp, R. (2001). Well-Being. *Stanford Encyclopedia of Philosophy* http://plato.stanford.edu/-entries/well-being/.

Cummins, R. A. (1995). On the Trail of the Gold Standard for Subjective Well-Being. *Social Indicators Research* 35: 179–200.

(2000). A Homeostatic Model for Subjective Quality of Life. *Proceedings, Second Conference on Quality of Life in Cities*. Singapore: National University of Singapore: 51–9.

(2005). Moving from the Quality of Life Concept to a Theory. *Journal of Intellectual Disability Research* 49(10): 699–706.

Daniels, N. (2000). Normal Functioning and the Treatment-Enhancement Distinction. *Cambridge Quarterly of Healthcare Ethics* 9(3): 309–22.

Emerson, E., R. Madden, H. Graham, G. Llewellyn, C. Hatton, and J. Robertson (2011). The Health of Disabled People and the Social Determinants of Health. *Public Health* 125(3): 145–7.

Felce, D. (1997) Defining and Applying the Concept of Quality of Life. *Journal of Intellectual Disability Research* 41(2): 126–35.

Garvin, D. A (1988). *Managing Quality*. New York: Freedom Press.

Hatton, C. (1998). Whose Quality of Life Is It Anyway? Some Problems with the Emerging Quality of Life Consensus. *Mental Retardation* 36(2): 104–15.

Hensel, E. (2001). Is Satisfaction a Valid Concept in the Assessment of Quality of Life of People with Intellectual Disabilities? A Review of Literature. *Journal of Applied Research in Intellectual Disability* 14(4): 311–26.

Hinchcliffe, G (2005). Capabilities, Learning and Value http://www.philosophy-of-education.org/pdfs/Sunday/Hinchliffe.pdf (retrieved May 2013).

Janssen, C. G. C., C. Schuengel, and J. Stolk (2005). Perspectives on Quality of Life of People with Intellectual Disabilities: The Interpretation of Discrepancies between Clients and Caregivers. *Quality of Life Research* 14(1): 57–69.

Janssen, C. G. C., G. J. Vreeke, S. Resnick, and J. Stolk (1999). Quality of Life of People with Mental Retardation; Residential versus Community Living. *The British Journal of Developmental Disabilities* 45(1): 3–15.

Janssen, K. G. J., M. A. Geesink, C. G. C. Janssen, and A. Došen (1995). Kwaliteit van het bestaan: visies van volwassenen met een licht verstandelijke handicap binnen een SGLVG-centrum. *Nederlands Tijdschrift voor Zwakzinnigenzorg* 21(3): 147–63.

Nussbaum, M. C. (1993) Social Justice and Universalism: In Defense of an Aristotelian Account of Human Functioning. *Modern Philology* 90, Supplement: 46–73.

(2006). *Frontiers of Justice: Disability, Nationality, and Species Membership.* Cambridge, MA: Harvard University Press.

(2011). *Creating Capabilities. The Human Development Approach.* Cambridge MA: The Belknap Press.

Perry, J., and D. Felce (2002). Subjective and Objective Quality of Life Assessment: Responsiveness, Response Bias, and Resident: Proxy Concordance. *Mental Retardation* 40(6): 445–56.

(2005). Correlation between Subjective and Objective Measures of Outcome in Staffed Community Housing. *Journal of Intellectual Disability Research* 49(4): 278–87.

Reinders, H. S. (2008). *Receiving the Gift of Friendship: Profound Disability, Theological Anthropology, and Ethics.* Grand Rapids, MI: Eermands Publishing.

Rosati, C. (1996). Internalism and the Good for a Person. *Ethics* 106(2): 297–326.

Schalock, R. L. (1990). Attempts to Conceptualize and Measure Quality of Life. In R. L. Schalock, and M. J. Begab (eds.), *Quality of Life: Perspectives and Issues.* Washington, DC: American Association on Mental Retardation, 141–8.

(1996). Reconsidering the Conceptualization and Measurement of Quality of Life. In R. L. Schalock (ed.), *Quality of Life Volume I: Conceptualization and Measurement.* Washington, DC: American Association of Mental Retardation, 123–39.

(2004). The Concept of Quality of Life: What We Know and Do Not Know. *Journal of Intellectual Disability Research* 48(3), 203–216.

(2005). Guest Editorial. Introduction and Overview. *Journal of Intellectual Disability Research* 49(10): 695–8

Schalock, R. L., G. S. Bonham, and C. B. Marchand (2000). Consumer-based Quality of Life Assessment: A Path Model of Perceived Satisfaction. *Evaluation and Program Planning* 23: 77–87.

Schalock, R. L., I. Brown, R. Brown, R. A. Cummins, D. Felce, L. Matikka, K. D. Keith, and T. Parmenter (2002). Conceptualization, Measurement, and Application of Quality of Life for People with Intellectual Disabilities: Report of an International Panel of Experts. *Mental Retardation* 40(6): 457–70.

Schalock, R. L., and D. Felce (2004). Quality of Life and Subjective Well-Being: Conceptual and Measurement Issues. In E. Emerson, T. Thompson, T. Parmenter, and C. Hatton (eds.) *International Handbook of Methods for Research and Evaluation in Intellectual Disabilities.* New York: Wiley: 267–8.

Schalock, R. L., and M. A. Verdugo Alonso (2002) (eds.). *Handbook of Quality of Life for Human Service Practitioners.* Washington: American Association on Mental Retardation.

Schalock, R. L., and M. J. Begab (1990) (eds.) *Quality of Life: Perspectives and Issues.* Washington DC: American Association on Mental Retardation.

Sen, A. (1982). *Choice, Welfare and Measurement.* Oxford: Oxford University Press.

(1999). *Development as Freedom.* New York: Anchor Books.

Verdugo, M. A., R. L. Schalock, K. D. Keith, and R. J. Stancliffe (2005). Quality of Life and Its Measurement: Important Principles and Guidelines. *Journal of Intellectual Disability Research* 49(10): 707–17.

Vreeke, G. J., C. G. C. Janssen, S. Resnick, and J. Stolk (1996). De kwaliteit van het bestaan van mensen met een verstandelijke handicap. Zoektocht naar een adequate benadering. *Nederlands tijdschrift voor opvoeding, vorming en onderwijs* 12(1): 2–16

9

Living a Good Life … in Adult-Sized Diapers
ANNA STUBBLEFIELD

The right to communication is the right to hope…. I am jumping for joy knowing I can talk, but don't minimize how humiliating it can be to know people jump to the conclusion I am mentally disabled. If people understand the punishment of perceiving other people as inhuman, then things will get better.

– DMan Johnson[1]

I cannot count the number of times I have heard people say, "If I end up for some reason having to use diapers, shoot me." Never mind that astronauts wear diapers during take-off and reentry, when they have to remain at their stations for hours. Never mind that on long road trips, I am jealous of my friends who use diapers – *they* aren't worrying about how many miles until the next rest stop. Toilet use symbolizes adulthood and independence in our culture, while diaper use symbolizes incompetence and dependency.

[1] From a presentation made as a member of a panel on "The United Nations Convention on the Rights of Persons with Disabilities: What Does It Mean to Guarantee Freedom of Expression?" at the Society for Disability Studies annual meeting in June 2010. Prior to gaining – at the age of twenty-eight – access to a form of alternative communication that worked for him, Johnson had lived his life under the diagnosis of profound mental retardation. In the spring of 2011, Johnson's access to his means of communication was taken from him, and he is once again treated as severely intellectually impaired by those who have control over his life. This chapter is dedicated to him, in hope that he will one day regain his voice and his freedom.

Thinking about adult diaper use raises a juxtaposition of attitudes in regard to physical impairment and intellectual impairment that deserves examination. On one hand, those who are afraid of wearing diapers or requiring assistance with bodily waste excretion conflate physical impairment and intellectual impairment: the inability to manage one's excreta without assistance implies infancy. On the other hand, disability rights scholars and activists have challenged the equation of physical impairment with intellectual impairment: requiring assistance with personal hygiene does not diminish one's standing as a competent adult.

Lost somewhere between these positions is the status of people labeled as severely intellectually impaired. They are deeply feared by those who fear disability, because they appear to confirm the latter's worst nightmares of complete incompetence. And disability rights scholars and activists have difficulty finding a place for them within the agenda of "nothing about us without us," because they appear unable to speak for themselves. (I suspect, too, that some disability rights scholars and activists fear them for reinforcing the enabled public's beliefs about disability and incompetence.)

So, as Licia Carlson has observed, people described as severely intellectually impaired end up in the work of ethicists and bioethicists as a marginal group, used to define the parameters of the human, of moral worth, and of ethical obligation (2010: 10). And those who defend their humanity – on the grounds that, despite their apparent limitations, they are nonetheless members of the human community and capable of participating, in their own ways, in relationships with others – are dismissed as sentimental or species-ist (2010: 122 and 137).

As thoughtful and carefully critical as Carlson's work is, she does not subject the concept of severe intellectual impairment to as radical a critique as it deserves. She astutely observes that the concept of intellectual disability has always been heterogeneous and that there has never been a consensus as to its definition (2010: 113). She discusses the prototype effect, whereby – differing in different contexts and historical eras – a particular image of a person with a certain version of intellectual disability is taken as representative of intellectual disability in general (for example, in the mid-1800s, the prototype was the child-like idiot; in the early twentieth century, it was the dangerous moron) (2010: 96–7). She analyzes how the portraits of "the intellectually disabled" that appear in ethics literature function as mirrors that reflect the fears of the philosophers who create them (2010: 189–94). But she does not make the crucial connection that the people who are labeled as the most significantly intellectually impaired are also the people who are the most significantly physically impaired. People labeled as severely intellectually impaired lack the physical ability to produce useful speech and also lack the motor skills necessary to demonstrate cognitive skills through pointing or signing. In most cases, their motor skills are so poor that they cannot master basic life activities that might signal some level of cognition. This includes the physical ability to signal the need to use the bathroom and to control their bowel and bladder muscles enough (either in terms of preventing those muscles from relaxing at the wrong time or being able to intentionally make those muscles relax at the right time) to use a toilet.

But that means that the very people labeled as severely intellectually impaired are people whose physical impairment is so significant that it is impossible to determine the extent, if any, of their intellectual impairment (Stubblefield 2009, 2011). What follows from this? First, the tidy distinction that philosophers such as Jeff McMahan want to draw between being significantly physically disabled but still having the "human qualities" necessary for a good life as opposed to being significantly intellectually disabled and therefore lacking those qualities is blurred (McMahan 2009: 243ff.). Second, the distinction that disability rights activists wrestle with between people with disabilities who can speak for themselves and those who supposedly lack the intellectual ability to do so becomes unstable.

A group of people has emerged whose experiences challenge the ways significant intellectual impairment is typically discussed. These people spent the first part of their lives – in most cases into their teens or adulthood – labeled as severely intellectually impaired, because they were mute and unable to point or manipulate objects accurately enough to demonstrate understanding on intelligence tests. They subsequently gained access to communication by learning to type with one finger with support to assist them in managing body regulation and motor control challenges. In this way, they could demonstrate intelligence once masked by their significant physical disabilities.

For example, Anne McDonald was an Australian woman who had cerebral palsy and who lived in an institution until she was eighteen years old. Based on intelligence tests administered when she was three and twelve years old, she was labeled as profoundly mentally retarded. At age fourteen, she learned to type with physical support to stabilize her arm. At age eighteen, she successfully sued the state to free herself from guardianship and went on to graduate from college and become an international advocate for disability rights. In a newspaper piece, McDonald observed that she had the body of a three-month-old – she could not walk, talk, feed herself, or use a toilet – and that led doctors, psychologists, and institution staff to perceive her as having the mind of a baby as well (2007).

Like sign language when it first emerged and like the finger spelling used by Helen Keller, McDonald's method of communication (called "supported typing" or "facilitated communication" (FC)) has been controversial. Developed in Australia in the late 1970s, it was introduced in the United States in 1990. Between 1990 and 1995, nine U.S. studies involving experienced FC users and experienced facilitators yielded evidence that the facilitators (the people providing support) were inadvertently influencing what the FC users typed. The researchers concluded that the FC users were not the authors of their typed communications and were therefore severely intellectually impaired after all (Stubblefield 2011).

Since 1995, however, twelve studies have been published that identified and corrected research flaws in the original studies and yielded evidence that FC is a valid means of communication (Stubblefield 2011).[2] Furthermore, a growing number of people who first typed with the support provided by FC have moved on to typing with no physical support. In published statements, they have said that they could not have accomplished independent typing without first having the support of FC and also that when they used FC, they – not their facilitators – authored their communication. Former FC users who achieved independent typing and who have written about their experiences include Birger Sellin (1995), Sue Rubin, Lucy Blackman, Alberto Frugone, Jamie Burke, and Richard Attfield (Biklen 2005). Rubin, who wrote an Academy Award–nominated documentary about herself called *Autism Is a World*, states:

> I sometimes feel as if I am the eighth wonder of the world as people stare and marvel at my irregular behaviors which lead to poor assumptions that I am simply mentally disabled with little or no intellectual functioning. My appearance is very deceptive, and day after day I am working, as an advocate for all autistic individuals, to let the world know that we are intelligent.... Being looked upon as feebleminded is something I have been forced to endure my entire life. What an extremely difficult hole to have to climb out of, to fight for your own intelligence and capabilities. (2005: 95 and 107)

The existence of a group of people who have the personal experience of being treated as severely intellectually impaired but who have acquired the means to share their experiences muddies the waters around discussion of "significant intellectual disability." We acquire a new priority for the disability rights agenda in regard to people labeled as severely intellectually impaired: to ensure that they get access to the means of communication they need to speak for themselves. Even if a workable method of communication has not yet been found for any particular person, that person should nonetheless be treated as

---

[2] No studies involving experienced FC users and experienced facilitators and showing FC to be invalid have been published since 1995.

having the potential to use language. McDonald, Rubin, and the others found a form of communication that worked for them only after years of other attempts had failed. Because it is possible for people to possess intellectual skills that they are unable to demonstrate as a result of physical challenges, we should never conclude that any particular person is failing our tests because of lack of intellectual ability rather than because of a physical impairment. The most we can conclude is that thus far we have not yet succeeded in finding a means of support for that person.

It might be argued that McDonald, Rubin, and others like them who have accessed communication are exceptions. McDonald addressed this objection in a speech she gave at the Australian Parliament House in 2008:

> I spent my childhood and adolescence in a state institution for severely disabled children. I was starved and neglected. A hundred and sixty of my friends died there. I am a survivor ... I wasn't exceptional in anything other than my good luck.
>
> I went to the Supreme Court and won the right to manage my own affairs. Unfortunately, that didn't mean that the institution offered the *other* residents the right to manage *their* own affairs. I was an exception ... I tried to show the world that when people without speech were given the opportunity to participate in education we could succeed. I went to Deakin University and got myself a degree. That, too, was seen as an exception.... People thanked me for being an inspiration; however, they didn't understand why there weren't more like me. They continued to act as if speech was the same thing as intelligence, and to pretend that you can tell a person's capacity by whether or not they can speak.
>
> If you let other people without speech be helped as I was helped they will say more than I can say. They will tell you that the humanity we share is not dependent on speech. They will tell you that the power of literacy lies within us all. They will tell you that I am not an exception.... Many are left behind. We still neglect people without speech. We still leave them without a means of communication. It

should be impossible to miss out on literacy training, but thousands … still do. (2008)

People labeled as severely intellectually impaired are treated as infants throughout their lives. The word *infant* denotes a baby, but also, in legal terminology, a person who has not achieved legal majority. It is note-worthy that the Latin root of the word *infant* means "without speech." People labeled as severely intellectually impaired are without speech in two ways: they are functionally mute and cannot use alternative methods of communication without support, but they have also been denied access to communication. If people cannot communicate, is it because they are impaired or because they have been deprived of the necessary support? Is it a medical problem or a social problem? The experiences of people who use facilitated communication – the one group of people who can legitimately speak on behalf of "the severely intellectually impaired" – suggest that the infantilization of people labeled severely intellectually impaired is one of the most serious acts of able-ist injustice (Stubblefield 2011). Rather than being so impaired that they fall outside of the disability rights agenda of "nothing about us without us," people labeled as severely intellectually impaired stand at the very heart of it.

The response I often receive when I make these claims is that I am reinforcing the idea that intelligence is crucial to quality of life. Objectors argue that I am too focused on how supposedly severely intellectually impaired people are intelligent after all, rather than giving an argument for why people who are "actually" severely intellectually impaired nonetheless deserve to be granted full human status.

My aim is to transcend that dichotomy, and in doing so, I take inspi-ration from Martin Buber. In *Between Man and Man*, he observes that to recognize another being as "Thou" rather than "It" involves adopt-ing a receptive attitude toward that being: connection between two beings does not require an exchange of words or ideas. According to Buber, when I am open to another as an I to a Thou, there is "genuine dialogue – no matter whether spoken or silent – where each of the participants really has in mind the other or others in their present and particular being and turns to them with the intention of establishing a living mutual relation between himself and them" (1949: 19). For Buber, this requires what he calls "becoming aware": recognizing that the other is present to me in a way that allows for us to enter into genuine dialogue with each other. "The limits of the possibility of dialogue," writes Buber, "are the limits of awareness" (1949: 10).

"Becoming aware" in Buber's sense requires understanding that there are many ways of experiencing the world and many forms of knowledge, and we miss that when we define competence too narrowly, in ways that require physical skills in order to demonstrate intellectual skills. This is a "two sides of the same coin" argument. On one side is a narrow definition of intelligence that excludes knowledge that is not acquired or expressed verbally or that cannot be boiled down to the correct answer on a test. On the other side is the assumption that a person who cannot speak or cannot control his body enough to pass an intelligence test or to independently engage in basic life activities must be intellectually impaired. An environment that is enabling for people who appear to be severely intellectually impaired is one in which their competence is presumed and in which those who support them make it their first priority to help them find an open-ended, language-based means of communication. But the attitude that allows for that is the same attitude that recognizes that human knowledge and connection transcend the verbal.

"Becoming aware" is the understanding that there *is* a person there, even before a means of verbal communication is found (and even if a means of verbal communication is never found), combined with the understanding that we can never legitimately assume that a person who appears to be severely intellectually impaired is unable to use language. Buber writes: "For no man is without strength for expression, and our turning towards him brings about a reply, however imperceptible, however quickly smothered, in a looking and sounding forth of the soul that are perhaps dissipating in mere inwardness and yet do exist" (1949: 22). Embracing the sounding forth of a soul means honoring the nonverbal knowledge and connection that is always already there, while seeking untiringly to give that soul access to the fullest means of expression.

The "Thou-ness" of people labeled as severely intellectually impaired is denied by philosophers and bioethicists who believe they lack the capacities necessary for a good human life. For example, according to Jeff McMahan, "higher cognitive capacities" are required for human goods such as intimate personal relations based on deep mutual understanding, achievement of difficult and valuable goals, and knowledge (2009: 247).

McMahan constructs his list of the goods that make life worth living in a way that excludes the forms of those goods that are accessible to all human beings, regardless of access to language-based communication and/or cognitive capacity. First, McMahan takes it as self-evident that relationships that involve verbal interaction and the sharing of ideas are more worthwhile than those based on receptivity to each other, comfortable familiarity, physical closeness and care, and nonverbal or one-sided verbal interaction. This claim is not self-evident, however.

Dave Hingsburger illustrates "becoming aware" and entering into "genuine dialogue" with people labeled as severely intellectually impaired in his book *First Contact*. Upon graduating from college, he took a job as a staff person at an institution housing people with developmental disabilities. He was assigned to what was referred to by the staff as the "mat ward," where people who could not speak and could not do much with their bodies lived. He admits to being frightened by this assignment.

His first day, he assisted another staff person in feeding the residents. Hingsburger recalls:

> Her touch was caring. Her attention solely upon each person we fed. She knew their names. She swapped food around – knowing who liked what, who hated what, who wanted more, who wanted

> less.... Then we got to Bobby.... We fed Bobby and when he was
> done she said, "Shall we show him, Bobby?" As she said it she
> pulled a small object out of her apron. With a snap of her wrist an
> oriental fan opened up. Without looking at me, she said, "Dave,
> meet Bobby." Then she leaned over and began to slowly wave the
> fan above his face, the edges of the fan coming close but not touch-
> ing his cheek. Bobby's eyes changed. It was like a small light went
> on inside of him. He knew we were there. With struggle his lips
> curled and he giggled. The sound was unmistakable. He was lying
> there and laughing in the wind. I bent down to look in his face and
> for a second our eyes caught. He saw me. I knew it. I saw him. He
> knew it. (2000: 3–4)

Hingsburger goes on to say that he was shaken by this experience.
"Somehow it was easier to believe that those damaged bodies, those
damaged minds, felt nothing, knew nothing. It was all so tragic. I felt
pity."

But, as Hingsburger notes, "Pity is prejudice masked as sympathy"
(2000: 4). He goes on to describe Patsy. He taught Patsy to do a simple puzzle when the other staff members taunted him that he could
not succeed because she was "unteachable." Hingsburger is ashamed
to admit that after she learned, neither he nor anyone else did anything
more to challenge her – she simply resumed the life of total inactivity
she had led before, the only difference being that as she lay on her
bed all day, she now spun a puzzle piece she had insisted on retaining
(2000: 9–10).

Hingsburger writes: "What I did to Patsy was horrible. I made contact without realizing what I was doing, and then I walked away. I used
her to prove a point and in doing so, Patsy revealed herself to me.
Instead of feeling honoured. Privileged, even. I ignored what had happened [sic]" (2000: 16–17).

Hingsburger recounts that he finally came to understand making
contact with a woman named Helen. On a trip to a mall, Helen was
approached by a lady at a fragrance counter who sprayed some perfume for her to smell. Hingsburger writes:

[T]hen the most amazing thing happened. Helen, whose body confined her, fought gravity. She lifted herself into the scent. Drank in the smell. Then burst into a grin. I had never seen Helen smile. Truth to tell, we all thought that her disability disallowed her from showing expressions. With that one smile we knew that her grim face expressed, not disability, but a grim existence....

Then the woman who had shot the perfume into the air was excited. "Let's see if she likes this one," she said grabbing another bottle and expertly whisking away the other scent. Helen moved a bit, but not like the first time. Again another scent was tried, and again Helen responded.

For the first time I realized that there was someone home inside Helen. The scent knocked at Helen's door and Helen answered. We went back from the outing understanding Helen in a very different way. If she was in there, if there was a person there, why hadn't we met her before? We had never tried....

But we had met Helen through joy. This was unexpected. Our prejudice told us that disability was tragedy. Our pity told us that she was a lesser being whose life we wouldn't want. Our eyes told us that we were wrong. Helen was home, waiting for pleasure, capable of joy, in love with the smells of her world. Sure Helen was different, but her difference didn't matter in the way that we thought it did. Her difference just gave her a different way to appreciate life, the world around her, and the relationships she had been waiting for 28 years to have....

With Helen, her "self" guided us. Her very personality informed us and helped us change the world. Helen could tell us the food she liked – we had been cooking too blandly, smells had been boiled away. A touch of curry to her meal gave Helen new pleasure. We learned to let her smell her food before she ate it ... we began cooking more fragrant foods. As much as possible, given the Canadian climate, Helen's bedclothes hang out in the fresh air to dry. And as for outings – I'll tell you that I know pretty much where Helen will be every Friday afternoon. She will be sitting in the bakery while they prepare cinnamon buns. Looking into her face, there in that place smelling of baking bread and cinnamon and sugar, Helen is lying in the lap of God. (2000: 22–6)

The insights that Hingsburger shares in *First Contact* require the caveat that Hingsburger did not know about facilitated communication, which might have worked for Bobby, Patsy, and Helen. Having made contact with Helen, Hingsburger and the other staff at the residence where she lived took steps to improve her quality of life based on what she had shown them, but they did not have the knowledge to try to find out if her physical impairments masked an ability to use language. Nonetheless, Hingsburger captures what it means to enter into a living mutual relation with another being, regardless of verbal interaction:

> When considering making contact with people who … are considered to be so significantly mentally disabled that they are in a "vegetative" (that's what it's called) state – there is a huge obstacle. Prejudice. Yours. Mine. Ours. Against them. The difficulty here is that prejudice will feel like pity. You may be overwhelmed by a sense of hopelessness first and then, if you examine the feeling long enough, terror.
>
> They can't be "like us" because then the logical extension of that is that they must be "feeling in there" and what they are feeling in there is what we'd be feeling in there – desperation, hopelessness, isolation, loneliness. The misuse of your sense of identification with the person inside that body will lead you to think horrible thoughts.
>
> Dangerous even.
>
> "I'd rather be dead than be like that."
>
> "If I was like that I'd like to be smothered."
>
> Well, back off. This isn't about *you*. Catching a first glimpse of a soul inside a body that is so different than your own can be frightening, true.… The temptation is to engage in an incredible waste of time and psychological energy – spending time imagining what it would be like to *be you* inside them. How egocentric is that?
>
> The issue is coming to understand and to get to know what it's like to be them, in them. That's the joy of contact, of connection. (2000: 11–12)[3]

[3] For another detailed account of contact – of "genuine dialogue" – between enabled people and people considered severely intellectually impaired, see David Goode's *A World Without Words* (1994).

If a person happens to have only nonverbal relationships with other human beings, that does not necessarily make his or her life so impoverished as to be not worth living. McMahan makes unfounded assumptions about what relationships are like for people who cannot speak, the people he describes as "radically cognitively limited." Not having had the experience of being such a person himself, he has no basis for his claims.

McMahan's inclusion of "the achievement of difficult and valuable goals" in his list of crucial human goods is similarly presumptuous. McMahan qualifies the achievement of goals with a notion of what is "valuable" that is loaded to disqualify what might be important goals to people with such significant physical impairments that they are labeled as severely intellectually impaired. I take it from the context of the quote that he would consider publication of an important work of philosophy valuable, but not learning to use utensils to feed oneself. Yet if the latter is important to the person who has worked to achieve it and it was a challenge to achieve, then there is no reason to believe that that person did not experience the same amount of stimulation from the challenge of acquiring the skill and the same amount of satisfaction from success that McMahan presumably experiences from being a philosopher.

Similarly, McMahan defines knowledge too narrowly. In her memoir *Life Behind Glass*, Wendy Lawson, an autistic woman, describes standing on a hot sidewalk for an hour and a half, watching a cicada emerge from the hole where it had lived as a larvae and transform from "brownish-green bug into a beautiful bright green and gold, singing creation." Lawson continues:

> I was so excited to catch this experience and be in on this creature's birth…. One neighbour was passing by in her motor car when she saw me looking up into the tree and flapping my hands with excitement. She stopped and came over.
>
> She thought maybe I needed help or my cat was stuck up the tree. When I told her what I was doing she looked at me in amazement….

> I have since heard that people thought my standing in the heat for one and a half hours to watch an insect was a crazy thing to do. I think it is they who are crazy. By choosing not to stand and watch, they missed out on sharing an experience that was so beautiful and exhilarating. A miracle can be happening all around us and no one is aware of it. (1998; 115)

Very few people in the world possess the knowledge of having seen the birth of a cicada. Lawson is a literate person, not "radically cognitively impaired," yet the knowledge she acquired that morning is a kind of knowledge that a person with significant intellectual impairments could acquire, not unlike Helen's fine-grained olfactory knowledge. Temple Grandin, an autistic woman with a doctoral degree in animal behavior who is the world's foremost expert on cattle behavior and the construction of cattle-handling facilities, attributes her ability to create environments in which cattle feel calm to her ability to see – her knowledge of – the world from a "cow's eye" point of view (Grandin and Johnson 2006). What she learned in graduate school put Grandin into the position of being able to use her knowledge to help both cattle and humans, but she did not learn to appreciate a cow's eye view of the world in graduate school: she learned it sitting in a cow pasture with the cows. And even if she had not had the skills or opportunity to attend graduate school – or any school – and even if she did not have the means to share what she knew with anyone else, she still would possess her knowledge of cows.

This is the problem with the notion of the "idiot savant." If a person cannot speak and requires assistance with basic life activities, but plays piano beautifully or draws perfectly detailed pictures of buildings after seeing them only briefly or works complicated mathematical problems in his or her head, the standard response has been to discount that individual's knowledge. But this is arrogant. Knowledge is knowledge, regardless of how it is packaged. If someone cannot speak and cannot do much with his or her body and has not been provided with access to a workable form of communication, no one knows what he or she might know. To assume that someone knows nothing is unfounded, and – as DMan Johnson states in the quote that serves as an epigraph to this chapter – is an act of cruelty.

Philosophers like McMahan who define knowledge too narrowly in denying it to people labeled as severely intellectually impaired should heed the words of Albert Einstein, who was – let us not forget – considered learning disabled when he was a child: "The true sign of intelligence is not knowledge but imagination." Those who deny that people labeled with severe intellectual impairments possess the capacity for meaningful relationships, the achievement of worthwhile goals, and knowledge demonstrate only their own lack of awareness and imagination.

Impairments – including the severe physical impairments that cause people to be labeled as severely intellectually disabled – do not inevitably prevent a person from having a good life. Impairments are additional challenges in life, but facing additional challenges does not *necessarily* decrease quality of life. If that were so, then Olympic athletes striving to break records and scientists trying to unravel the mysteries of the universe would have to be deemed as having a decreased quality of life compared to that of the typical person. People with impairments have documented various ways in which they found that the challenges associated with their impairments improved their lives.

For example, in *Waking: A Memoir of Trauma and Transcendence*, Matthew Sanford (2006) shares his experiences after becoming paraplegic as the result of a car accident when he was thirteen years old. He writes that he spent the first twelve years with paraplegia operating under the model presented to him during his rehabilitation: that he had to use his willpower and the part of his body that still worked – his arms and shoulders – to overcome the fact that his lower body was effectively dead. According to Sanford, this way of thinking about his impairment cut himself off from most of his body. When he began to study yoga in his mid-twenties, he began to realize that he could still "hear" the paralyzed part of his body and that he could connect with that and integrate his mind and his body. He has gone on to become an acclaimed yoga practitioner and instructor, sharing his insights with both enabled and disabled students. He is also a husband and a father. Is this a "better life" than he would have had if the accident had not occurred? Not necessarily. Is it a "worse life"? Not necessarily.

Writing about being diagnosed with ALS at the age of twenty-one, Stephen Hawking observed:

> Not knowing what was going to happen to me, or how rapidly the disease would progress, I was at a loose end. The doctors told me to go back to Cambridge and carry on with the research I had just started in general relativity and cosmology. But I was not making much progress, because I didn't have much mathematical back-ground. And, anyway, I might not live long enough to finish my PhD. I felt somewhat of a tragic character.... Before my condition had been diagnosed, I had been very bored with life. There had not seemed to be anything worth doing. But shortly after I came out of hospital, I dreamt that I was going to be executed. I suddenly rea-lised that there were a lot of worthwhile things I could do if I were reprieved. Another dream, that I had several times, was that I would sacrifice my life to save others. After all, if I were going to die any-way, it might as well do some good. But I didn't die. In fact, although there was a cloud hanging over my future, I found, to my surprise, that I was enjoying life in the present more than before. (http://www. hawking.org.uk/living-with-als.html)

In a *New York Times* interview forty-eight years later, Hawking reit-erated that "I'm happier now than before I developed the condition" (Dreifus 2011).

In *Love, Sex, and Disability: The Pleasures of Care*, Sarah Smith Rainey argues that, in couples composed of a nondisabled partner and a part-ner with impairments that require a significant amount of personal assistance, the provision of care enhances intimacy. Contrary to typical assumptions and the ways such care is often portrayed in the media, the provision of care does not necessarily detract from the relationship: instead, the couples she interviewed found that it helped them to feel more open with each other in a way that typical couples often do not. The communication required to support basic life activities – especially in regard to taboo issues such as personal hygiene, bodily waste elimination, and pain management – led to better communication and therefore enhanced closeness and pleasure during sexual interaction (2011, chapter 7).

It does not follow from these examples that everyone with an impairment feels the same. What these examples do suggest, however, is that – as in anyone's life – whether we thrive on or are snowed under by challenges depends on our personality and what we – and those around us – make of the challenges that come to us. Calculations about whether disability increases or diminishes happiness must therefore be agnostic: I cannot prove that the experience of impairment in every case is likely to enhance quality of life, but neither can anyone prove the opposing claim that the experience of impairment will detract from quality of life.

Objectors might ask: If there is a probability or even possibility of improvement in our lives as a result of impairment, why do we avoid causing impairment in others when possible?

We avoid causing impairment because it is not fair to knowingly and intentionally add or risk adding additional challenges to someone's life without his or her consent. Responding to a challenge often ultimately proves beneficial and worthwhile, but engaging a challenge of any kind brings pain. The benefit derives from the struggle. To add or risk adding an extra challenge where one did not previously exist – where the impairment is not simply part of who one is from conception – is not a decision that we can justifiably impose on someone else, just as it is wrong to force people to push themselves athletically if that is not their choice ("When you win the Olympics, you'll thank me" just does not cut it). But we have to be careful about how we approach avoiding the risk of impairment, because there are costs associated with avoiding risk. It is one thing to avoid taking thalidomide during pregnancy or to buckle your child in a safety seat in the car or to remove lead paint from your home. Taking these measures does not decrease the quality of life of the child. It is another thing to never allow your child to play on the climbing equipment at the playground to avoid the risk that he or she might fall and acquire an impairment.

In a video entitled "One Question," thirty-five people labeled with intellectual impairments were asked to answer the question: "What would you change about yourself?" Twenty percent of the respondents said they did not want to change anything about themselves. Another 20 percent wanted to "be nicer," or "not so bossy," or "control my anger." Another 20 percent wanted, more generically, to "be a better person," or "be happier," or "change my attitude." Five people wanted to change their appearance – to be "sexier" or "more attractive," to have more muscles or a full head of hair. One wanted to drive a car, one to get a college education, one to get a new job. One woman wanted to have a baby, one woman wanted to get married (Di Salvo 2011). Worth noting about this video is that the answers the respondents gave are the same sorts of answers that any random group of thirty-five people would give. Only one respondent mentioned anything remotely related to intellectual impairment: he wished he had a better memory. If we heed – as we should – the experiences of people with impairments, then we must conclude that disability is not a deciding factor in the overall quality of a person's life. Disability is only one among the many aspects of life, and happiness results from embracing all the various challenges that come to us and using them to develop ourselves and to live fully – happiness is not determined by whether or not we have an impairment.

Quality of life, however, is definitely influenced by how people treat us. A review of the writings of people labeled as severely intellectually impaired prior to gaining access to a means of communication yields no claims that I could find (which does not mean there are none) that the writers find the significant physical disabilities that earned them that label to be beneficial. In two books, for example, the contributors express great frustration at how their bodies work (Gillingham and McClennen 2008; Young 2011). It is noteworthy, however, that their frustration is expressed primarily as aggravation at having bodies that work so poorly that people perceive them as severely intellectually impaired and infantilize them. In the words of Jenn Seybert, who gained access to communication at the age of twenty-four:

> My life without communication was 24 years of a living hell. Imagine yourselves sitting in your seats and having your thoughts constantly interrupted by thoughts of terror, your own voice sounding like a thunder of garbled words being thrown back at you, and other folks screaming at you to pay attention and finish your task. You find your body and voice do unusual things, and you realize you aren't in control. People are screaming at you to stop the aggression, and they stick a raisin or lemon juice in your mouth, depending on your response. Now add to this that you cannot talk ... maybe a few words ... nothing consistent with language. With all this in mind, welcome to the world of a person with autism who is also nonverbal.
>
> My life was always upside down. Nothing made sense. I kept trying to please but was not able to let anyone know what I was trying to say. We are a confusing lot. We are able to have intelligent brains, but our outward appearance is looked at as severely retarded. (Gillingham and McClennen 2008: 115ff)

Despite their extreme frustration, however, the contributors express the belief that their lives have value. Sarah Stup began using supported typing in 1991 at the age of eight. In response to a lecture in a high school science class about genetic issues and fetal testing for Williams syndrome and Down syndrome, which Stup believed took a negative tone toward people with disabilities, Stup wrote in a letter to the teacher that:

> I love science but hate it that you think I am not a good student. You wish I was dead. Williams syndrome and Downs [*sic*] syndrome might be bad genes but the people are not bad. Autism is awful but I am not awful. You forgot to tell my class that real people do live inside who are needing people to quit staring and start politely making friends. (Young 2011: 121–2)

Stup has also written:

> When young, I could not speak and was a student in a school with kids who were broken, like me. We were scared because others didn't know that inside bodies that didn't work were kids with wishes and hopes … I felt awful being alone and silent. My voice or body did not do what I wanted.… Your world hurt my ears with loud throwing echos that stayed inside my head. I needed to do weird stuff to protect me. Don't hate autism, my shield and enemy both, because I need it to protect me from the pain of your world.
>
> Autism is part beast and part human with people trying to tame the naughty animal. The beast has talent but can't always put on a good show. The beast scares you and the human is sad and lonely. Love my beast. Beast keeps me safe. Find me inside the beast. I am the soul. (Young 2011: 125)

Wally Wojtowicz, Jr., who began using FC in 1992 at the age of twenty-five, writes:

> God's kindness is manifested in each of us, not only in the normal. God's blessings are equally shared and enjoyed by all whether we recognize them or not. God made us, meaning all of us, in his likeness, image, body, and spirit. (Young 2011: 254)

And Barb Rentenbach, who began using FC in 1992 at the age of nineteen, observes:

> It is in our best interest to remember that we are all the same. People are flecks of god. Each God fragment dispersed through space/time has a slightly different shape. One shape is not superior to another. All are necessary to complete the perfect, infinite, God puzzle. (Young 2011: 254)

Chammi Rajapatirana, who began using FC in 1991 at the age of seventeen, offers the following poem (Young 2011: 94):

The Potter
The Potter who spoiled
My poor body

> Paused to pour
> Poetry into my
> Heart
> I pour it out

Most strongly, people who have experienced being labeled as severely intellectually impaired emphasize how having access to communication and being able to change how people perceive them contributes to their quality of life. As Seybert writes: "When people are supported to emerge from behind the mask of 'disability' and are able to reveal their true selves, they become the beautiful butterflies God meant them to be" (Gillingham and McClennen 2008: 120). Rather than representing the limit of the social model of disability – because their impairments are so severe – the experiences of people labeled as severely intellectually impaired reinforce the social analysis of disability: how people are viewed and treated is crucial to quality of life. The rightful position of people labeled as severely intellectually impaired is at the center of the disability rights agenda, rather than the margin. Stup writes:

> People with disabilities are patiently waiting for access to you.... We are not real citizens and participants until you allow us to bring our disabilities into your places and then find our gifts inside. Reach out by getting past your fear of imperfection. Please be with us to realize we are worth knowing. Disabilities can make you sad and uncomfortable. Many of you pray not to be like us, and to see us in your places puts you too close to what seems to be a sad life. Pity sounds like caring but it is really fear. We are sad to see fear on your faces instead of friendship. Peace comes when it is passed to all people – not one is unworthy. People with disabilities need access to you, not just your buildings. Do you need ramps to get over your fear of imperfection? (Young 2011: 125)

I have a dear friend who was labeled as severely intellectually impaired well into adulthood, when he finally acquired access to a means of communication. Because of the particular way his body functions, he finds it best to manage bodily waste elimination by wearing diapers.

Changing his diapers is not something he can do for himself, so when I am spending time with him and providing the support he needs, that is a task I undertake. What's a little diaper changing between friends, after all?

One day, when things were a bit more messy than usual, he asked me in embarrassment, "How can you stand my impairments?" He may have meant that question rhetorically, but I thought it merited a response, because it cuts to the heart of what it means to have a good human life in relation to disability.

I told him my answer would be threefold. First, I pointed out that I clean myself after my bodily waste eliminations, so it is not as if I never deal with human excreta. The distinction that we draw between managing our own excreta and managing the excreta of others is artificial. It is a product of cultural conditioning to be comfortable with our own shit while finding the shit of others disgusting. Just ask a nurse: it is not impossible to get past this particular aspect of our cultural conditioning. Society would be more enabling for everyone if we did not create psychological obstacles like this for ourselves in the first place.

Second, I observed that bodily waste elimination is as necessary to human physical functioning as the beating of one's heart. After surgery, patients are monitored to make sure that bowel and bladder function resumes, and that is a crucial measure of how well the body is recuperating. If your body is not eliminating waste, you are either dead or well on the way. So, I told my friend, when I am helping you in the bathroom, I am pleased to be presented with evidence that you are alive and well.

Finally, I drew his attention to the fact that we met each other because I move in certain circles that are defined by disability. Had he not had his impairments, it is unlikely that we would have met. And even if we had, he would not have been the same person. I acknowledged that if he were so lucky as to find a magic lamp and a genie who would grant him a wish, I could understand that he would want to eliminate those impairments going forward – they are inconvenient at best and, in many ways, have been the cause of much distress in his life. But I said that I hoped for my own sake that he would not wish to never have experienced those impairments, because wishing that would be wishing away our friendship.

Needing adult-sized diapers can be the means to good things in life. Being willing to wipe someone's ass without infantilizing him can be the means to good things in life. Disability is neither inherently a tragedy nor inherently a boon. Disability just *is* – a part of the human condition. Whether we make of disability a tragedy or a boon or – like life itself – a mixed blessing is up to individuals with impairments and the people they encounter and the social environments in which they live.

Disability is a fundamental human characteristic. To fear disability is to fear our humanity. And that fear of who we are – of our potential – underlies the many ways we devalue disabled lives. We tend to think of "human potential" in terms of those characteristics that we perceive as desirable: unusually excellent academic performance, outstanding physical skills. But few of us achieve unusual excellence in anything. On the other hand, the likelihood for all of us is that sometime during our lives, later or sooner, we will achieve our potential to experience disability. In light of the centrality of disability to the human experience, we should embrace disability and ensure that all people are enabled rather than disabled by how they are treated by others. To appreciate disability is to embrace our humanity, in both senses of the word: our human condition and our highest ideals of moral obligation.

References

Biklen, Douglas. 2005. *Autism and the Myth of the Person Alone* (New York: New York University Press).

Buber, Martin. 1949. *Between Man and Man* (London: Kegan Paul).

Carlson, Licia. 2010. *The Faces of Intellectual Disability: Philosophical Reflections* (Bloomington: Indiana University Press).

Di Salvo, Anthony (director). 2011. *One Question.* Viewed online October 21, 2012 at *http://sproutflix.org/content/one-question*.

Dreifus, Claudia. 2011. "A Conversation with Stephen Hawking: Life and the Cosmos, Word by Painstaking Word." May 9, *New York Times*. Viewed online October 21, 2012 at *http://www.nytimes.com/2011/05/10/science/10hawking.html?pagewanted=all*.

Gillingham, Gail and Sandra McClennen. 2008. *Sharing Our Wisdom: A Collection of Presentations by People on the Autism Spectrum* (Autism National Committee).

Goode, David. 1994. *A World Without Words* (Philadelphia, PA: Temple University Press).

Grandin, Temple and Catherine Johnson. 2006. *Animals in Translation: Using the Mysteries of Autism to Decode Animal Behavior* (New York: Scribner).

Hingsburger, Dave. 2000. *First Contact: Charting Inner Space* (Angus, Ontario: Diverse City Press).

Lawson, Wendy. 1998. *Life behind Glass: A Personal Account of Autism Spectrum Disorder* (London and Philadelphia, PA: Jessica Kingsley Publishers).

McDonald, Anne. 2007. "The Other Story From a 'Pillow Angel': Been There. Done That. Preferred to Grow." *Seattle Post-Intelligencer*, June 15.

2008. "Rowing Upstream." Viewed October 21, 2012 at: http://www.annemcdonaldcentre.org.au/rowing-upstream-0.

McMahan, Jeff. 2009. "Radical Cognitive Limitation." In Kimberley Brownlee and Adam Cureton, eds., *Disability and Disadvantage* (Oxford: Clarendon Press), 240–59.

Rainey, Sarah Smith. 2011. *Love, Sex, and Disability: The Pleasures of Care* (Boulder, CO: Lynne Rienner Publishers).

Rubin, Sue. 2005. "Conversation with Leo Kanner." In Douglas Biklen, ed., *Autism and the Myth of the Person Alone* (New York: New York University Press), 82–109.

Sanford, Matthew. 2006. *Waking: A Memoir of Trauma and Transcendence* (Pennsylvania, PA: Rodale Books).

Sellin, Birger. 1995. *I Don't Want To Be Inside Me Anymore: Messages from an Autistic Mind* (New York: Basic Books).

Stubblefield, Anna. 2009. "The Entanglement of Race and Disability," *Metaphilosophy*, 40(3–4) (July): 531–51.

2011. "Sound and Fury: When Opposition to Facilitated Communication Functions as Hate Speech," *Disability Studies Quarterly*, 31(4) (November): *http://dsq-sds.org/article/view/1729/1777*.

Young, Sally. 2011. *Real People, Regular Lives: Autism, Communication & Quality of Life* (Autism National Committee).

10

Ill, but Well: A Phenomenology of Well-Being in Chronic Illness

HAVI CAREL

Sweet are the uses of adversity,
Which like the toad, ugly and venomous,
Wears yet a precious jewel in his head.
   (William Shakespeare, *As You Like It*, Act II, Scene i, ll.12–14).

INTRODUCTION: WHAT CAN 'FLU TELL US?

I have never been so ill in my life. Lying in my bedroom for more than three weeks, half dozing, half hallucinating, and in continuous pain, I vowed never to forget how terrible I felt. But I forgot. When I recovered, it was as if the whole episode became some distant, half-buried memory. Even as I try to recall the experience of incapacitation, nausea, aching, and weakness, I am already elsewhere. It seems so far away. When I was ill, the feeling of sickness and weakness was so overwhelming, so total. And now I can recall only a shadow of this feeling. This bizarre ability to set illness aside, to forget episodes of acute distress and to return to normal life, is a core feature of chronic illness and perhaps of human psychology more generally. What does this odd phenomenon reveal about living with chronic and severe limitations?

Long-term illness is often episodic in nature. It is also global in reach. But the two characteristics are not mutually exclusive. Chronic illness is, as Merleau-Ponty called it, a "complete form of life" (1962:

107). As such it contains within it all the familiar tensions and extremes we know from other forms of life. Illness is a theme that can envelop one's whole life. But it can also – and often does – recede into the background in a way unimaginable to the healthy outsider. How could I forget that a whole month was taken away from me, wasted lying in sweaty bedclothes doing nothing, and what's worse, capable of doing nothing? That I was unable to eat, have a coherent conversation, and perhaps most painfully, that I could not care for myself? And yet, I have forgotten. The momentary and world-shattering sensation of incapacity, of being unable to do, and hardly be, has become a faint memory for me, the person who lived through this illness in its sharp and unrelenting acuteness.

This chapter explores these two dimensions of chronic illness – its *global* and *fluctuating* nature – in order to reveal the completeness of this form of life. I use the phenomenological approach, which focuses on first-person experiences in the aim of discerning and ordering these experiences, while refusing to subsume any experience under a pre-scriptive formulation. The experiences of illness are as varied as people are. Phenomenology offers a philosophical foundation that respects idiosyncrasy but searches for shared features of illness. Section 1 outlines a phenomenological approach to illness. Section 2 focuses on two important questions about ill health. The first question is: Does illness affect one's well-being, and if so, in what ways? I explore some of the empirical evidence on the relationship between health and happiness to suggest that, surprisingly, the answer to the question is no and offer several explanations for this. I do this by examining first-person reports of ill people, to see what they say about their own happiness and lives. This demonstrates the usefulness of phenomenology, which, in this case, helps us understand how it is possible for ill health not to affect one's well-being. The second, related, question is: Given that illness does not make us less happy, why do we conceive of it as one of the most terrifying evils that can befall a person? I turn to recent work in empirical psychology to suggest some answers to this question. In the final section I suggest, following some remarks by Julia Annas, that happiness is an achievement that requires thought, planning, and work, and that this view of happiness contributes to our understanding of why illness does not significantly affect long-term well-being. I conclude that illness provides us with a context and opportunity for the kind of reflection that is the condition for and prelude to happiness on Annas's account; in this sense her account of happiness provides philosophical grounding for the view that illness does not affect well-being.

HOW CAN WE STUDY THE EXPERIENCE OF ILLNESS?

Before we can assess the impact of chronic ill health on well-being, we need to understand better the phenomenon itself. Can we give a general characterization of the experience of illness? Is there such a unified experience? The experience of illness varies from one person to another, as well as depending on cultural context, social influences, historical situation, and so on. Even for the same person, an experience of a symptom or aspect of her illness may vary across time. Experiencing a symptom for the first time is very different to experiencing it once diagnosis is made, or after many years of coexisting with a chronic condition. So how can we talk about the (or even "an") experience of illness or of disability? Surely that would be like talking about "the" experience of love or of parenthood – how is it possible to generalize such an experience? Because the experience of illness is so diverse and multidimensional, we need a descriptive method that does not try to subsume the richness and diversity of experience under predetermined conceptual categories. We also need a method that recognizes and values first-person reports and appreciates how crucial they are in the case of illness and disability. I suggest that phenomenology offers the most apt philosophical method for achieving just this.

What is phenomenology? It is a descriptive method used by philosophers interested in focusing on human experience and its conditions of possibility. It turns its attention from the object of experience (which we normally focus on when engaging with an object) to the acts of consciousness involved in experiencing, such as those involved in perception, imagination, and memory. Phenomenology investigates general modes of experience, revealing the fundamental philosophical categories involved in experience such as intentionality, embodiment, and being-in-the-world (Heidegger 1962; Husserl 1999; Merleau-Ponty 1962). It is not an empirical mode of investigation, but a philosophical, and on some accounts, transcendental, way of studying consciousness and its relationship to the world.

An example may help clarify the particular kind of descriptive philosophy phenomenology is. In his study of the phenomenology of our internal sense of time, Husserl addresses the question: What must be in place in human consciousness to enable us to hear a melody? He suggests that consciousness requires the temporal structure of retention and protention. Retention enables us to retain the memory of the notes just played, against which we hear the present tone. Protention stretches into the future, presenting us with a sense of anticipation or expectation of what the coming notes might be. The frustration or fulfillment of this expectation determines, in part, the kind of melody we hear. As Husserl writes in *On the Phenomenology of the Consciousness of Internal Time*, "the tone begins and 'it' steadily continues. The now-tone changes into a tone-having-been; the *impressional* consciousness, constantly flowing, passes over into ever new *retentional* consciousness" (1991: 31). The conclusion Husserl draws from this example is that consciousness requires retention and protention to hear a melody, rather than a succession of discrete notes. This investigation is not empirical in nature, but transcendental – examining the conditions of possibility for hearing a melody.

We can see that phenomenology engages in the study of consciousness in a very different way to that of empirical psychology or other

sciences. And we can see how phenomenology may illuminate particular aspects of human experience, such as perception or memory. But
can phenomenology be of use in the study of a concrete, socially and
culturally situated, and varied experience such as the experience of
illness? Can illness be abstracted to some core transcendental features
that are experienced by all and only cases of ill health? S. Kay Toombs,
a philosopher suffering from multiple sclerosis who has written extensively on the phenomenology of illness, suggests precisely that. She
searches for the eidetic (essential) features of illness, which characterize all illness, over and above the particular features of specific diseases
(1987: 229). Toombs suggests that in the same way that a cuboid has
essential features, such as having six sides and being rectangular and
extended in space, illness has essential features (1987: 229). Toombs's
aim is to find these eidetic features of illness, which transcend peculiar
and particular features of different disease states and constitute the
meaning of illness as lived. On her view, these unvarying characteristics of particular disease states are analogous to eidetic characteristics
of illness, and uncovering these enables a shared world of meaning, so
those who are not ill (health professionals, family, friends) can better
understand this experience. The practical usefulness of this approach is
clear: it can improve patient-physician communication, increase com-
pliance and trust, assist in medical teaching and training, and enable
patients to better understand and order their own experiences (for an
overview of these practical applications, see Carel 2010; for a patient
toolkit based on phenomenology, see Carel 2012).

So what are the essential features of illness? Toombs describes five
such features: loss of wholeness, loss of certainty, loss of control, loss
of freedom to act, and loss of the familiar world (1987: 229ff.). These
are further broken down into features such as bodily impairment; profound sense of loss of total bodily integrity; the body can no longer be
taken for granted or ignored; the body thwarts plans, impedes choices,
renders actions impossible; disruption of fundamental unity of body
and self. Further features include experiencing the body as other than

me; loss of faith in body; perceiving the body as threat to self; radical loss of certainty; experiencing the illness as capricious interruption; loss of control; unpredictability. And finally, the patient is isolated from the familiar world and unable to carry on normal activities; the future is truncated. For Toombs, regardless of what particular disease one suffers from, these features will be present and thus serve to reveal the experience of illness beyond its surface features, which vary from one case to another. As she writes: "the eidetic characteristics of illness transcend the peculiarities and particularities of different disease states and constitute the meaning of illness-as-lived. They represent the experience of illness in its qualitative immediacy" (1987: 229).

Other authors point to different features of illness that can be explored phenomenologically. Fredrik Svenaeus offers a unique account of medicine's aim, using a hermeneutic phenomenological approach to describe medicine as an interpretive practice (2001). This emphasis on hermeneutic aspects of the patient-clinician encounter, as well as on the interpretative work involved in diagnosis and in other epistemic aspects of medical work, draws on Gadamer's account to provide a view of illness as based in social and interpretative practices of generating meaning. Svenaeus suggests viewing illness as an experience of uncanniness, or "unhomelike being in the world" (2000a). Such a characterization of illness sees it as an experience of "a constant sense of obtrusive unhomelikeness in one's being-in-the-world," in which our transcendence into the world becomes incoherent and loses its sense of order and meaningfulness (Svenaeus 2000a: 10–11). This arises from the changed conditions of embodiment, and the loss of attunement, or harmony, between one's body and the environment. On this view the role of medicine should be to deal with the unhomelikeness of illness, or to help the ill person find their way home, back to a homelike being-in-the-world (Svenaeus 2000a: 10–11). Thus medicine becomes "the art of providing a way home for the patient" (Svenaeus 2000a: 14). The phenomenological approach supports Susan Sontag's (1978) claim that illness is not merely a metaphor, or indeed a narrative or a story. Illness is primarily a bodily experience that gains meaning from social and cultural context, but is first and foremost lived as a bodily experience of suffering and limitation.

Phenomenological concepts such as being-in-the-world, authenticity, anxiety, uncanniness, and the body-as-lived have been used to analyze philosophically the experience of illness (Carel 2008; Svenaeus 2000b; Toombs 1987, 1999, 2001). Viewing illness as transforming one's entire being-in-the-world, including one's relationship to the environment, social and temporal structures, and one's identity, has been useful for capturing the holistic and all-pervasive nature of illness. Some authors have tried to identify health with authenticity and illness with inauthenticity, although this approach has been widely criticized (Keane, 2013; Svenaeus 2000b). Philosophical work on anxiety has been extremely productive in developing an account of "existential feelings" and of the ways anxiety (and other mental disorders) involves pervasive symptoms that cut across the psyche/soma distinction (Carel 2013; Ratcliffe 2008). The distinction between the biological body ("objective body") and the body-as-lived ("subjective body") has been utilized to express the difference between disease and illness, as well as to account for the difference in perspective between physician and patient (Carel 2008; Toombs 1987). And some work has been done to bring together biological and phenomenological understanding of trauma in order to develop a holistic account of the ways such events affect human beings (Getz, Kirkengen, and Ulvestad 2011). This brief overview of the ways phenomenological methods and concepts have been used to illuminate the experience of illness and its distinctness from disease gives a flavor of this rich and creative approach. However, much work remains to be done. Further work is needed to understand specific aspects of the experience of illness, or to describe particular conditions and situations of illness. In addition, no recent account has attempted to reconcile the conflicting findings of existing qualitative studies of the experience of illness (although Thorne and colleagues published a meta-study in 2002). And the plurality of concepts, traditions, approaches, and accounts have been criticized as too promiscuous to really count as a unified qualitative research methodology (Earle 2011). These challenges remain and are yet to be tackled in future work.

Another type of challenge has been voiced by authors writing on the phenomenology of illness who have argued against the idea that illness experiences have general and universal essential features, as Toombs (1987, 2001) suggests. On their view, the specificity of particular conditions and the ways they are debilitating, as well as the concrete context in which illness is experienced, cannot be stripped away from the experience of illness. This view is critical of Husserl's construal of phenomenology as a transcendental science of consciousness, claiming that the abstraction of concrete contents of an individual life removes much of what is essential to it (Merleau-Ponty 1962). This view suggests using phenomenology to study the specific details of particular illness situations (e.g., "the experience of stroke in middle-aged men"). This has been developed into a qualitative research method, but has also come under criticism for losing sight of phenomenological principles of thought and becoming indistinctive from other methods of qualitative research that also rely on first-person reports (Earle 2010). Other aspects of the experience of illness that have been studied phenomenologically have been the patient-physician relationship (Carel and Macnaughton 2012; Toombs 1999, 2001), temporal experience in illness (Toombs 1990), the phenomenology of mental disorder (Ratcliffe 2008, Stanghellini 2004), and the role of medicine (Svenaeus 2000a, 2000b, 2001; Toombs 1999).

INSIDER AND OUTSIDER PERSPECTIVES ON ILLNESS

I get into a taxi. It is late at night and I am tired; I have just come back from a conference. I carry with me a small oxygen cylinder, which I use when walking. The sound of the oxygen streaming through the tubes is clearly audible in the quiet night. The taxi driver is silent for a few moments, but I brace myself for the inevitable question. By the time we reach the second roundabout, he asks: "What is that?" "Oxygen," I reply and explain I have a chronic lung condition. He pauses for a moment and then says: "I feel sorry for you." It turns out that he is a devout Muslim and is well intentioned; when I leave the taxi, he promises to pray for me. I am not offended; I am a veteran of chronic illness, and have had many such (and worse) exchanges before. But I think long and hard about this phrase, this sentiment: "I feel sorry for you." Feeling sorry for someone indicates that this person has suffered an unjust harm or deserves pity. And it is a very common response to witnessing an illness or disability. Indeed, disability activist Harriet Johnson (2003), who suffered from a degenerative neuromuscular disease, wrote poignantly about how people come up to her on the street and say, "if I had to live like you I think I would kill myself."

However, as it turns out, disabled and chronically ill people rarely take their lives, and seem to have similar levels of well-being to those of healthy people (Gilbert 2006: 153).[1] Dozens of studies report no difference in levels of reported well-being between groups of people with a variety of medical conditions and healthy controls. For example, Angner and colleagues (2009) studied 383 adults in the community, examining the relationship between subjective health (as assessed by the individual), objective health (as assessed by an objective measurement such as comorbidity count), and happiness (subjective well-

---

[1] It is important to note that *well-being* in this context denotes subjectively measured well-being, or level of happiness. For a period, discussions focused on whether well-being is subjective or objective, and how we should measure it. Should we measure some objectively observable feature of behavior, such as amount of smiling or brain activity, or should we simply ask people how they feel? More recently many prominent researchers in psychology and happiness studies agree that only the subjective measurement makes sense and corresponds, roughly, to what we mean in everyday talk when we refer to happiness or well-being (Lyubomirsky 2007: 34). As Gilbert writes: "the attentive person's honest, real-time report is an imperfect approximation of her subjective experience, but it is the only game in town" (2006: 70). This is now more or less the received view.

being). They conclude that "medical conditions are associated with lower happiness scores only if they disrupt daily functioning or are associated with social stigma" and give two such examples – pain and urinary incontinence – in which happiness is affected by the condition (2009: 510). Another study compared a group of hemodialysis patients with healthy controls and found that both groups overestimated the impact of hemodialysis on well-being. In fact, both groups reported a similar level of well-being (Riis et al. 2005: 6). Similar findings have been reported by Chwalisz, Diener, and Gallagher (1988), Chaung and colleagues (1989), and de Haes and van Knippenberg (1985). De Haes, Van Knippenberg, and Neijt find that "Psychological symptoms do not automatically accompany physical distress" (1990: 1036). In a literature review of quality of life in cancer patients de Haes and van Knippenberg conclude that "in general the results from comparative studies are meagre and do not support the assumption that cancer or cancer treatment lead to a significantly lower quality of life" (1985: 815). These studies show little correlation between objective health and well-being, although NICE clinical guideline 91 summarizes evidence for some links, in particular in the first year following diagnosis of a chronic condition (p. 27). However, even if chronic illness and impairment overall do not reduce levels of well-being, we are still keen to avoid illness and consider good health a primary good. In other words, we try to avoid falling ill and to promote good health, but when we do fall ill this does not seem to affect our well-being in the long term (although a short-term negative effect does occur).

A common pattern is one of temporary lowering of well-being around the time of symptom appearance or diagnosis, with levels of well-being recovering to their previous baseline level within about a year (cf. Lyubomirsky 2007: 50). This can be explained by appealing to the phenomenon known as "hedonic adaptation": the way we adapt to – and therefore cease to feel the impact of – changes to circumstances like the car we drive, size of house, and even marital status (Lyubomirsky 2007: 47ff.). Hedonic adaptation also works when the changes are negative, for example, falling ill, having to adjust to continuous medical treatment, and loss of mobility (Riis et al. 2005). As Angner and colleagues (2009) note, insofar as a medical condition impacts well-being at all, it does so for a relatively short period of time after diagnosis or symptom appearance. More generally and more strongly, some findings show that overall life circumstances (which include upbringing, marital status, income, health, and so on) together account for only 10 percent of our happiness (Lyubomirsky 2007: 20). This view, known as *set point theory*, holds that the stable component of well-being is largely determined genetically (Lykken and Tellegen, 1996). Set point theory views the effects of life events as "transitory fluctuations about a stable temperamental set point or trait that is characteristic of the individual" (Lykken and Tellegen 1996: 189). Lykken and Tellegen go so far as to claim that the well-being of one's identical twin is a better predictor of one's self-rated happiness than one's own education, income, or status (1996: 189).

How can we explain this discrepancy between our intuition that illness is a terrible thing, and the data showing that when we are stuck with it, we quickly adjust? Two issues require an explanation. First, why does illness not affect long-term well-being? Second, if illness does not make people unhappy, why do healthy people view illness as a purely negative event? One way of accounting for this tension is attending to the difference between outsider assessments of ill health made by healthy people and insider assessments made by ill people. The difference is big and can be presented by using the following example. In a study of European quality of life assessments, Dolan (1997) identified eighty-three states of illness that healthy interviewees characterized as worse than death. In contrast, people who actually live with these conditions report a similar level of well-being as their healthy counterparts. There is clearly a marked difference, indeed a gulf, between how these states of illness are experienced firsthand and how observers perceive them.

Here are a few reasons such a gulf exists. First, healthy people have only sketchy ideas about what it would be like to live with an illness or impairment. Without firsthand acquaintance with the details, their view would probably be based on popular representations of illness, biased by the "focusing illusion," and would be limited and anecdotal. Healthy people would think of the illness or impairment as the defining feature of such a life, and therefore over weight it (Schkade and Kahneman 1998). Their knowledge of the actual impact of a particular condition on their life would be limited, so their ability to estimate this impact or to imagine ways of coping with it would suffer as a result. Moreover, healthy people also fail to anticipate the ways ill people adapt to poor health (Riis et al. 2005) and therefore fail to consider that such an adaptive process may enable them to be happy despite poor health.

So the sentiment expressed by my taxi driver and those described in Johnson's report is one of an outsider. Outsiders do not have access to the experience of illness or disability; they only have access to their imagined experience. And as psychologists such as Daniel Gilbert and Jonathan Haidt argue, work in empirical psychology shows that our ability to imagine counterfactual situations is limited and hampered by general psychological deficiencies. The relevant deficiencies are: limited imagination (the ability to imagine what a counterfactual situation would be like), flawed memory (defects in recall and recognition), limited ability to remember what a period of sickness was like, and the lack of ability to recognize past experiences of resilience and coping in difficult circumstances. In addition, people are unrealistically optimistic and tend to overestimate the possibility of good things happening to them in the future (Weinstein 1980). Healthy people spend less time imagining themselves as old and unwell, or diagnosed with a serious illness, than they do imagining themselves playing post-retirement golf in the Florida sunshine.

As Gilbert claims, imagination fails us in several ways. First, there is the focusing illusion, about which Gilbert writes:

[W]hen sighted people imagine being blind, they seem to forget that blindness is not a full-time job. Blind people can't see, but they do most of the things that sighted people do ... and thus they are just as happy as sighted people are.... when sighted people imagine being blind, they fail to imagine all the other things that such a life might be about, hence they mispredict how satisfying such a life can be. (2006: 104)

We have little capacity to imagine a complex situation that is remote from our own life (e.g., living with diabetes), because, for one, we do not have the required detail to hand. Without having firsthand or at least secondhand knowledge of the complexity of ensuring stable blood sugar levels, the frequent need to draw one's own blood, the calculation of insulin amounts needed prior to having a snack, and so on, it is impossible to even begin to imagine what such a life might be like. I moved from an abstract understanding of diabetes (understanding the disease mechanism and the need for insulin injections) to a startling recognition of my ignorance when I spent a day with a diabetic friend. The reality of the disease was very different and much more complex than my poorly imagined understanding of the disease in abstraction.

We also have limited ability to remember past events and feelings. In contrast to our sense of confidence about our memories, it transpires that we are much less able to remember what a situation was like, what an experience felt like at the time, or what we thought and felt in the past. As Gilbert writes:

The elaborate tapestry of our experience is not stored in memory.... Rather, it is compressed for storage by first being reduced to a few critical threads ... or a small set of key features. Later, when we want to remember our experience, our brains quickly reweave the tapestry by fabricating – not actually retrieving – the bulk of the information that we experience as memory. (2006: 79)

We do not remember full scenarios, in the way a film or a recording takes down all (or most) relevant data. Our memories do not preserve wholly intact clips of past events. Memory preserves core features of the situation (e.g., it was dark; I felt frightened; harsh words were said) rather than the episode in its entirety. Important information is discarded and then reconstructed again when we recall the situation. So remembering is not so much remembering as fabricating. And of course that means that our ability to remember what it was like when we were sick or in hospital is compromised.

The practical reason human memory has evolved to work this way is maximal efficiency: by storing only core features of a situation, we make considerable savings on memory storage space. And it is probably a good enough mechanism for most events. It guarantees personal identity, ensures that salient events are remembered well (even if not accurately), and that crucial warnings (e.g., don't eat that plant, don't walk by the lion den) are remembered and heeded. It also guarantees that we remember the way to the waterhole, who our relatives are, and so on. But the factual and emotional details of noncrucial events are not important in an evolutionary sense. They are therefore forgotten and, when recalled, fabricated. Gilbert (2006) gives as an example an experiment in which participants are shown a picture of a room. The picture is then removed and participants are asked to recall the shape and color of the clock that was on the wall in the picture. The majority of participants manage to describe the clock. However, there was no clock on the wall in the picture and participants confabulate one based on other clocks they have seen and remembered in the past. Gilbert sums this by saying: "memories – especially memories of experiences – are notoriously unreliable" (2006: 40). Overconfidence with respect to memory has also been shown to be particularly misleading in situations of danger or high emotions. High levels of adrenalin or feelings of panic interfere with cognitive function and make memories of an unusual or negative situation even less trustworthy. For example, eyewitness misidentification is argued by *The Innocence Project* to be extremely rife and "the single greatest cause of wrongful convictions" (cf. Cutler and Penrod 1995). Similarly, particular states, such as intense physical activity, can reduce recall and recognition ability (Hope et al. 2012). So we have three reasons to distrust the intuitions of healthy people about illness: they do not have the relevant information, cannot imagine life with illness in detail, and have only rudimentary memories of their own periods of illness. Now we can turn to the second question identified earlier, and ask: How can we explain the lack of impact ill health has on well-being?

RESILIENCE IN ILLNESS

Overall, we are more resilient than we think. Adverse life events such as illness, accidents, divorce, and loss of a loved one seem to be overemphasized as life destroying by people asked to think about them. Illness is no exception to the general finding, replicated in many studies and with respect to different kinds of events: we erroneously think that negative events will affect us more intensely and for longer than they actually do (Gilbert 2006: 152; Haidt 2006: 136ff.; Lyubomirsky 2007). As Haidt notes, people systematically underestimate their ability to cope with adverse circumstances and have no way of predicting the personal growth, resilience, and development that often follow a period of great difficulty. In fact, he goes so far as to present an "adversity hypothesis": "people need adversity, setbacks, and perhaps even trauma to reach the highest levels of strength, fulfilment, and personal development" (2006: 136). Haidt calls this consequence of experiencing adversity "posttraumatic growth" and notes three mechanisms that enable such personal growth in the face of adversity.

First, having to confront a challenge, in the form of an accident, divorce, losing one's job, or an illness reveals hidden abilities and experiencing these changes one's self-image. "One of the most common lessons people draw from bereavement or trauma is that they are much stronger than they realized, and this new appreciation of their strength then gives them confidence to face future challenges" (Haidt 2006: 139). This is not just a form of self-deception; studies show that people who have suffered hardship recover more quickly when faced with future adversity (Haidt 2006: 139).

The second factor is the improvement to relationships noted in such circumstances, in which people are forced to speak frankly about important issues, such as death and disease, and are forced to ask for help from family and friends. The lack of intimacy that is possible in routine social encounters becomes untenable and an opportunity emerges for authentic relationships to become stronger and for honesty and intimacy to be sought with clarity and intensity. As Bronnie Ware, a palliative care nurse, writes about caring for a dying woman: "once we reached this level of honesty, our conversations flowed unhindered. There was no time for holding back.... With death on her doorstep, Elisabeth, too, enjoyed the openness of our constant exchanges" (2012: 149). Actor Christopher Reeve, who became paralyzed from the neck down in a sports accident, famously said that he did not appreciate other people nearly as much as he does now, when severely disabled (quoted in Gilbert 2006). When adversity strikes, Haidt notes, it "strengthens relationships and opens people's hearts to one another" (2006: 139).

The third factor is the change to priorities and values, which makes people who undergo adversity focus on the present. This has been noted in many qualitative health care studies of people who have become ill (Brennan 2012; Frank 2002). The unpredictability of the course of illness leads some to adopt a perspective of living in the present and refraining from looking toward the future, making long-term plans, or having rigid goals (Michael 1996). One of the reported changes to their lives is the refocus on the present (which we all had as children, but we mostly lose as adults) that leads to great enjoyment of and attention to one's current experience. In the case of illness in particular, because of physical and mental limitations, pain, limited mobility, fatigue, and sometimes a poor prognosis, the emphasis on what is still possible to enjoy is often described by ill people as a positive way of dealing with the effects of illness. But this is often the result of a long process of adjustment and reflection.

The challenge in the case of illness, in particular when prognosis is poor, is clear. Resilience needs to be developed in response to a considerable challenge. If we return to the phenomenological concepts discussed in the first section, we can think about illness as modifying one's entire being-in-the-world. A localized response will not suffice in such cases. Illness changes everything about individuals' lives – their relationship to their environment, social relations, their relationship with their own body, their goals and plans, and their relationship to their future. Moreover, the challenge of illness is often to make peace, or to learn to live well with, facts that we would dearly wish to be otherwise. As I wrote in my book, *Illness*:

> The future no longer contains the vague promise of many more decades. Death is no longer an abstract, remote notion. The soft-focus lens is replaced by a sharp magnifying glass through which terminal stages of illness can be viewed in nauseating detail. The future curls in on itself and at once becomes both exposed and radically curtailed. (2008: 123)

The response to this challenge is to take notice of time and to turn from taking time for granted as a resource that can thoughtlessly be spent, to appreciating it, cherishing it. The result is more awareness of the present moment and an increased ability to experience the details of what seem like mundane moments:

> Time did change for me. I began to take it much more seriously. I began to make a point of enjoying things thoroughly: memorizing sensations, views, moments. Partly in preparation for days to come in which I may not be able to leave the house or my bed, but also in order to feel that I have taken the time to really sense, really experience pleasurable things. I wanted to feel that I am living life to the full in the present. That I *am* now. (2008: 123)

When the future becomes uncertain, or becomes certainly bad, it releases us from its usual intense grip. We normally worry a lot about the future, plan, strategize, strive toward goals. When this element is weakened, many ill people find that turning to the present enables them to slow down, appreciate the moment, and cease worrying about what may happen. The fragility and preciousness of the present become more visible and more appreciated. And this can lead to flourishing in unexpected ways. As Nietzsche notes about his own lengthy period of illness, physical frailty has a regenerative effect:

> It was as if I discovered life anew, myself included; I tasted all the good things, even the small ones, as no other could easily taste them – I turned my will to health, to life, into my philosophy ... the years when my vitality was at its lowest were when I stopped being a pessimist. (2004: 8)

Other thinkers, like Epicurus, argue passionately in favor of living in the present as the key to well-being. For Epicurus, the achievement of well-being is removing all sources of anguish and pain. Once this state has been attained, nothing more can be added to one's well-being. It is already perfectly tranquil (*ataraxia*), perfectly painless (*aponia*). But in order to achieve tranquility, an important temporal focus must be achieved first. We must remove our unhealthy connections to the past (regret, longing, bitterness, loss) and the future (anxiety, obsession, worry, desire). Such detachment from the past and the future brings with it an ability to concentrate on the present – what is happening now, what is being experienced now. Learning to free oneself from the past and the future in order to fully concentrate on the present is an important part of well-being. Epicurus recommends that it be followed by an effort to bring pleasure and joy into the present, and finally, realizing that the quality of the present moment does not depend on how long it lasts, or how many desires it fulfills. A moment can be simple, quaint, unremarkable but for its joy. Adversity, in its many shapes and forms, can be a powerful reminder of the value of such a moment. As Epicurus sums it up: "you are not in control of tomorrow and yet you delay your opportunity to rejoice" (1994: 36).

This focus on the present is particularly important in the case of illness. Privileging the present can make a significant change to the experience of illness. It enables us to locate the source of mental anguish in the past: memories of things she could once do can cause an ill person great suffering. Similarly, the future causes us great anxiety in illness: we fear future suffering and death. Focusing on the present can help us distance ourselves from both past and future, and this can be a way to distill a moment (or a string of moments) of well-being. Focusing on present abilities, joys, and experiences instead of worrying about a past that no longer exists (my previous healthy self, regrets about its loss and longing for it) and a future that does not yet exist (the imagined future suffering that may or may not happen) is a way of avoiding some of the suffering caused by illness.

Gilbert offers another psychological mechanism that explains resilience in illness, namely, rationalization. People consider their situation relative to that of others in the relevant reference group in an attempt to minimize the perceived adversity of their situation by contextualizing it and comparing it to the situation of those in a similar predicament. For example, in a study by Taylor and colleagues (1986) 96 percent of cancer patients claimed to be in better health than the average cancer patient. People with life-threatening illnesses are particularly likely to compare themselves with those who are in worse shape and this protects them from thinking that their own state is substantially worse off than that of the healthy.

Also, many qualitative studies of the experience of a variety of illnesses have identified central positive themes that emerge from coping with illness. For example, themes such as being courageous, regaining control of an altered life course, reshaping the self, self-transcendence, empowerment, and discovery, are often described by interviewees suffering from an illness (Thorne and Paterson 1998). Although suffering from a serious condition and having to contend with illness and a poor prognosis, the "posttraumatic growth" expressed by such themes and the positive psychological response to illness go some way toward explaining how well-being is possible even within the context of a serious illness. As Helson (1964) notes, well-being is comprised of multiple components, and it is possible that a reduction in one area (health) is compensated for by an increase in another area (personal growth, intimacy, relationships), so the overall level of well-being remains the same. Helson's observation ties in with a general view of illness as non-linear, changeable experience. Paterson (2001) developed a "shifting perspectives" model of chronic illness in which illness comes into the foreground during the initial phase of illness, but then recedes into the background, coming back into the foreground during episodes of symptom exacerbation or disease progression. This model enables us to see how illness may fade into the background and accounts for lengthy periods in which it may play no substantial role in one's life.

A final way of explaining resilience in illness relates to the ways we experience our body. It has become a kind of accepted truth that the body in health is "transparent" (Sartre 2003), "hidden" (Keane 2013), or even "absent" (Leder 1990), and this has often been contrasted with illness, in which the body becomes cumbersome, aberrant, and is thematized mainly through negative medical attention (Toombs 1987). I would like to suggest that this rift in bodily experience has perhaps been overstated. In fact, the healthy body contains its own opaqueness and glimpses of the experience of illness, although radical and disruptive, can be seen in everyday bodily failure. The upshot of this is that if we cease to understand bodily experiences of illness and of health as radically different, we may find it easier to accept that illness undergoes a normalizing effect over time. This, in turn, makes illness more tolerable and those who are ill more resilient. This sits well with several ideas discussed earlier, such as hedonic adaptation, the focusing illusion, and the empirical findings that ill health does not affect well-being over time, beyond an initial period of disruption and then adjustment. If we place bodily experiences of illness and of health on a continuum, rather than contrasting them sharply, we may find that resilience is an expression of this continuity. Perhaps bodily experiences that initially seem bizarre and extraordinary become quotidian once they are added to our bodily and experiential repertoire. The same applies for loss of abilities and possibilities. Perhaps we similarly adjust to such losses by shrinking our perceived horizon of possibilities. To exemplify this point, here are two first-person accounts of such a process. The first is a multiple sclerosis patient, reflecting on the fact that he can no longer use his legs to walk, run, or even stand. These abilities, he says, lost much of their importance and are "no longer within the sphere of possibility and are therefore not missed as though they were possible" (Schneider 1998: 71). In my account of my illness I wrote:

> My body adapted with astonishing alacrity to new limitations. My mind quickly forgot how things were before. Within a year my physical habits were entirely different. Whereas in the first months my body would attempt a brisk pace, hurrying up stairs, physical impatience, these movements have been erased from my bodily repertoire. While my memory still contained images of mountain views and the inside of a gym, I could no longer remember what it felt like to run, to work out, the euphoric sensation of healthy exertion, the effortlessness of being young and healthy. New habits were formed and a new way of negotiating the world was incorporated into my physicality. Blissful forgetfulness of the pleasures of physical movement accompanied them. (2008: 30)

It is not so clear that the healthy body is as transparent or as absent as scholars have postulated in the philosophical literature. The body continuously emerges for us in everyday activities. It may not be the thematic focus of our activity or attention, but it will still provide constant reminders of itself through hunger, fatigue, failure to concentrate, inability to learn a new task (e.g., how to juggle or do a headstand). The body is constantly there for us not merely as a peripheral enabling background, but as the medium of our experiencing, which necessarily includes a self-reflexive dimension, although this can recede into the background. When we experience the beauty of an icy winter landscape, the feeling of cold is part and parcel of this experience. When we weep at a melodrama in front of the TV, the visceral sense of sadness is an inseparable part of the experience. Other, more obvious, examples may include the many kinds of bodily enjoyment available to us: food, sex, warmth, restfulness, dancing, running, hugging and so on are cases in which bodily experience comes to the fore.

The body is not transparent in health. And nor is it entirely opaque or obstructive in illness. Bodily enjoyment is often still possible, at least in some form, and the increased opacity that characterizes illness may be mitigated by other things. Several authors in the phenomenology of illness have emphasized the opacity and limitations of illness (Svenaeus 2001; Toombs 1987). But it is also important to acknowledge the possibility of continued, or regained, normalcy, and the periods of stability that often characterize chronic illness. This has been captured in the notions of "health within illness" (Lindsey 1996) and "well-being within illness" (Carel 2007), which aim to make space for the possibility of being well and happy within the broader context of having a chronic condition or impairment. Even if the body in illness becomes more opaque and more cumbersome, this opacity has the same changeability and varied inflections as the putative transparency of health. I am not belittling the effects of ill health, the suffering, loss of freedom, or indeed shock and shattering of life's hopes and expectations. I am pointing out that these negative effects are temporary and are often mitigated by life's other goods, such as good relationships, intimacy, finding joy and solace in new activities, and our incredible ability to adapt to what might seem at the outset as an intolerably cruel turn of fate.

CONCLUSION: WELL-BEING AS ACHIEVEMENT

This chapter posed a question, namely, how is well-being possible within the confines of poor health, an uncertain prognosis, and limitation of one's freedom? I suggested that two "enigmas of health" (to paraphrase Gadamer) arise from this question. First, why don't ill people become markedly unhappy as a result of their illness? Second, given that we have robust evidence showing that well-being is not impacted by ill health, why do we fear illness and see it as such an evil when we are healthy? I then sought to explain the discrepancy by looking carefully at what takes place when insiders and outsiders view illness and disability. I proposed phenomenology as a useful tool for philosophically describing the first-person experience of illness. Several concepts – being-in-the-world, authenticity, anxiety, uncanniness, and the body-as-lived– were introduced and the importance of the first-person account of illness was demonstrated. I then suggested some explanations for the remarkable resilience people show in the face of illness (and other trauma).

To conclude this chapter, let us now turn to the philosophical question, what *is* well-being? Philosophers have proposed many definitions of well-being, flourishing, and happiness (for a selection of philosophical writings on happiness see Cahn and Vitrano 2008). We find Aristotle defining flourishing objectively, as *eudemonia*, a life that consists of cultivating virtue, where virtue is objective. We find psychologists turning to subjective measurements of well-being as definitive, and arguing that "no one but you knows or should tell you how happy you truly are" (Lyubomirsky 2007: 34). We find behavioral economists developing sophisticated methods of showing that sometimes even the subject herself is subject to bias and illusion when she tries to judge her own well-being (Schkade and Kahneman 1998). And we find that even our own attempts to predict what will make us happy are hampered by the limits and fallibility of our memory and imagination (Gilbert 2006). All this does not seem to leave us in a very comfortable, or consistent, position with respect to the notion of happiness.

I would like to suggest that we put to one side these conflicting definitions and methodologies and turn, in phenomenological spirit, to what ill and disabled people themselves say about well-being within the constraints of illness. Here is what disability activist Harriet Johnson (2003) thought:

> Are we "worse off""? I don't think so. For those of us with congenital conditions, disability shapes all we are. Those disabled later in life

adapt. We take constraints that no one would choose and build rich and satisfying lives within them.

And here is what I wrote about illness and the sense of helplessness that characterizes being ill:

> I cannot change reality; my illness is here to stay. But I can control some of the elements making up my life. I can, for example, control my thoughts (to some extent); I can control my reactions; I can cultivate the happy aspects of my life and I can say no to distressing thoughts and actions. I can choose what to do with the time I have and I can reject thoughts that cause me agony. I can learn to think clearly about my life, give meaning even to events beyond my control and modify my concepts of happiness, death, illness and time. (2008: 129)

These passages seem to suggest that well-being in the context of illness is neither something that is impossible, nor something that can be taken for granted. Rather, cultivating well-being within illness and learning to live well with physical and mental constraints is an *achievement* and should be both recognized and celebrated as such. Julia Annas suggests that happiness is "the task of forming my life as a whole in and by the way I act" (2008: 242). If we take seriously the phenomenological approach to illness and the robust evidence that ill people (and others who face adversity) are no less happy than other people, we can conclude that paying close attention to such claims may yield important insights about the experience of illness. If happiness is an achievement that requires thought, planning and work, this view contributes to our understanding of why illness does not affect long-term well-being. Illness provides us with a context and opportunity for the kind of reflection and revaluation that are the condition for and prelude to happiness on Annas' account. So it is no wonder that ill people find ways of being happy even within the constraints of illness.

FUNDING

This chapter was written during a period of research leave funded by the Leverhulme Trust. I thank the Trust for awarding me a fellowship and supporting my research. I also thank Jerome Bickenbach for helpful comments on the chapter.

References

Angner, E., N. R. Midege, K. G. Saag, and J. Allison (2009). Health and Happiness among Older Adults: A Community-Based Study. *Journal of Health Psychology* 14(4): 503–12.

Annas, J. (2008). Happiness as Achievement. In S. M. Cahn and C. Vitrano (eds.), *Happiness*. Oxford & New York: Oxford University Press, 238–45.

Brennan, J. (2012). Transitions in Health and Illness: Realist and Phenomenological Accounts of Adjustment to Cancer. In H. Carel and R. Cooper (eds.), *Health, Illness and Disease*. Durham, NC: Acumen.

Cahn, S. M., and C. Vitrano (2008). *Happiness*. Oxford & New York: Oxford University Press.

Carel, H. (2007). Can I be Ill and Happy? *Philosophia* 35(2): 95–110.

    (2008). *Illness*. Stocksfield: Acumen.

    (2010). Phenomenology and its Application in Medicine. *Theoretical Medicine and Bioethics* 32(1): 33–46.

    (2012). Phenomenology as a Resource for Patients. *Journal of Medicine and Philosophy*. DOI: 10.1093/jmp/jhs008.

    (2013). Bodily Doubt. *Journal of Consciousness Studies*. 20(7-8): 178–197.

Carel, H., and J. Macnaughton (2012). "How do you feel?": oscillating perspectives in the clinic (with J. Macnaughton), *Lancet* 379(9834): 2334–2335 (23 June) DOI:10.1016/S0140-6736(12)61007-1

Chaung H. T., G. M. Devins, J. Hunsley, and M. J. Gill (1989). Psychosocial Distress and Wellbeing among Gay and Bisexual Men with Human Immunodeficiency Virus Infection. *American Journal of Psychiatry* 146(7): 876–80.

Chwalisz, K., E. Diener, and D. Gallagher (1988). Autonomic Arousal Feedback and Emotional Experience: Evidence from the Spinal Cord Injured. *Journal of Personality and Social Psychology* 54(5): 820–28.

Cutler, B. L., and S. D. Penrod (1995). *Mistaken Identifications: The Eyewitness, Psychology, and Law*. New York: Cambridge University Press.

Carel

Dolan, P. (1997). Modelling Valuations for EuroQoL Health States. *Medical Care* 35(11): 1095–108.

Earle, V. (2010). Phenomenology as Research Method or Substantive Metaphysics? An Overview of Phenomenology's Uses in Nursing. *Nursing Philosophy* 11(4): 286–96.

Epicurus. (1994). *The Epicurus Reader.* B. Inwood and L. P. Gerson (eds.). Cambridge, MA: Hackett.

Frank, A. (2002). *At the Will of the Body.* New York: Mariner Books.

Getz, L., A. L. Kirkengen, and E. Ulvestad (2011). The Human Biology – Saturated with Experience. *Tidsskrift for Den Norske Legeforening* 7: 683–7.

Gilbert, D. (2006). *Stumbling on Happiness.* London: Harper Press.

Goldberg, D. et al. (2009). Depression in Adults with a Chronic Physical Health Problem: Treatment and Management. National Clinical Practice Guideline Number 91.

de Haes, J. C. J. M., and F. C. E. van Knippenberg (1985). The Quality of Life of Cancer Patients: A Review of the Literature. *Social Science and Medicine* 20(8): 809–17.

de Haes, J. C. J. M., F. C. E. van Knippenberg, and J. P. Neijt (1990). Measuring Psychological and Physical Distress in Cancer Patients. *British Journal of Cancer* 62: 1034–8.

Earle, V. (2010) Phenomenology as Research Method or Substantive Metaphysics? An Overview of Phenomenology's Uses in Nursing. *Nursing Philosophy* 11(4): 286–96.

Haidt, J. (2006). *The Happiness Hypothesis.* London: William Heinemann.

Heidegger, M. (1962 [1927]). *Being and Time.* Trans. J. Macquarrie and E. Robinson. Oxford: Basil Blackwell.

Helson, H. (1964). *Adaptation-Level Theory: An Experimental and Systematic Approach to Behaviour.* New York: Harper and Row.

Hope, L., W. Lewinski, J. Dixon, D. Blocksidge, and F. Gabbert. (2012). Witnesses in Action: the Effect of Physical Exertion on Recall and Recognition. *Psychological Science.* ISSN 1467–9280 10.1177/0956797611431463.

Husserl, E. (1999 [1950]). *Cartesian Meditations.* Trans. D. Cairns. Dordrecht: Kluwer.

Husserl, E. (1991 [1966]). *On the Phenomenology of the Consciousness of Internal Time.* Trans. J. B. Brough. Dordrecht: Kluwer.

The Innocence Project. http://www.innocenceproject.org/ (accessed on 19 March 2012).

Johnson, H. M. (2003). Unspeakable Conversations. *New York Times.* February 16, 2003.

Keane, N. (2013). The Hiddenness of Health. In D. Meacham (ed.), *Medicine and Society: New Continental Perspectives*. Dordrecht: Springer. (in press).

Leder, D. (1990). *The Absent Body*. Chicago, IL: University of Chicago Press.

Lindsey, E. (1996). Health within Illness: Experiences of Chronically Ill/ Disabled People. *Journal of Advanced Nursing* 24: 465–72.

Lykken, D., and A. Tellegen (1996). Happiness is a Stochastic Phenomenon. *Psychological Science* 7(3): 186–9.

Lyubomirsky, S. (2007). *The How of Happiness*. London: Piatkus Books.

Merleau-Ponty, M. (1962 [1945]). *Phenomenology of Perception*. Trans. C. Smith. New York & London: Routledge.

Michael, S. R. (1996). Integrating Chronic Illness into One's Life. *Journal of Holistic Nursing* 14(3): 251–67.

Nietzsche, F. (2004). *Ecce Homo*. Oxford: Oxford University Press.

Paterson, B. (2001). The Shifting Perspectives Model of Chronic Illness. *Journal of Nursing Scholarship* 33(1): 21–6.

Ratcliffe, M. (2008). *Feelings of Being: Phenomenology, Psychiatry and the Sense of Reality*. Oxford: Oxford University Press.

Riis J., J. Baron, G. Loewenstein, and C. Jepson (2005). Ignorance of Hedonic Adaptation to Haemodialysis: A Study Using Ecological Momentary Assessment. *Journal of Experimental Psychology: General* 134(1): 3–9.

Sartre, J. P. (2003 [1943]). *Being and Nothingness*. London: Routledge.

Schkade, D. A., and D. Kahneman (1998). Does Living in California Make People Happy? A Focusing Illusion in Judgments of Life Satisfaction. *Psychological Science* 9(5): 340–6.

Shakespeare, W. (2007). As You Like It. In *The RSC Shakespeare: The Complete Works*. Basingstoke: Palgrave Macmillan.

Ware, B. (2012). *The Top Five Regrets of the Dying: A Life Transformed by the Dearly Departing*. London: Hay House UK.

Schneider, C. E. (1998). *The Practice of Autonomy*. New York: Oxford University Press.

Sontag, S. (1978). *Illness as Metaphor*. New York: Farrar, Straus & Giroux.

Stanghellini, G. (2004). *Disembodied Spirits and Deanimated Bodies*. Oxford: Oxford University Press.

Svenaeus, F. (2000a). Das Unheimliche – Towards a Phenomenology of Illness. *Medicine, Health Care and Philosophy* 3: 3–16.

(2000b). The Body Uncanny – Further Steps Towards a Phenomenology of Illness. *Medicine, Health Care and Philosophy* 3: 125–37.

(2001). *The Hermeneutics of Medicine and the Phenomenology of Health*. Dordrecht: Kluwer.

Taylor, S. E., R. L. Falke, S. J. Shoptaw, and R. R. Lichtman (1986). *Journal of Consulting and Clinical Psychology* 54(5): 608–15.

Thorne, S., and B. Paterson (1998). Shifting Images of Chronic Illness. *Image: Journal of Nursing Scholarship* 30(2): 173–8.

Thorne, S., B. Paterson, S. Acorn, C. Canam, G. Joachim, and C. Jillings (2002). Chronic Illness Experience: Insights from a Metastudy. *Qualitative Health Research* 12(4): 437–52.

Toombs, S. K. (1987). The Meaning of Illness: A Phenomenological Approach to the Patient-Physician Relationship. *The Journal of Medicine and Philosophy* 12: 219–40.

(1990). The Temporality of Illness: Four Levels of Experience. *Theoretical Medicine* 11: 227–41.

(1999). *The Meaning of Illness: A Phenomenological Account of the Different Perspectives of Physician and Patient.* Amsterdam: Kluwer.

(2001). The Role of Empathy in Clinical Practice. *Journal of Consciousness Studies* 8(5–7): 247–58.

Ware, B. (2012). *The Top Five Regrets of the Dying.* London: Hay House.

Weinstein, N. (1980). Unrealistic Optimism about Future Life Events. *Journal of Personality and Social Psychology* 39: 806–20.

11

Natural Diversity and Justice for People with Disabilities

CHRISTOPHER A. RIDDLE

"Human dignity," writes Martha Nussbaum, "is equal in all who are agents."[1] Everyone is said to deserve equal respect from societal laws and institutions. She argues that the primary target of a theory of egalitarian justice ought to be the protection of freedoms so central that without them, an individual's life is not worthy of human dignity.[2] She argues for the centrality of notions of dignity and respect in articulating a conception of social justice.[3] The conception of dignity at play here espouses a principle of human beings as an end, and not merely a means to another's end.[4]

Not everyone of course, places such primacy on dignity. Some suggest that while dignity is a notoriously slippery and multidimensional notion, it can retain its usefulness with further theorizing and clarification.[5] Still others suggest that the notion of human

---

[1] Martha Nussbaum, *Creating Capabilities: The Human Development Approach* (Cambridge: The Belknap Press of Harvard University Press, 2011), 31.

[2] Ibid.

[3] Ibid., 26.

[4] Ibid., 25; Martha Nussbaum, *Frontiers of Justice: Disability, Nationality and Species Membership* (Cambridge: The Belknap Press of Harvard University Press, 2006), 36 and 70; Martha Nussbaum, *Women and Human Development* (Cambridge: Cambridge University Press, 2000), 74.

[5] Doris Schroder, "Dignity: Two Riddles and Four Concepts," *Cambridge Quarterly of Healthcare Ethics* 17, 2 (2008): 237.

dignity offers little by way of moral justification or guidance.[6] Ruth Macklin for example, suggested that we can do away with dignity altogether.[7]

A different objection has recently come to the forefront, however. *Contra* those who dissent in the abovementioned manner, this objection acknowledges the importance of dignity, but suggests that the capabilities approach is not the proper means to ensure it. At the foundation of the capabilities approach is the protection of areas of freedom (or capabilities) "so central that their removal makes a life not worthy of human dignity."[8] Thus, dignity plays an integral role in the establishment and justification of the capabilities approach.

The abovementioned objection is not launched because the capabilities approach is thought of as prima facie, the incorrect currency of egalitarian justice. Nor is it because the central capabilities thought to be of utmost importance are deemed misrepresentative of what it means to live a life worthy of human dignity. Instead, the emphasis has been placed upon the operationalization of the capabilities approach. More specifically, it has been suggested that the capabilities approach stigmatizes individuals in both the assessment of need, and provision of resources and accommodation, thus undermining an essential aspect of one's human dignity.

In this chapter I suggest that one of the primary measures of the success or failure of a conception of egalitarian justice ought to be its ability to avoid the *further* stigmatization of vulnerable populations when making assessments of need *and* implementing measures to address that need.[9] I refer to the ability to not further stigmatize individuals on the basis of naturally acquired skills or endowments

---

[6] Udo Schüklenk and Anna Pacholczyk, "Dignity's Wooly Uplift," *Bioethics* 24, 2 (2010): ii.

[7] Ruth Macklin, "Dignity is a Useless Concept," *British Medical Journal* 237, 7429 (2003): 1419–20.

[8] Nussbaum, *Creating Capabilities*, 31.

[9] I owe the emphasis on "further" to Andrew D. F. Ross.

when addressing need as *stigma sensitivity*. I suggest that despite the clear strengths of the capabilities approach, it nevertheless fails to be as stigma sensitive as alternative conceptions. One might deduce (and correctly so) from this statement that stigma sensitivity is not an all-or-nothing attribute. Conceptions can be more or less stigma sensitive. Thomas Pogge suggests the capabilities approach suffers from what he refers to as "the vertical-inequality problem,"[10] Elizabeth Anderson suggests alternatively that capabilities possess more stigma sensitivity than resource-based conceptions of justice.[11] My interpretation of capabilities falls somewhere between Pogge's and Anderson's. I suggest this low level of sensitivity ought to be taken seriously within justice discourse and that consequently, we must reformulate the capabilities perspective to be a more stigma-sensitive egalitarian theory in an attempt to promote an adequate minimal conception of justice.

I suggest that when examining competing claims of justice, attention ought to be paid to how we might begin to operationalize redistributive measures and assess need in a society where these values of equality and justice are endorsed. I make a modest and I think self-evident claim that, when comparing two otherwise equally desirable conceptions of justice, priority ought to be given to the conceptualization that is more stigma sensitive – that stigmatizes those in need less than other, competing claims. I then defend a more ambitious claim, suggesting that strict opportunity-based accounts of distributive justice increase the likelihood of further marginalizing individuals on the basis of naturally acquired skills or endowments.

---

[10] Thomas Pogge, "Can the Capability Approach be Justified?," *Philosophical Topics* 30, 2 (2002): 204; Thomas Pogge, "A Critique of the Capability Approach," in *Measuring Justice: Primary Goods and Capabilities*, ed. Harry Brighouse and Ingrid Robeyns (Cambridge: Cambridge University Press, 2010), 44.

[11] Elizabeth Anderson, "Justifying the Capabilities Approach to Justice," in *Measuring Justice: Primary Goods and Capabilities*, ed. Harry Brighouse and Ingrid Robeyns (Cambridge: Cambridge University Press, 2010), 95–7.

DEFINING THE CAPABILITIES APPROACH

Prior to engaging with Pogge and Anderson, let me attempt to clearly articulate what it is I am referring to when I say "the capabilities approach." There of course, have been numerous proponents of this approach. It was first introduced by Amartya Sen, who suggested that a focus on the possession of goods or resources was inadequate.[12] Instead, he argued that what really mattered was what people were able to be or do as a result of possessing goods or resources. According to Sen, "the conversion of goods to capabilities [opportunities to pursue various valuable life states] varies from person to person substantially, and the equality of the former may still be far from the equality of the latter."[13] We can see the truth of this statement by examining the life of an individual with a severe disability. The costs of living are often drastically increased for disabled individuals as basic functions such as navigating their built environment comes at a much greater expenditure of resources.[14] Therefore, an adequate distribution must take into account what people are capable of doing with the resources at their disposal, and not simply what goods they might avail themselves of.

Thus, we must shift our attention from goods or resources to what these goods can do to and for human beings.[15] The primary focus ought to be individuals' capability to function.[16] These capabilities should be pursued by each and every person and, as mentioned previously, the

---

[12] Amartya Sen, "Equality of What?," in *Equal Freedom: Selected Tanner Lectures on Human Values*, ed. S. Darwall (Ann Arbor: University of Michigan Press, 1995), 328.

[13] Ibid., 329.

[14] See, for example, a study completed by Wiebke Kuklys that demonstrates this fact in *Amartya Sen's Capability Approach: Theoretical Insights and Empirical Applications* (Berlin: Springer-Verlag, 2005), 83–7.

[15] Sen, "Equality of What?," 329.

[16] Jonathan Wolff and Avner De-Shalit, *Disadvantage* (Oxford: Oxford University Press, 2007), 8.

goal of such an approach is to treat each person as an ends, and never as a mere means to the ends of another.[17] The capabilities approach has two primary components. Briefly, *functionings* are things and/or activities that people have a choice between. A *capability* is a set of functionings an individual has a choice over. Therefore, one's capability set represents one's freedom to choose alternative lives to lead.

Martha Nussbaum, the other main proponent and founder of the capabilities approach, suggests that "one way of thinking about the capabilities list is to think of it as embodied in a list of constitutional guarantees."[18] One's capability set is the set of substantial freedoms genuinely and securely available to pursue. The end state of a realized capability is a functioning. There are various valuable functionings in life and the capabilities approach, at least according to Nussbaum, is resolutely pluralistic about value.[19]

Jonathan Wolff and Avner De-Shalit agree, and argue first, that disadvantage is plural and is in one sense, a matter of low functioning.[20] Second, they suggest that not only is disadvantage related to the actual functionings achieved, but more importantly, that a vital aspect of advantage and disadvantage is one's prospect of achieving or sustaining a particular level of functioning.[21] This notion introduces security as it relates to functioning – or security as it relates to achievement rather than merely the ability to achieve. One way of being disadvantaged is when one's functionings become insecure involuntarily (or when one must make one functioning insecure to ensure another). The assurance of "expected functioning" or "expected utility" can reduce individual responsibility, however.[22] Wolff and De-Shalit address the need for individuals to be responsible for their actions by suggesting that the idea of

[17] Nussbaum, *Women and Human Development*, 5.
[18] Nussbaum, *Frontiers of Justice*, 155.
[19] Nussbaum, *Creating Capabilities*, 18.
[20] Wolff and De-Shalit, *Disadvantage*, 24.
[21] Ibid., 65.
[22] Ibid., 75.

"capability" is too vague when attempting to address such consider-ations, and that instead it should be replaced with the idea of "genuine opportunities for secure functionings," thus ensuring individuals are held accountable for their own actions while also providing security.[23]

Various other capable theorists have advanced, defended, or mod-ified the capabilities approach.[24] However, I do take Nussbaum's ver-sion of the capabilities approach to be primary in this examination, and return to it now. I focus primarily on Nussbaum partly for reasons of necessary limitations, but mainly because she is far more explicit than most with reference to both the philosophical assumptions and importance of the approach, as well as how this approach addresses problems of disability.

Nussbaum defends her list of basic capabilities by appealing to a criterion of what it means to be "truly human." More specifically, she asks:

> What are the features of our common humanity, features that lead us to recognize certain others, however distant in their location and their forms of life, as humans, and on the other hand, to decide that certain other beings who resemble us superficially could not possi-bly be human?[25]

Take the following examples to illustrate this process. Were we to encounter a set of creatures that resemble humans physically, but that had eternal life, or perhaps did not attach any value to life whatsoever and wanted to die as quickly as possible, we would likely consider them

---

[23] Ibid., 80.

[24] The most important of which I take to be: Jennifer Prah Ruger, *Health and Social Justice* (New York: Oxford University Press, 2009); Jennifer Prah Ruger, "Toward a Theory of a Right to Health: Capability and Incompletely Theorized Agreements," *Yale Journal of Law and Humanities* 17, 2 (2006): 273–326; Elizabeth S. Anderson, "What is the Point of Equality?," *Ethics* 109, 2 (1999): 287–337.

[25] Martha Nussbaum, "Aristotelian Social Democracy," in *Liberalism and the Good*, ed. R. Bruce Douglas, Gerald M. Mara, and Henry S. Richardson (New York: Routledge, 1990), 219.

so distinct from us because of these peculiarities that they could not possibly count as human. The fact that we face death and generally all wish to live, coupled with the fact that we would deem any creature who did not face death or wish to live as being so distinct from us it did not qualify as a human being, gives us reason to include life on the basic capability list.[26]

Take one last example to highlight the process Nussbaum uses to articulate her basic capability list. She suggests that we regard an inability to laugh to signify some sort of deep disturbance in a child.[27] Moreover, were we to imagine a society comprised entirely of individuals lacking the ability to laugh and find humor in things, we would find such a society strange or perhaps even frightening.[28] Therefore, according to Nussbaum, the capabilities of humor and play ought to be included on the list because they are part of what it means to be distinctly human. Nussbaum offers similar rationale for specifying the other eight capabilities as well.

In shoring up these justifications, she also consistently speaks of living a life worthy of human dignity.[29] More specifically, she asks us what conditions must be met to say that one is living a life worthy of human dignity. That said, it is not my intention to justify, defend, or critique the methods employed by Nussbaum to arrive at her conception here. I simply mention such things by way of background for what follows.

Ultimately, through such a process, Nussbaum arrives at a list of ten basic capabilities required for one to live a life worthy of human dignity:

1. *Life.* Being able to live to the end of a human life of normal length; not dying prematurely, or before one's life is so reduced as to be not worth living.

---

[26] Ibid.
[27] Ibid., 222.
[28] Ibid.
[29] Nussbaum, *Frontiers of Justice*, 74.

2. *Bodily Health.* Being able to have good health, including reproductive health; to be adequately nourished; to have adequate shelter.

3. *Bodily Integrity.* Being able to move freely from place to place; to be secure against violent assault, including sexual assault and domestic violence; having opportunities for sexual satisfaction and for choice in matters of reproduction.

4. *Senses, Imagination, and Thought.* Being able to use the senses, to imagine, think, and reason – and to do these things in a "truly human" way, a way informed and cultivated by an adequate education, including, but by no means limited to, literacy and basic mathematical and scientific training. Being able to use imagination and thought in connection with experiencing and producing works and events of one's own choice, religious, literary, musical, and so forth. Being able to use one's mind in ways protected by guarantees of freedom of expression with respect to both political and artistic speech, and freedom of religious exercise. Being able to have pleasurable experiences and to avoid nonbeneficial pain.

5. *Emotions.* Being able to have attachments to things and people outside ourselves; to love those who love and care for us, to grieve at their absence; in general, to love, to grieve, to experience longing, gratitude, and justified anger. Not having one's emotional development blighted by fear and anxiety. (Supporting this capability means supporting forms of human association that can be shown to be crucial in their development.)

6. *Practical Reason.* Being able to form a conception of the good and to engage in critical reflection about the planning of one's life. (This entails protection for the liberty of conscience and religious observance.)

7. *Affiliation.*
   A. Being able to live with and toward others, to recognize and show concern for other human beings, to engage in various forms of social interaction; to be able to imagine the situation of another. (Protecting this capability means protecting institutions that

constitute and nourish such forms of affiliation, and also protecting the freedom of assembly and political speech.)

   B. Having the social bases of self-respect and nonhumiliation; being able to be treated as a dignified being whose worth is equal to that of others. This entails provisions of nondiscrimination on the basis of race, sex, sexual orientation, ethnicity, caste, religion, national origin.

8. *Other Species.* Being able to live with concern for and in relation to animals, plants, and the world of nature.
9. *Play.* Being able to laugh, to play, to enjoy recreational activities.
10. *Control over One's Environment.*

   A. *Political.* Being able to participate effectively in political choices that govern one's life; having the right of political participation, protections of free speech and association.

   B. *Material.* Being able to hold property (both land and movable goods), and having property rights on an equal basis with others; having the right to seek employment on an equal basis with others; having the freedom from unwarranted search and seizure. In work, being able to work as a human being, exercising practical reason and entering into meaningful relationships of mutual recognition with other workers.[30]

I hope this serves as an adequate cursory glance at the capabilities approach. I intend to explore more details as the necessity arises throughout the remainder of the text.

ACKNOWLEDGING NEED AND DIFFERENCE AND PROMOTING DIGNITY

After having briefly examined some further intricacies of the capabilities, we can now examine the capabilities approach and how it goes

---

[30] Ibid., 76–8.

about examining need. There has been a long and rich history addressing the difficulty associated with celebrating difference and recognizing need. This discussion has been perhaps made most famous by Martha Minow. In 1990 she introduced a now famous question she called "the dilemma of difference."[31] More pointedly, the dilemma of difference concerns two interrelated questions. First, when does treating people differently emphasize difference and result in stigmatization? Second, when does treating people similarly result in insensitivity to difference and stigmatize and hinder them on that basis? She is concerned that "when we identify one thing as unlike the others, we are dividing the world; we use our language to exclude, to distinguish – to discriminate."[32] This stigma, according to Minow, can be magnified both by ignoring difference and by focusing on it.[33] Put more simply, the dilemma of difference is a choice between integration and separation – between special treatment and similar treatment.[34] In the present context, the questions are concerned with whether negative stereotypes are reinforced through a commitment to equality, or if on the contrary, differences are accommodated because of the fulfillment of a vision of equality.[35]

In a rather obvious way, there are better or worse ways to go about accounting for difference. The most famous, and perhaps now even cliché, example is the citing of fifteenth-century English poor laws that focused on a distinction between the worthy and unworthy poor. These laws of course, made people with disabilities the object of pity and charity. This miniature version of a welfare state saw redistribution

---

[31] Lorella Terzi has suggested that the capabilities framework might altogether overcome the tension Minow raises in the dilemma of differences in "Beyond the Dilemma of Difference: The Capability Approach to Disability and Special Educational Needs," *Journal of Philosophy of Education* 39, 3 (2005): 443–59.

[32] Martha Minow, *Making All the Difference: Inclusion, Exclusion, and American Law* (Ithaca, NY: Cornell University Press, 1990), 3.

[33] Ibid., 20.

[34] Ibid., 20–1.

[35] Ibid., 21.

take the form of local collection and dissemination of resources to only those deemed worthy – the impotent poor: the elderly, widows, and the sick or disabled. Others who were victims of what we might now call bad option luck[36] were deemed unworthy of charity and were left to their own devices to overcome the hardships that were perceived to be brought about by their own action or inaction.

That said, I think it is important to bear in mind that, as Carl Knight suggests, "the social stigma of compensation would almost always be outweighed by the benefits of compensation."[37] Anderson acknowledges this point as well when she states, "[o]f course, merely noticing that someone is being unjustly treated can be wounding to the victim."[38] She continues to acknowledge that this is a difficulty all theories of justice will inevitably face. But, "[i]n general, people would prefer that they not suffer injustice, than that their plight be ignored."[39] This point is made of course, not to diminish the significance of stigma sensitivity, but to instead emphasize the importance of not *further* stigmatizing individuals on the basis of naturally acquired skills or endowments.

An old Finnish proverb states, "*kun menee sutta pakoon, tulee karhu vastaan.*" Roughly translated into English, this means, "when escaping a wolf, one will run into a bear." This wisdom is of course meant to suggest that sometimes avoiding one particular danger or undesirable outcome may very well lead to a far worse outcome.[40] I think this adage can

---

[36] For more on the distinction between brute and option luck, see Ronald Dworkin, "What is Equality? Part 2: Equality of Resources," *Philosophy and Public Affairs* 10, 4 (1981): 293; Ronald Dworkin, *Sovereign Virtue: The Theory and Practice of Equality* (Cambridge: Harvard University Press, 2000), 73–83.

[37] Carl Knight, "In Defence of Luck Egalitarianism," *Res Publica* 11, 1 (2005): 64.

[38] Anderson, "Justifying the Capabilities Approach," 96.

[39] Ibid.

[40] In an important way we can regard this as an example of what Wolff might call an inverse-cross-category risk – when steps taken to secure one functioning may put other functionings at risk. See Jonathan Wolff, "Disability among Equals," in *Disability & Disadvantage*, ed. Kimberly Brownlee and Adam Cureton (Oxford: Oxford University Press, 2009), 120.

lend great insight into our redistributive planning. At a certain point, one necessarily runs a risk of others using an acknowledgment of difference against those the egalitarian planner is attempting to promote justice for. Redistributive measures must be taken to avoid stigmatization, and in an attempt to mitigate that stigmatization and low social standing, what is important is achieving an adequate redistribution while minimizing the stigmatizing effects on the relevant agents. As previously mentioned, my modest claim here is that, *caeteris paribus*, priority ought to be given to the conceptualization of egalitarian justice that is more stigma sensitive. If there is indeed a genuine risk of stigmatizing individuals through a redistributive scheme, it seems to be a relatively minor one in comparison to the benefits accrued as a result of taking this risk. Put more simply, even if individuals were stigmatized as a result of such a redistribution, it would nevertheless likely be a favorable one.

POGGE AND THE VERTICAL-INEQUALITY PROBLEM

Despite the fact that the stigma associated with compensation would almost always be outweighed by the benefits of the compensation that generated that stigma, it is important to note and promote the most stigma-sensitive conception of egalitarian justice. Put simply, Thomas Pogge thinks we are in error to suggest the capabilities approach is as sensitive to differing natural endowments as alternative approaches.

Recall, Sen suggested a shift in our attention from goods or resources to what goods can do to and for human beings.[41] He suggested that the primary focus ought to be individuals' capability to function.[42] These capabilities should be available to be pursued by each and every person and the goal of such an approach is to treat each person, regardless

---

[41] Sen, "Equality of What?," 328.
[42] Wolff and De-Shalit, *Disadvantage*, 8.

of resource level or native endowment, as an ends, and never as a mere means to the ends of another.[43]

Pogge has suggested that by making this shift from resources to capabilities, the capabilities approach suffers from what he calls the *vertical-inequality problem*. If we employ my phrase, Pogge would be suggesting the capabilities approach is less stigma sensitive than a resource-based approach.

He suggests that by shaping institutional arrangements in such a manner that the distribution of resources in society compensates for natural inequalities in endowments, capability theorists are committed to making interpersonal comparisons and judging humans beings as better or worse than others.[44] He suggests that capability theorists are committed to regarding human diversity in vertical terms.

Elsewhere I have suggested that it is helpful to view the various aspects of the capabilities approach as residing on two spectrums – a vertical and a horizontal. Like Pogge, I thought it was helpful to use the imagery of a vertical spectrum to assist in visualizing what the capability theorist was doing when assessing need. I suggested that assessing need is particularly difficult for the capability theorist because individuals' abilities to secure capabilities cannot be represented as one distinct position on the vertical spectrum. Instead, I suggested that we must represent individuals on this spectrum through a multitude of *potential* positions. Ultimately, I concluded that the capability theorist must introduce a metric to properly assess need in light of the criticism I offer.[45]

Putting aside this skepticism about the ability of the capabilities approach to adequately assess need, Pogge's suggestion is that the very fact that individuals are situated on a vertical spectrum is troubling.

He suggests that the capability theorist must regard individuals as having less or more of a particular endowment and situate individuals on

---

[43] Nussbaum, *Women and Human Development*, 5.

[44] Pogge, "Can the Capability Approach be Justified?," 204–5.

[45] For more on this see Christopher A. Riddle, "Indexing, Capabilities, and Disability," *Journal of Social Philosophy* 41, 4 (2010): 527–37.

a vertical spectrum accordingly. He suggests the capabilities approach is committed to viewing diversity as consisting of a natural hierarchy of persons with more or less natural endowments.[46]

Pogge argues that it is precisely because capability theorists have acknowledged that people vary drastically, and that people ought to be compensated for how natural inequalities manifest themselves socially, that they are committed to regarding human natural diversity as residing on a vertical spectrum – in vertical terms.[47]

Conversely, as resource theorists make no such compensatory guarantees, they have no use for the notion of greater or lesser natural endowments, and are thus not committed to a value question in assessing difference. In other words, resource theorists are free to endorse a horizontal conception of natural diversity.

He highlights this distinction with the following example of horizontal reasoning. He claims that if we celebrate natural diversity and acknowledge how our lives are enriched by this variety, we are not committed to viewing the diversity associated with eye color, for example, in better or worse terms. We can see persons as different without committing ourselves to the view that having brown eyes is better or worse than having blue ones.

Pogge does take a step back to acknowledge that there certainly are some forms of diversity that are, and ought to be, regarded in vertical terms. He suggests that "we speak of bad posture, bad health, and bad memory and thereby explicitly deny that these are no worse than their 'good' counterparts."[48] He expands this discussion to include many of the things we commonly regard as worse: "to be dim, obese, balding, frail, tone-deaf, or short."[49] He acknowledges that some of these

---

[46] Pogge, "Can the Capability Approach be Justified?," 205–6.
[47] Ibid., 204–5.
[48] Ibid., 205.
[49] Ibid. By no means do I wish to imply that Pogge's list places proper valuations on the things he includes. I simply use his examples to illustrate the intended point.

valuations are cultural, and there are some that we may even wish to eradicate at some point. Nonetheless, Pogge does not suppose that we would wish to be in a world where no one was free to admire or value some particular natural feature of another.[50]

This caveat aside, Pogge does not think that this "partial verticality" needs to undermine "the shared public sense that human natural diversity *overall* is horizontal."[51] He goes on to clarify further. He claims that musical people, for example, "tend to attach great importance to being musical, and athletes to be athletic, brainy people to brains, and most notoriously – beautiful people to being beautiful."[52] Even though one might admire the musicality of another, one can simultaneously recognize that one has other desirable traits. For example, while the brainy individual might admire the musicality of the musical person, we recognize that the musical person may very well admire the brain of the brainy person, or perhaps the athletic abilities of the athlete. Nonetheless, the fact that musical people tend to value musicality reinforces our reluctance to trade or to envy others.[53]

Thus, under a resource-based conception, Pogge concludes that we will possess an awareness of diversity and have a bias in favor of our own endowments. And, according to Pogge, "[l]ooking at each person's full set of endowments from a shared social point of view we can sustain the conception of natural inequality as horizontal."[54] Instead of viewing humankind's difference in terms of better or worse valuations, we can instead, view it as a wonderful natural diversity to be celebrated.[55]

[50] Ibid.
[51] Ibid.
[52] Ibid.
[53] Ibid.
[54] Ibid., 206.
[55] Ibid.

While resource-based approaches are supported by being able to conceptualize diversity in horizontal terms, the capabilities approach, as mentioned, requires diversity to be understood in vertical terms.[56] By capability theorists affirming that institutions ought to possess a bias in favor of particular people because of a lack of natural endowments, an implicit judgment is being made suggesting that the endowments in question should be regarded as deficient or inferior. The conclusion is often made that not only are these individuals less endowed with respect to a particular form of functioning, but that indeed, they are less well overall.[57] I refer to this point later. But furthermore, to add insult to injury, the judgment being made is not simply an expression of a personal preference another individual has, but Pogge claims that the judgment is made from a position of overlapping consensus – from a shared public criterion.[58]

Pogge does concede that this concern for the less naturally endowed is noble, but suggests that this return in thinking to a natural hierarchy, in fact, constitutes a social loss.[59] His concern is that those who are singled out under this compensatory scheme are characterized as naturally disfavored or worse than others. This judgment of course prevents individuals from coming forward proudly and insisting on additional resources.[60]

In an important way, we can relate this to discussions about the proper allocation of blame for disability or inability. The argument Pogge is making suggests that blame for one's disability will be put back on the individual under the capabilities framework, instead of on society, as social model proponents fought so hard to achieve during the early stages of the disability rights movement.

[56] Ibid.
[57] Ibid.
[58] Ibid.
[59] Ibid.
[60] Ibid.

ANDERSON AND THE VERTICAL-INEQUALITY PROBLEM

Having said that, Anderson astutely summarizes the primary differ-ence between resources theorists and capabilities theorists, and in so doing, summarizes the nature of the debate about stigma sensitivity. Recall:

> [t]he fundamental difference between capability theorists and resource theorists lies rather in the degree to which their princi-ples of justice are sensitive to internal individual differences, and environmental features and social norms that interact with these differences.[61]

Resourcism relies on the basic structure to provide a standardized package or bundle of goods or resources designed to be all-pur-pose means, allowing individuals to realize their particular desired ends.[62]

In contrast, capabilities theorists call for the basic structure to amend the standard package and to be certain it aligns with differing natural endowments to ensure individuals are not unfairly disadvan-taged by requiring greater resources to achieve similar ends as oth-ers. These resources are "adjusted to that person's individual ability to convert resources into relevant functionings, and sensitive to environ-mental factors and social norms that also affect individuals' conver-sion abilities."[63] According to Anderson, the so-called hallmark of the capability approach, then, is its "sensitivity to variations in the abilities of individuals to convert resources into functionings, which may be affected by internal variations, environmental features, and prevailing social norms."[64]

[61] Anderson, "Justifying the Capabilities Approach," 87.
[62] Ibid.
[63] Ibid.
[64] Ibid.

We can see by what Pogge has said thus far, and by how Anderson has characterized the capabilities approach, that the primary question dividing resourcists and capabilities theorists is whether a conception of justice ought to be sensitive to these variations in natural endowment.[65]

Contra Pogge, Anderson suggests that if we think justice requires sensitivity to the diverse natural endowments of individuals, not only in terms of redistributive claims, but also in terms of avoiding the further stigmatization of individuals – being stigma sensitivity – then we ought to favor a capabilities approach. In other words, Anderson defends the capabilities approach against Pogge's claim that it is not as stigma sensitive as resource-based conceptions of justice.

Anderson suggests that Pogge has mischaracterized the capabilities approach. I agree with her. She claims that Pogge moves too fast from the capabilities theorists' concern about natural endowments to a commitment of "attributing the blame for shortfalls in equal functioning to individuals' innate endowments."[66]

In fact, capabilities theorists view a person's capabilities much more holistically. Here we can invoke imagery from discussions about the definition of disability. While Pogge is attributing a strict medial model way of understanding disability and the disadvantage associated with disability,[67] Anderson is suggesting that capabilities theorists in fact endorse a view of disability and disadvantage much more akin to an interactional model.

Anderson suggests that an individuals' capabilities are best understood as a "joint product of her internal endowments, her external resources, and the social and physical environment in which she lives."[68] This understanding is similar to the current conceptualization

---

[65] Ibid.

[66] Ibid., 96.

[67] I think this error is similar to one made by Dworkin and highlighted by Shelly Tremain in "Dworkin on Disablement and Resources," *Canadian Journal of Law and Jurisprudence* 9, 2 (1996): 344.

[68] Ibid.

of disability endorsed by most disability theorists. Interactionalist theorists suggest that "disability ought to be regarded as a complex interaction between the traits inherent to a person (or one's impairment), and how these traits manifest themselves in the environment they find themselves in (the disabling facts of one's impairment)."[69] In light of this, we can conclude that Anderson, like interactionalist theorists, vehemently denies that capabilities theorists must necessarily attribute any failures to function to a presumed inferiority due to the innate, different natural endowments of individuals.[70]

Capabilities theorists do not hold the position that lacking of a natural endowment, such as high intelligence, is in itself grounds to warrant compensation. Instead, they call for an assessment of how society treats people lacking such an endowment, either through the built environment, the social and political institutions, or the attitudinal barriers they encounter.[71] Therefore, unlike Pogge's claim, capabilities theorists are not committed to a vertical viewing of natural endowments.

LIVES WORTH LIVING AND FAILURES OF BASIC JUSTICE

Thus, we see that Anderson's defense of the capabilities approach relies on her identifying a mischaracterization of the approach by Pogge. As I stated previously, I think this is an astute observation. That said, I think Anderson has missed another failing of Pogge's that rebuts his critical claims even further.

Recall, Pogge views the fundamental difference between the capabilities approach and a resource-based approach to be the capabilities

---

[69] Christopher A. Riddle, "Defining Disability: Metaphysical not Political," *Medicine, Health Care, and Philosophy* (2013).

[70] Ibid.

[71] Ibid., 97.

approach's position on providing accommodation to those disadvantaged in terms of natural endowments.[72] Previously we saw Anderson identify a misrepresentation related to this point. I fear that Pogge has mischaracterized the capabilities approach with reference to this distinction in another way still.

He suggests that in order for an individual to justify her claim as one of justice, she is forced to demonstrate that not only is she worse off with reference to a particular natural endowment than those around her (undoubtedly a move that will result in a diminution of her social basis of self-respect), but she is forced to make a much stronger claim as well. This further claim is even more damaging. Pogge highlights the additional claims she must make in the following passage:

> [I]t is not enough for her to point to one respect in which she is worse off than most others. For there are many other respects in which the addressees of her claim have special limitations, needs, or handicaps, other respects in which she may be better endowed than those she is addressing.[73]

He goes further to suggest that, for her to have a legitimate claim that she is owed compensation as a matter of justice, "she must present her special limitation, need, or handicap as one that outweighs all other particular vertical inequalities and entitles her to count as worse endowed all things considered."[74]

It is the final clause that Pogge inserts that leads to his misrepresentation of the capabilities approach. In other words, the capabilities theorist does not invoke the "all things considered" clause that Pogge attributes to her.

Pogge continues by asking: Who in their right mind would possibly want to have to claim that their endowments were inferior, overall, to

[72] Pogge, "Can the Capability Approach be Justified?," 206.
[73] Ibid.
[74] Ibid.

those of most everyone else?[75] Pogge thinks it is obvious that no one would want to be "officially signaled out by [their] society for special compensatory benefits reserved for the 'worse endowed.'"[76]

Were this signaling out what a capabilities theorist required for one to receive the special compensation Pogge is concerned with, it would be most troubling and he would be correct in expressing a concern about the lack of stigma sensitivity displayed by the capabilities approach. Luckily for capabilities theorists, Pogge is wrong about what is required of an individual to claim special compensation under the capabilities approach.

I will explain how he is wrong by first, addressing generally what is required under the capabilities approach to justify compensation. I will then move to discussing more particular characteristics of the capabilities approach that lead me to hold this belief. Before transitioning into my own minor critique of the capabilities approach, I revisit Pogge's misrepresented version of the capabilities approach to highlight briefly where it went wrong.

In general terms, the capability approach requires no such (explicit) holistic judgment to be made about how a lack of a particular endowment relates to the larger question of overall well-being or opportunity to flourish. This is because the capabilities approach, by its very nature, views all the aspects of well-being that it stresses as being non-fungible and constitutive of living a life worthy of human dignity.

Recall, Nussbaum argues that it is possible to specify the *entirety* of functionings or activities that constitute a good life and promote "human flourishing."[77] Here I added emphasis to *entirety* because Nussbaum argues that all of the capabilities on her list of central human capabilities are "implicit in the idea of a life worthy of human dignity."[78] In other words, all the capabilities Nussbaum specifies are

---

[75] Ibid.

[76] Ibid., 207.

[77] Ruger, "Toward a Theory of a Right to Health," 290–91.

[78] Nussbaum, *Frontiers of Justice*, 70.

held to be constitutive of human flourishing. Though Nussbaum, Sen, and Wolff's various incarnations of the capabilities approach differ in many respects, a common thread between them all is that they view the elements of a life worth living as plural and not singular. Nussbaum further characterizes this pluralism when she explicitly states that one is in error to single out any particular capability as any more or less constitutive of what it means to flourish as a human.[79] The important upshot about this belief is that "if people are below the threshold on any one of the capabilities, that is a failure of basic justice, no matter how high up they are on all the others."[80] In other words, individuals are not "made to say that [they are] overall worse endowed than others,"[81] as Pogge would have us believe.

Individuals instead can simply rely on the fact that more generally, a lack of security over a particular functioning is viewed as constituting a failure of basic justice. Individuals in positions like the one described will be granted special compensation, not because they must present a particular limitation as damaging to their well-being as a whole, but because these capabilities are non-fungible, and a failure to secure one, for whatever reason, constitutes failure of basic justice. These interpersonal comparisons of well-being that Pogge is concerned about need not arise in the assessment of justice under a capabilities framework. What is more, as Anderson rightly highlighted, capabilities theorists are not committed to viewing disadvantage as stemming innately from natural endowments, but instead, focus on the complex relationship between these endowments and how they interact with the environment, political and legal structures, and attitudinal barriers.[82]

Thus, the onus is doubly shifted away from the individual to express her need in such a manner that justifies a claim to justice. First, she need not express how any special limitation of hers relates

---

[79] Ibid., 84.
[80] Ibid., 167.
[81] Pogge, "Can the Capability Approach be Justified?," 206.
[82] Anderson, "Justifying the Capabilities Approach," 97.

to larger questions of well-being. This is because capabilities theorists are committed to viewing any failure to secure a functioning, whether solely a result of a special limitation or a result of how that limitation manifests itself socially, as a failure of basic justice, thereby warranting redistribution.

Second, in a related manner, in making the assessment associated with a special limitation, capabilities theorists are not committed to viewing the origins of that limitation as stemming from the individual. Capabilities theorists can instead view such limitations in social terms.

These two features highlight how Pogge misrepresented the capabilities approach, as well as demonstrate how stigma-sensitive the capabilities approach is.

OPPORTUNITY-BASED PERSPECTIVES AND STIGMA SENSITIVITY

While to this point I have supported Anderson's defense of the capabilities approach, and indeed, even offered further support of my own against the critical remarks of Pogge, I do not think the capabilities approach can go without criticism.

My criticism can be characterized as one that tends to revolve around a more general observation concerning the broader goals of approaches to justice. More specifically, my concern is that the focus on responsibility that often comes part-in-parcel with liberal theories of justice may be a conceptual undoing. That said, I do want to limit the scope of my discussion here to strictly focus on capability theory and the alternative of resourcism as I have discussed thus far.

Implicit within an opportunities perspective is a necessary judgment about whether an individual has utilized the resources provided to her adequately to satisfy a basic minimum. This is to say, when we make judgments about the opportunities available to people or the securing of opportunities, we make intrusive evaluations regarding how that individual has lived his or her life and has utilized (or can utilize) available resources. I contend that this is *potentially* problematic.

Perhaps evaluating the alternative – resource-based conceptions – is a good place to start to highlight this concern. Resource theorists advocate allocating a bundle of all-purpose means to individuals. Most resource-based approaches invest little concern in how the utilization of those resources affect the individual making the choices about what to do or not do with those goods.

Contrast this with capabilities approaches that focus on the securing of opportunities. In assessing the opportunities available to any particular individual, there is a back story that has to be constructed that explains how that individual has arrived at his or her current state of affairs. After all, it is possible that an individual may have otherwise had an opportunity, but opted to squander it in favor of an activity she deemed more fruitful. A focus on opportunity involves implicit judgments about the kinds of actions individuals have performed surrounding the securing of that opportunity.

Not only are we making judgments about the background conditions informing one's set of opportunities, but also about the ability of that individual to secure that opportunity. After all, something is not a genuine opportunity if it cannot be secured in practice.[83] So when we ask questions about opportunities, we make an evaluative judgment about individuals' abilities and background conditions informing those opportunities.

In other words, we are asking whether a state of affairs could potentially manifest itself if conditions $x, y,$ or z were met. If these states cannot manifest themselves, we look to the individual (at least partially) to explain this inability.

As Anderson stated before, we do not have to allocate entire blame to an individual for this inability as capability theorists. But the point is,

---

[83] Wolff and De-Shalit, *Disadvantage*, 80.

evaluations of this nature, whether focused solely on the individual or not, look to the individual, or her particular circumstances, to explain why an opportunity is not a genuine one. Conversely, there is no such evaluation made with a starting-line conception, as no evaluations of this nature are made *ex-post*.

In a distinct, but I think, still useful discussion, T. M. Scanlon has suggested that "[t]he conclusion that a person is responsible ... for what he or she did leaves open what kind of appraisal, if any, is therefore in order – whether what the person did was praiseworthy, blameworthy, or morally neutral."[84] It is this appraisal that Scanlon highlights that leads to a potential lack of stigma sensitivity. If appraisals are made that focus on why individual *A* has a particular opportunity available to her, while *B* fails to have that same opportunity, we run the risk of stigmatizing individuals further. If we praise one for seizing an opportunity and frown upon another for squandering theirs, we risk further marginalizing an already disenfranchised individual. We run this risk because we make intrusive judgments about responsibility and the abilities of the people we are assessing. We necessarily make these judgments because we have to assess the security of an opportunity. We do this to ensure our distribution satisfies our robust conception of well-being.

CONCLUDING REMARKS

It appears that a focus on starting-line principles, like those espoused by the majority of resource-based theorists, avoids the potential further stigmatizing on the basis of natural endowments or talents. While resourcism is preferable in this instance solely on an stigma-sensitivity

[84] T. M. Scanlon, "Justice, Responsibility, and the Demands of Equality," in *The Egalitarian Conscience: Essays in Honour of G. A. Cohen*, ed. Christine Sypnowich (Oxford: Oxford University Press, 2006), 76.

metric (due to avoiding opportunity-based discussion), I do not think it satisfies the *caeteris paribus* feature as discussed at the outset of this chapter – it is not otherwise equal – and thus, should not be given equal regard as a conception of justice.

That said, while we have seen that a focus on opportunity leads to a *potential* further stigmatizing of individuals, and that an emphasis instead on starting-line principles reduces this possibility, we have yet to say anything about end-state principles. That is, what about principles of justice that advocate for the attainment of a particular state of affairs, rather than merely the opportunity to secure that state? I suggest, that for reasons very similar to those expressed earlier concerning starting-line principles endorsed by resource theorists, that end-state principles are also likely to be more stigma sensitive than opportunity-based conceptions of justice.

After all, if we are concerned with simply the attainment of state *A*, and we are directed to disregard all factors pertaining to why an individual succeeded or failed at attaining that state, then we seem to avoid the messy judgments that come with opportunity-based discussions. If we deem a particular state of affairs, *A*, so valuable that regardless of the choices exercised surrounding *A*, it ought to be assured, then we run little risk of making intrusive judgments about individuals with reference to responsibility.

In this chapter, I advanced a principle that I feel should be weighed in assessing conceptualizations of distribution justice. More pointedly, I suggested that one of the primary measures of the success or failure of a conception of egalitarian justice ought to be its ability to avoid the further stigmatization of vulnerable populations. I referred to the ability to not further stigmatize individuals on the basis of naturally acquired skills or endowments as stigma sensitivity. I suggested that all things being equal, when comparing two equally desirable conceptions of justice, priority ought to be given to the conceptualization that is more stigma sensitive – that stigmatizes those in need less than other, competing claims.

I then proceeded to examine a criticism made by Pogge that sug-gested the shift away from resources to capabilities has resulted in the viewing of natural endowments in a vertical manner. Subsequently, Pogge suggested a capabilities approach failed to be as stigma sensitive as opposing, resource-based conceptions.

In addressing this claim, I endorsed a counter-remark made by Elizabeth Anderson. I then suggested, that in addition to Anderson's claim against Pogge, that he had mischaracterized the capabilities approach in another way still. Thus, the capabilities approach was defended from an attack by resourcism on both accounts: the explicit criticism tackled by Anderson, and the second misrepresentation that led to an implicit judgment.

Finally, I suggested that while the capabilities approach was not guilty of being less stigma sensitive for either the explicit or implicit reasons offered by Pogge, that opportunity-based accounts like the capabilities approach do in fact, have the potential to further stigmatize individuals. This is because, among other reasons, judgments about opportunities require an intrusion into individual lives to make assessments of the kind necessary to advance an opportunities-based perspective.

References

Anderson, Elizabeth. "Justifying the Capabilities Approach to Justice." In *Measuring Justice: Primary Good and Capabilities*, ed. Harry Brighouse and Ingrid Robeyns, 81–100. Cambridge: Cambridge University Press, 2010.

"Justifying the Capabilities Approach to Justice." In *Measuring Justice: Primary Good and Capabilities*, ed. Harry Brighouse and Ingrid Robeyns. "What is the Point of Equality?" *Ethics* 109, no. 2 (1999): 287–337.

Dworkin, Ronald. *Sovereign Virtue: The Theory and Practice of Equality*. Cambridge, MA: Harvard University Press, 2000.

"What is Equality? Part 2: Equality of Resources." *Philosophy and Public Affairs* 10, no. 4 (1981): 283–345.

Knight, Carl. "In Defence of Luck Egalitarianism." *Res Publica* 11, no.1 (2005): 55–77.

Kuklys, Wiebke. *Amartya Sen's Capability Approach: Theoretical Insights and Empirical Applications.* Berlin: Springer-Verlag, 2005.

Macklin, Ruth. "Dignity is a Useless Concept." *British Medical Journal* 237, no. 7429, 2003.

Minow, Martha. *Making All the Difference: Inclusion, Exclusion, and American Law.* Ithaca, NY: Cornell University Press, 1990.

Nussbaum, Martha. *Creating Capabilities: The Human Development Approach.* Cambridge, MA: The Belknap Press of Harvard University Press, 2011.

Frontiers of Justice: Disability, Nationality and Species Membership. Cambridge, MA: The Belknap Press of Harvard University Press, 2006.

Women and Human Development. Cambridge: Cambridge University Press, 2000.

"Aristotelian Social Democracy." In *Liberalism and the Good,* ed. R. Bruce Douglas, Gerald M. Mara, and Henry S. Richardson, 203–52. New York: Routledge, 1990.

Pogge, Thomas. "A Critique of the Capability Approach." In *Measuring Justice: Primary Good and Capabilities,* ed. Harry Brighouse and Ingrid Robeyns, 17–60. Cambridge: Cambridge University Press, 2010.

"A Critique of the Capability Approach." In *Measuring Justice: Primary Good and Capabilities,* ed. Harry Brighouse and Ingrid Robeyns. "Can the Capability Approach be Justified?." *Philosophical Topics* 30, no. 2 (2002): 167–228.

Rawls, John. *A Theory of Justice.* Cambridge, MA: Harvard University Press, 1971.

Riddle, Christopher A. "Defining Disability: Metaphysical not Political." *Medicine, Health Care, and Philosophy* 16, no. 3 (2013)

"Indexing, Capabilities, and Disability." *Journal of Social Philosophy* 41, no. 4 (2010): 527–37.

Ruger, Jennifer Prah. *Health and Social Justice.* New York: Oxford University Press, 2009.

"Toward a Theory of a Right to Health: Capability and Incompletely Theorized Agreements." *Yale Journal of Law and Humanities* 17, no. 2 (2006): 273–326.

Scanlon, T. M. "Justice, Responsibility, and the Demands of Equality." In *The Egalitarian Conscience: Essays in Honour of G. A. Cohen,* ed. Christine Sypnowich, 70–87. Oxford: Oxford University Press, 2006.

Schroder, Doris. "Dignity: Two Riddles and Four Concepts." *Cambridge Quarterly of Healthcare Ethics* 17, no. 2 (2008): 230–8.

Schüklenk, Udo and Anna Pacholczyk. "Dignity's Wooly Uplift." *Bioethics* 24, no. 2 (2010): ii.

Sen, Amartya. "Equality of What?." In *Equal Freedom: Selected Tanner Lectures on Human Values*, ed. S. Darwall, 307–30. Ann Arbor: University of Michigan Press, 1995.

Terzi, Lorella. "Beyond the Dilemma of Difference: The Capability Approach to Disability and Special Educational Needs." *Journal of Philosophy of Education* 39, no. 3 (2005): 443–59.

Tremain, Shelly. "Dworkin on Disablement and Resources." *Canadian Journal of Law and Jurisprudence* 9, no. 2 (1996): 343–59.

Wolff, Jonathan. "Disability among Equals." In *Disability & Disadvantage*, ed. Kimberly Brownlee and Adam Cureton, 112–37. Oxford: Oxford University Press, 2009.

Wolff, Jonathan and Avner De-Shalit. *Disadvantage.* Oxford: Oxford University Press, 2007.

12

Inclusion and the Good Human Life

FRANZISKA FELDER

The UN Convention on the Rights of Persons with Disabilities (2006) as well as other conventions and agreements (e.g., UNESCO 1994) mark a paradigm shift in approaches to people with disabilities: from viewing them as objects of charity, treatment, and social protection to subjects with rights who are capable of claiming those rights and making decisions for their own lives as well as being active members of society and different communities. In Article 19, the UN Convention for instance explicitly states the right to full inclusion and participation in the community in which disabled people live.

In this chapter, I do not directly address the UN Convention nor do I deepen the question of how these rights to inclusion and participation look. Instead, my focus is more specific. I want to highlight the relationship between inclusion and a good human life. Following this task, however, implies that there is conceptual clarity about what we mean by inclusion. But this is not the case. As John Wilson (2000) pointed out, the concept of inclusion lacks the necessary conceptual lucidity; it is a vague term, loaded with numerous economic, social, political, and cultural connotations and used in a broad range of fields, in different disciplines as well as practical and political contexts. The lack of clarity and distinctness in conceptualization has vast practical and political consequences. Without a clear definition and a coherent theoretical core, the concept of inclusion is of very limited practical, political, and empirical use. Additionally, if we do not interrogate the moral significance of inclusion, we do not know what exactly a right to inclusion should cover.

For these reasons, I start by scrutinizing the nature and moral relevance of the idea of inclusion. I then try to connect the notion of inclusion to a concept of a good human life. The idea I defend takes it that a good life consists of engagement in worthwhile activities and having the capability to develop them. Inclusion, being both part and prerequisite of a good human life, requires shared social activities that occur in communities or in society. In distinguishing two spheres of inclusion – inclusion into communities and inclusion in a society (with its diverse institutions) – I rely on a distinction put first forward by early German sociologists like Ferdinand Tönnies (1957) or Max Weber (1922). I take it that these two spheres of inclusion help us to situate different contexts of inclusion and facilitate the understanding of the different mechanisms and interactions that are important to understand the processes of inclusion or exclusion. Additionally, I take it that inclusion has to do with "identification" of others as a legitimate part of a whole – whether this is a group or a society. And moreover, inclusion is bound to social interaction in a very broad sense. In other words, inclusion calls for social intentionality from the partners in social interaction.

As I move to clarify the value of inclusion, I suggest that its potential lies in delivering and ensuring development, freedom, and recognition. I specifically shift attention to the significance of freedom and recognition. If we then turn to the connection of inclusion and the good human life, we can see the relationship between these different ideas. I show that the connection between inclusion and its different elements on one hand and the idea of a good human life on the other hand first lies in that inclusion is a constitutive part of a good human life and second in the fact that, to be included, humans need recognition, development, and freedom. In other words, normative preconditions need to be fulfilled if we speak of inclusive processes that lead to a good life or a component of it. Inclusion thus incorporates different normative claims – recognition and freedom being the most important ones – but is not reducible to one of them alone.

DEFINING INCLUSION

In a very general sense, inclusion means inclusion in a form of social life (Ikäheimo 2009: 85). The term *social life* refers to abstract notions like inclusion in economic or political life as well as to inclusion in close relationships, such as friends and families. Inclusion thus has connections to concepts such as social citizenship (Marshall 1950), as well as to important moral concepts such as friendship (Aristotle 2009).

I start with a quite evident observation that we can roughly distinguish two distinct and yet overlapping spheres of inclusion, namely inclusion into society and inclusion into communities. The distinction between community and society and different aspects that go along with it has shaped sociology since its beginnings, mainly because of the works of early German sociologists, principally Ferdinand Tönnies (1957). The intuition behind the distinction concerns the point that the structure and form inclusion takes is dependent on the kind of *relationship* involved. Undoubtedly, there is a crucial difference between interpersonal relationships and those that reside at a more abstract level, namely the level of society. Being included in the former contexts – communities – requires mutual recognition between different members of the community in question. It also involves feelings of belonging as well as a certain kind of interpersonal respect between the members. There is no question that there are many forms and shapes of such communities. They range from family and close friendships to sports teams or choirs or even such loose communities as fan clubs. People evidently belong to many different communities, and some of them can be overlapping (e.g., a close friend can also be a member in the same chess club). Social actions that constitute inclusion in communities are largely dependent on the affiliation of people to these communities. According to Andrew Mason (2000), one of the few philosophers from a liberal political background who has tried to define the term, a community is a group of people who share values and a way of living, identify themselves to the group, and recognize each other as members of the group. This descriptive concept of community contrasts with a normative account of community. The latter is a concept of community in which different members display solidarity and mutual concern for one another and between whom there is no systematic exploitation or injustice.

For the moment, it is this former concept that is of interest. It turns out that if we take all elements Mason claims to be essential elements of a definition of inclusion– shared values, shared way of life, identification to the group, and mutual recognition – very few groups count as communities because only in very closed societies do people actually share a lifestyle – and not merely values and tastes. In other words, a definition of community that applies only to groups that share a way of life is too narrow. I therefore suggest that we should concentrate on shared values, identification, and mutual recognition respectively as the essential elements of a definition of community.

Inclusion in communities contrasts with inclusion in society. The term *society* stems from the Latin word *societas*, which derived from the noun *socius* (meaning comrade, friend, or ally). According to Adam Smith, a society "may subsist among different men, as among different merchants, from a sense of its utility *without any mutual love or affection* (highlights FF), if only they refrain from doing injury to each other" (2010 [1759]: 192). As I already mentioned, in a society people recognize each other as "abstract others" instead of "concrete others." Additionally, societies are not only built by their people – in democratic societies, by their citizens – but also by different institutions, among them the state.

If we look at different institutions in a society, we can see the problems that disabled people face in trying to be included on a societal level. For instance, we know from the literature that disabled people face many challenges with regard to education and employment (Burchardt 2000b, Burchardt 2005, Rigg 2005), health services or social support (Lippold and Burns 2009), transport, access to buildings, communication devices, or technical aids. They also face challenges concerning housing, leisure, and their overall social and political life (McBryde Johnson 2004), to name just a few examples (WHO 2011). These challenges shed light on the fact that disability is a dynamic process between the individual and his or her environment or circumstances, including social relationships, and the structures of the society disabled people live in (Burchardt 2000a; Minow 1990). The institutions of a society and their effects on people's lives and, more particularly, on their inclusion, are thus not reducible to interpersonal relationships and vice versa.

THE MORAL SIGNIFICANCE OF INCLUSION

When we turn to the moral meaning of inclusion, we have to ask: Why does it, from a moral point of view, matter to individuals – whether they are disabled or not – to be included? I suggest that inclusion contributes to and at the same time requires development, freedom, and recognition. It is thus in a sense necessary to be included to gain freedom and recognition and to develop as a human being. And at the same time, development, freedom, and recognition contribute to different and more elaborated forms of inclusion. For instance, to be included in an educational context, children need a certain cognitive development (they should be educable, in other words). And on the other hand, education leads to different forms of inclusion and further development. So, in a sense, development is a precondition for inclusion and at the same time a result of inclusion. In what follows, I concentrate specifically on recognition and freedom. It is the aim of the following section to not only highlight what we should understand by recognition and freedom in the context of inclusion. It also builds the bridge to the next section where I concentrate on the relationship between inclusion and the good human life.

Recognition

On a very basic level, the relationship between recognition and inclusion is of anthropological significance. The relationship builds on the basic idea that human individuals structurally rely on others to develop all or at least some of their cognitive, moral, and affective capacities. As it became evident from historical examples (which I offer shortly), recognition as a human being with certain basic needs (love and care, for instance) is indispensable for a healthy development.

It is possible to look at this anthropological relationship between inclusion and recognition from two sides: we can first see recognition (or identification as a member of the same human family) as a descriptive feature of inclusion into humanity that implies the essential intersubjective dependency of human beings. Charles Taylor's essay on the "Politics of Recognition" (1994: 26) argues that recognition is not only a courtesy we owe people, but is a vital human need, crucial for the capability of becoming a human agent in the full sense.[1] And second, as a normative reading, we can see that these relations of dependency are mainly about positive affirmation of certain identity features of individuals by other human beings and by institutions of society.

The attitudes of others are obviously important for inclusion. More specifically, these attitudes can be called "recognitive attitudes," in the sense that they need to reflect positive and affirmative attitudes toward the person claiming recognition. According to Axel Honneth (1995), these necessary recognitive attitudes can be divided into three aspects:

---

[1] This claim further elaborates his arguments made in *Sources of the Self* (1989), where he argues the self can only develop self-understanding and self-definition in relation with others within "webs of interlocution" (1989: 32).

love, respect, and esteem. Like Taylor, Honneth draws on Hegel and his emphasis on the vital importance of recognition for the formation of human identity. While Honneth argues that all three forms of recognition are vital, love is the most significant. It is conceptually and genetically prior to the need for respect (manifested in human rights) and social esteem. Love is therefore a form of recognition we must experience before we can experience respect and esteem.

I use Honneth's (1995) account of recognition for several purposes, most importantly because he developed a theory of recognition that explicitly connects his understanding of recognition to a theory of inclusion. For Honneth, the social meaning of inclusion depends on a sense of belonging on the side of the individual and a form of acknowledgment on the other side, whether it be other individuals, communities, or institutions. Also, Honneth's account of inclusion and recognition is useful as he distinguishes recognition of a human being as a "concrete other" and recognition of an "abstract other," for example, an individual as a citizen. This distinction is important as it supports my distinction of communal and societal inclusion.

Honneth's theory starts from an account of identity building as an ongoing, intersubjective process of struggling to acquire mutual recognition from one's partners in relations. Through such a process of struggle, individuals develop three different forms of relation to self through three types of social interaction. Individuals first gain self-confidence in primary, affective relationships. Second, they develop self-respect in legal relations of rights. Third, they build and increase their self-esteem in local communities, defined by shared value orientation. Self-confidence and self-esteem are the first and the third form of relations to oneself and the corresponding form of recognition – they involve the understanding of oneself in one's *concrete particularity*. Self-respect, on the other hand, involves a relation to oneself in an *abstract universality*.

Honneth's account of recognition as a necessary moral condition for inclusion relies on the following assumption: the possibility for realizing one's needs and interests in inclusion depends crucially on social relations that allow the development of self-confidence, self-respect, and self-esteem and thus special modes of self-relation. The three modes of self-relation can only be acquired and maintained intersubjectively, through being granted recognition by someone or something (an institution like the state, for instance). As a result, the conditions for self-realization result in dependency on the establishment of relationships of mutual recognition. These relationships include, first, close relations of love and friendship, second, legally institutionalized relations of universal respect for the autonomy and dignity of persons and third, networks of solidarity within which the particular worth of members of a community can be acknowledged.[2]

In addition to emotional care and legal recognition, individuals require social esteem that allows them to find a positive relationship toward their abilities and skills. Social esteem is measured by the extent to which individuals can contribute to various social objectives. Abilities and achievements of individuals are therefore judged intersubjectively according to how individuals can contribute to the implementation of culturally or socially based values.

Social appreciation does not extend to passive tolerance, but requires affective appreciation of the particular individual. This form of appreciation, according to Heikki Ikäheimo (2009), should not be reduced to instrumental valuing. It must include estimation of the intrinsic value of human beings.[3] To understand someone as a genuine contributor to a shared social value thus means to value this person in the *full sense*.

---

[2] These relationships are established and expanded through social struggles. They are moral in the sense that feelings of outrage and indignation are generated by the rejection of claims to recognition. In this sense they are normative judgments about the legitimacy of existing social arrangements.

[3] If someone is only appreciated as a slave, then the recognition he gains is only instrumentally valuable.

However, this third stage of recognition begs the question of which of the features and characteristics of people can be valued socially. This is of special importance as appreciation is measured in a social context and is therefore bound to a collective reference (Bedorf 2010: 58). Appreciation relies on the following intuition: as with the plans and objectives of people in general, not all features and characteristics of people are valuable and not all abilities people have are of such importance to them that they need (for reason of a healthy relation to self) appreciation. Quite the contrary: people usually want to gain social esteem for selected, specific properties and characteristics important *for them.*[4] If someone, for instance, wants to be appreciated for his musicality and is, instead, only esteemed for his cooking talent (something that this person does not really care for), this appreciation has no, or at least no substantial, effect on his self-respect.

We all want to be valued by others for our skills and features, as well as for the personal attributes we bring to a friendship. And we wish those characteristics and skills to be principal in our social interactions, "so that people leave the meeting thinking, 'She chairs the committee so well,'" not, "'She's so blind, and still she chairs this committee well'" (Scully 2008: 127). With respect to people with disabilities we often see the problem Scully mentions: many disabled people experience this form of recognition "despite their disability." In other words, they do not gain esteem for a sports performance as such, but only on the background of a specific, often undisclosed normality (or the idea thereof), such as normal sports, or (statistically or biologically) normal functioning.

So it turns out that precisely this third level of recognition is often a major problem for most people with disabilities – both in its social and in its individual dimension. Still commonly used terminology, for instance *invalid* (from Latin *invalidus* = worthless), show this lack of recognition in the language. Such terms indicate that disabled people

---

[4] Thanks to Susanne Schmetkamp for pointing this out to me.

are usually, perhaps sometimes because of an alleged incompetence, victims of misrecognition on this level that hinders their inclusion or symbolizes their exclusion. Although this kind of misrecognition is rarely consciously and directly intended and thus does not reflect discrimination in the direct and strict sense, many disabled people experience devaluation at this level, for instance by being ignored. They experience misrecognition in the form of a devaluation by nonperception (Honneth 2003). It is thus not surprising that these kinds of devaluation have serious effects on the psychological development of people (Calder 2011).

However, misrecognition in its various forms not only has consequences for the psychological development of persons, it also affects the political, cultural, and social status of humans. Contrary to Honneth's psychological model of recognition, Nancy Fraser suggests a status model of recognition. The status model not only looks at the interaction between individual identity forming and processes of recognition, but points to the harm done by misrecognition from the institutions of society. The politics attached to this view seeks to overcome status subordination by altering the values that regulate interaction and by trying to establish new values that promote inclusion. Fraser (2000: 116ff.) also points to the fact that the lack of inclusion can also be due to the lack of the necessary resources to interact with other people as peers. Where this happens, maldistribution constitutes an impediment to the inclusion of people. Whereas the recognition dimension corresponds to the status order in society, the distributive dimension corresponds to the economic structure of society, for instance, to labor markets.

Let me take up the example of work in order to show these relationships. Employees value work for a range of reasons, including intrinsic interest and sense of purpose, the ability to use skills and knowledge acquired over a lifetime, social status and self-respect, and social engagement with colleagues and workmates, customers and partners (Vickerstaff, Phillipson, and Wilkie 2011). Also, work is a value of high stakes, at least in Western societies. Research shows that people who are employed are more satisfied with their lives than unemployed people; this goes for the general population as well as for people with disabilities, for instance mental illnesses (Eklund, Hansson, and Ahlqvist 2004). It even seems that work can contribute to mental health as work provides a distraction from symptoms (Van Dongen 1996). Additionally, Strong (1998) showed how participation in meaningful work left clients to define themselves as capable and to develop roles and self-images that were not illness focused. Research also showed that work enhances the recovery process from psychiatric illness by providing experiences such as self-empowerment and self-actualization (Provencher et al. 2002). It is not clear which of the ingredients of competitive work leads to satisfaction – money earned, contact with other people, or the symbolic meaning of work. Research suggests that all aspects are likely to play a role (Eklund et al. 2004). These examples show how work affects the quality of life for humans and how unemployment not only leads to serious instances of social exclusion, but ultimately to a diminishment of important aspects of a good life, both in terms of lack of necessary goods for living, diminished or impoverished social standing, and psychological well-being.

It is thus recognition in its various forms that contributes to inclusion and, as we will see, to human well-being. Different instances of recognition are important in order to be included in different communities as well as diverse institutions of and processes in society, as Fraser (2000) points out. Additionally, different forms of inclusion also lead to different instances of recognition, as the example of inclusion in the workforce and its contribution to recognition as social appreciation suggests.

FREEDOM

The relationship between freedom and social inclusion is not apparent at first sight as inclusion seems to be more concerned with the relation between people, and between people and institutions within society. Consequently, social inclusion seems to have closer connections to ideas of solidarity, equality, and fraternity than to freedom. However, the importance of freedom for inclusion is clear when we consider that inclusion protects people's most basic interests and opens spaces of choice as to where and with whom one wants to be included (Buchanan et al. 2000: 291). If we mean by inclusion not only being part of a given framework that is not freely chosen, for instance, the family, the relationship between inclusion and freedom becomes apparent. Not surprisingly, many problems of deprivation disabled people experience arise from unfavorable or forced inclusion or exclusion. If we look at the freedom or opportunities a person has to choose a certain social relationships, unfavorable inclusion is seen as one source of deprivation (Sen 2000: 29).

The list of freedoms relevant to inclusion includes social opportunities for inclusion, institutional arrangements (within the market and the education system, for instance), the enhancement of social facilities and organizations, as well as the development of specific individual capabilities. The building and rebuilding of institutions is of special importance. As human beings in modern societies live in a world of institutions, the opportunities and prospects people have depend crucially on which institutions exist and how they operate and function, especially in how inclusive they are (Sen 2000: 33). Not only do institutions contribute to human freedom and opportunities, their roles can be evaluated in terms of how much freedom or opportunities they offer. It thus becomes evident that a lack of opportunities – due to different obstacles – can restrict inclusion in different domains and contexts in life.

The example of disability makes it clear that people can be exposed to a variety of obstacles and that their lack of social inclusion is not only due to limited internal resources, such as skills, talents, or physical strength, but also external constraints. Let me illustrate this point with an example. A person in a wheelchair develops the desire to join a chess club. In the execution of her plan, she can be exposed to different obstacles. First, her inclusion in the chess club may fail because the building in which the chess club trains is not accessible to her because of the lack of ramps or elevators. Second, she may not be included because, although she dreams of playing chess, she lacks the necessary cognitive or physical abilities to do so and to keep up with the group. Third, it is possible that although she has both the ability to play chess and to keep up with the team and access the building, no one is willing to play chess with her. This may be because they assume she does not have the necessary skills to play or because it is assumed (perhaps wrongly) that she needs too much help from others and nobody wants to be pushed into the position of having to assist her. In addition, combinations of, and mutual reinforcement between, the three obstacles are also possible.

Looking at the substantive freedom someone has, both in terms of opportunity and process aspects, different freedom-related contingencies are apparent (Sen 2009: 255ff.): the personal heterogeneity of people, such as age, gender, impairments, education or social background; variations in the social climate or in the social environment, such as health care or the education system that affect people differently; and differences in the physical or technical environment and infrastructure, such as the accessibility of technology or buildings. In addition, differences in relational terms, such as views of what kind and amount of resources are required to participate effectively in society, are related to freedom.

It transpires that only a small part of the freedom people can actually enjoy is dependent on their individual skills, inasmuch as individual abilities are themselves mediated in at least two respects to social forms. First, individual abilities or disabilities are socially valued. Second, the learning as well as the practice of social skills and functionings can be prevented or enabled by social relations or social institutions.

Moreover, social attitudes toward people and their skills have a major effect on what is seen as a disability in the first place. If a disability is understood solely as a lack of individual abilities or impairment, and not in its social dimension, then the social deprivation and exclusion disabled people experience will not be seen as a lack of freedom. Such people with disabilities do have a hypothetical freedom, but they are not in a substantial sense free because they experience social deprivation and exclusion (Hull 2007). Ultimately, certain contexts are closed to them. Again, this becomes most apparent in the case of inclusion in the labor market. If a disabled person never gets the opportunity to show his or her skills in a socially rewarding way, this counts as a lack of freedom for the affected person who undergoes a kind of stereotypical negative social assessment. This lack of freedom, however, cannot causally be attributed to the physical constraints under which the person suffers.[5]

The conventional view of disability, still prominent in political philosophy, is different from this view:

> Conventional views of disability, while acknowledging the social manifestation of many disadvantages and exclusion, tend to assume that, since they would not arise in the absence of functional limitation, those disadvantages must originate in functional limitation. This lends support to the view that disabled people should be grateful for any charitable measures granted in their favour but it is too swift and simple an assumption to make. (Hull 2007: 22)

A social-interactional view on disability focuses on the dynamics between internal resources and circumstances or external resources. In this view, both society and functional limitation are necessary conditions for disadvantage and exclusion. That this is a more accurate view on disability becomes evident if we think of physical disabilities.

---

[5] In a society where, for example, blind people are expected to learn to be either basket makers or physiotherapists and lack substantial opportunities to learn other professions, people without interests in one of these two professions are deprived. Moreover, this lack of opportunities also tends to solidify and perpetuate, ultimately legitimizing existing social conditions, even if they are unjust.

Many people in need of a wheelchair that makes them free to move around find their environment largely inaccessible. The disadvantage and the exclusion that arise from the inaccessible environment, with stairs instead of ramps, does not exist because of the functional limitation but because of the lack of it between individual characteristics and the built environment. Were ramps available people relying on wheelchairs could gain access to the building and the goods and opportunities provided there; without ramps they are deprived of the freedom to enter and to enjoy the benefits of entering.

INCLUSION AND THE GOOD HUMAN LIFE

I now try to connect the ideas developed so far. The question I want to address is the following: In what ways does inclusion contribute to a good human life? To answer this, I will not defend a specific account of human well-being or a good life, but will assume that human well-being consists of both subjective well-being and objective conditions that make a life go well. The latter in particular can be seen as preconditions that help us to lead a good life.

I want to suggest that we can distinguish a direct and indirect relationship between inclusion and the good life, reflecting a direct and indirect interest in inclusion. A direct relation to good life is the constitutive role inclusion plays in achieving the good human life. One can argue that a good, meaningful life consists in part of good interpersonal relationships and living with others. This becomes apparent when we look at friendship and why we seek it. The point is not that the benefits of inclusion in such a relationship would be external to friendship, but that elements such as trust, enjoyable companionship, support, and help are intrinsic parts of friendship. So being a friend requires the inclusion of someone else in building this kind of relationship and, at the same time, viewing the intrinsic parts of friendship as essential requirements. The direct relationship from inclusion to a good human life is linked to the fact that human beings are fundamentally social beings, and inclusion in relationships is part of the fabric and meaning of being human (Aristotle 2009). Thus the direct interest of inclusion links to the intrinsic and instrumental value of inclusion, which means that inclusion is both an end in itself and an instrumentality that generates well-being.

This direct relationship between inclusion and a good life reflects a *direct interest* in inclusion. Some human functionings are of such nature that our dependence on others is constitutive of flourishing and not merely contingent as causally or developmentally related to well-being. However, the necessity of being included not only covers the most basic need for survival, as the nature of human beings not only embraces the needy, vulnerable, and passive side of human existence, but also the active, goal-pursuing, and autonomous side of human life (Laitinen 2009: 14). Evidently, the need for inclusion covers both aspects. As Abraham Maslow (1970) pointed out, human needs begin with deficiency needs (needs that, if not met, present a very strong obstacle to life), yet having them met does not make a life good and meaningful. Humans also have growth needs that relate to individual self-realization. Unlike basic needs, these interests are pursued through optional goals or plans. And unlike deficiency needs, these interests can be substituted by other interests.

A supportive and inclusive environment is necessary for humans to develop at all (Clarke-Stewart and Apfel 1978). Thus, exclusion from these basic and close human relationships is a serious problem. When a supportive environment is absent or deprived, the observable results are constraints on cognitive, psychological, and physical development. This phenomenon, often observable with children growing up in institutions with severely deprived conditions,[6] is called *hospitalism*.

---

[6] Children in such circumstances lacked playthings and opportunities for motor activity and were restricted and lacked stimulation from and responsive contact with adults, not only parents.

René A. Spitz, a psychologist who gave this condition its name, writes:

> The term hospitalism designates a vitiated condition of the body due to long confinement in a hospital, or the morbid condition of the atmosphere of a hospital. The term has been increasingly pre-empted to specify the evil effect of institutional care on infants, placed in institutions from an early age, particularly from the psychiatric point of view. (1945: 53)

Spitz observed high death rates – in some institutions, 90 percent of the infants had died by the end of their first year – and even after having improved hygienic conditions, Spitz discovered that, practically without exception, children developed psychiatric disorders, became asocial and delinquent, and were less intelligent than children who did not grow up in institutional care.

We know from historical experience that disabled people suffered and still suffer from severe forms of exclusion grounded in a neglect of the direct interest in inclusion and its importance for a good human life. I wish to mention one striking and influential historical example that illustrates this point. In 1966, a book was published that shocked the U.S. public: *Christmas in Purgatory*, a photographic exposé of America's institutions for cognitively disabled people. The book was the result of a tour of five state-supported institutions in four Eastern states (the authors decided not to reveal any further detail, so the institutions are still unknown and the reader only knows the identity of the good examples). It contained a series of inhumane images captured by photographer Fred Kaplan using a hidden camera, with complementary description by researcher and educator Burton Blatt.

A series of revelations about conditions at one specific school, the Willowbrook State School in New York, and the release of the photographs in *Christmas in Purgatory* not only shed light on a group in U.S. society that was out of sight and out of mind, barred behind the walls of institutions in the late 1960s and early 1970s, but also highlighted the fact that these people had to live like animals, without social contact and interpersonal relationships. They were not included in any kind of caring relationships, had to sleep on the floor, and were almost naked when Kaplan took his photos. The public's reaction was one of revulsion, as the brutal conditions in which cognitively disabled people were forced to live were laid bare for all to see. The publication of the book and the following public outrage contributed much to litigation and subsequent laws and policies that stipulated the basis for a new understanding and appreciation for the basic humanity and rights to inclusion of disabled people in U.S. society.[7]

We can also see the *indirect interest* in social inclusion. This is the interest in inclusion as a precondition for a wide range of goods that are part of or the means for a good life. Here too the quest for inclusion includes a developmental perspective insofar as inclusion is a prerequisite for human development. As Lev Vygotskij (1979) pointed out, human beings only learn in active engagement with others. In other words, "we do not become persons like apples grow on trees; nor do we jump off Jupiter's ear in the full armour of personal competence, as Minerva did in mythology. It rather seems to be a truism that education and formation (*Bildung*) are necessary preconditions for personal competences like those of thinking or judging, planning and performing actions" (Stekeler-Weithofer 2007: 174).

Also, many pursuits and goals people choose are bound to a social context and hence to inclusion. Just imagine a person who loves dancing the tango. As dancing the tango is something that quintessentially needs to be done in pairs, inclusion in a relationship that allows you to dance is a necessary precondition to pursuing this chosen hobby. This is true not only for goals particular individuals adopt, like dancing the tango, but also for shared social goals or resources, like education and employment.

---

[7] Recent examples of similarly shocking revelations can be found at http://www.disabilityrightsintl.org/.

The indirect interest in inclusion refers primarily to the instrumental value of inclusion. It points to the fact that human beings need to be included to fulfill genuinely social roles and tasks, for instance being a friend or a parent, dancing the tango, or building a house. These tasks range from basic human needs (such as being loved by someone) to genuinely individual interests (such as dancing the tango). Nevertheless, not only communities, also society as a whole only exists because of or with coordinated work among institutions ultimately built by humans, their interactions, and relationships, which – taken together – make the fabric of social life possible.

Again, we can see the problems disabled people face in having their indirect interest in inclusion fulfilled. As a wide range of goods and actions – dancing the tango was an obvious example – require social action, social coordination, and ultimately social intentionality, people can only achieve the goods of participating in the action if they are included in the corresponding contexts or occupy a role attached to the action or the good.

CONCLUSION

The UN Convention on the Rights of Persons with Disabilities (2006), among other agreements and conventions, claims a right to inclusion and participation for disabled people. However, there is conceptual vagueness and ambiguity as to what we mean by the term *inclusion*. For this reason, this chapter started with examining the definition of inclusion, defending two spheres of inclusion. I claimed that we have to distinguish between inclusion into communities and inclusion into a society. The main difference is that in the former contexts, people relate as "concrete others," whereas societal inclusion is shaped by individuals meeting as "abstract others."

As to the moral significance of inclusion, I tried to defend three ideas, concentrating mainly on the first two: first, social inclusion is dependent on the positive attitudes of others – otherwise it would not be called *social* inclusion. Second, the more freedom a person has, the more contexts are open to choose from and vice versa. This consequently leads to more inclusion both in quantitative and (probably) in qualitative terms. Third, the complexity (or non-complexity) of a specific social context demands more or less complex levels of human development. For instance, if one wants to be included in an opera orchestra, one obviously needs more and different skills than if one wants to be included in, say, a playgroup of children.

When we interrogate the relationship between inclusion and the good human life, we can highlight two things: first, there is a direct interest in inclusion and a corresponding direct relationship between inclusion and a good human life. A good human life, as I understand it, consists of inclusion in society as well as communities. Moreover, inclusion is not only a necessary precondition for a *good* human life, it is also a crucial part of basic human thriving at all, at least at the very beginning of one's life and sometimes also in between and at the end of a human life. A loving and caring relationship between parents (or surrogating parents) and their children, for instance, is a necessary condition for a psychologically and physiologically healthy development.

Second, there is an indirect interest in inclusion and a corresponding indirect relationship between inclusion and a good human life. There are several relational features of social inclusion that are not in themselves good, but that may lead to good results. For instance, to be able to work, to have a good education, or to be mobile may not in itself be a necessary feature of a good life – and lacking it not intrinsically bad. But not having access to employment, education, or mobility, can lead to other deprivations. Significant inclusions and exclusions have, as a result, considerable instrumental importance. They may not improve one's life situation, but they can lead to a good life because of their causal connections. Also, a range of goods and actions that people strive for are only feasible with the help of or together with other people. In this sense of inclusion, social intentionality is a necessary element.

These patterns in the quest for inclusion help us to understand why a right to inclusion and participation is of such great importance for the good life of human beings, including – but not restricted to – disabled people.

ACKNOWLEDGMENT

Thanks to Barbara Schmitz and Carina Fourie for their useful comments on this chapter.

References

Aristotle. *Nicomachean Ethics.* Oxford: Oxford University Press, 2009.

Bedorf, Thomas. *Verkennende Anerkennung.* Frankfurt a. M.: Suhrkamp, 2010.

Buchanan, Allen, Dan W. Brock, Norman Daniels, and Daniel Wikler. *From Chance to Choice – Genetics and Justice.* Cambridge, MA: Cambridge University Press, 2000.

Burchardt, Tania. "The Dynamics of Being Disabled." *Journal of Social Policy* 29, no. 4 (2000a): 645–68.

Enduring Economic Exclusion: Disabled People, Income and Work. York: The Joseph Rowntree Foundation, 2000b.

The Education and Employment of Disabled Young People: Frustrated Ambition. York: The Joseph Rowntree Foundation, 2005.

Calder, Gideon. "Disability and Misrecognition." In *The Politics of Misrecognition,* edited by Simon Thompson and Majid Yar, 105–24. London: Ashgate, 2011.

Clarke-Stewart, K. Alison, and Nancy Apfel. "Evaluating Parental Effects on Child Development." *American Educational Research* 6, (1978): 47–119.

Eklund, Mona, Lars Hansson, and Carin Ahlqvist. "The Importance of Work Compared to Other Forms of Daily Occupations for Wellbeing and Functioning among Persons with Long-Term Mental Illness." *Community Mental Health Journal* 40, no. 5 (2004): 465–77.

Fraser, Nancy. "Rethinking Recognition." *New Left Review* no. 3 (2000): 107–20.

Honneth, Axel. *The Struggle for Recognition. The Moral Grammar of Social Conflicts.* Cambridge: Polity Press, 1995.

Unsichtbarkeit – Stationen einer Theorie der Intersubjektivität. Frankfurt a. M.: Suhrkamp, 2003.

Hull, Richard. *Deprivation and Freedom – A Philosophical Enquiry.* New York: Routledge, 2007.

Ikäheimo, Heikki. "Personhood and the Social Inclusion of People with Disabilities: A Recognition-Theoretical Approach." In *Arguing about Disability – Philosophical Perspectives,* edited by Kristjana Kristiansen, Simo Vehmas, and Tom Shakespeare, 77–92. London: Routledge, 2009.

Laitinen, Arto. "Recognition, Needs and Wrongness: Two Approaches." *European Journal of Political Theory* 8, no. 1 (2009): 13–30.

Lippold, T, and Jan Burns. "Social Support and Intellectual Disabilities: A Comparison between Social Networks of Adults with Intellectual Disability and Those with Physical Disability." *Journal of Intellectual Disability Research* 53, no. 5 (2009): 463–73.

Marshall, Thomas H. *Citizenship and Social Class and Other Essays.* Cambridge: Cambridge University Press, 1950.

Maslow, Abraham H. *Motivation and Personality,* third edition. New York: Harper & Row, 1970.

Mason, Andrew. *Community, Solidarity and Belonging: Levels of Community and Their Normative Significance.* Cambridge, MA: Cambridge University Press, 2000.

McBryde Johnson, Harriet. "Stairway to Justice." *The New York Times Magazine,* 2004.

Minow, Martha. *Making All the Difference – Inclusion, Exclusion, and American Law.* Ithaca, NY: Cornell University Press, 1990.

Provencher, Helene L., Robin Gregg, Shery Mead, and Kim T. Mueser. "The Role of Work in the Recovery of Persons with Psychiatric Disabilities." *Psychiatric Rehabilitation Journal* 26, no. 2 (2002): 132–44.

Rigg, John. "*Labour Market Disadvantage amongst Disabled People: A Longitudinal Perspective.*" London: Centre for Analysis of Social Exclusion, London School of Economics, 2005.

Scully, Jackie Leach. *Disability Bioethics – Moral Bodies, Moral Difference.* Plymouth: Rowman & Littlefield Publishers, 2008.

Sen, Amartya. *The Idea of Justice.* London: Allen Lane, 2009.

Social Exclusion: Concept, Application, and Scrutiny. Manila: Asian Development Bank, 2000.

Smith, Adam. *The Theory of Moral Sentiments.* London: Penguin Books 2010 [1759].

Spitz, René A. "Hospitalism – An Inquiry into the Genesis of Psychiatric Conditions in Early Childhood." *Psychoanalytic Study of the Child* no. 1 (1945): 53–74.

Stekeler-Weithofer, Pirmin. "Persons and Practices: Kant and Hegel on Human Sapience." In *Dimensions of Personhood*, edited by Heikki Ikäheimo and Arto Laitinen, 174–98. Exeter: Imprint Academic, 2007.

Strong, Susan. "Meaningful Work in Supportive Environments: Experiences with the Recovery Process." *American Journal of Occupational Theory* 52, no. 1 (1998): 31–8.

Taylor, Charles. "The Politics of Recognition." In *Multiculturalism: Examining the Politics of Recognition*, edited by Amy Gutman, 25–74. Princeton, NJ: Princeton University Press, 1994.

Tönnies, Ferdinand. *Community and Society*. East Lansing: Michigan State University Press, 1957.

UNESCO. *The Salamanca Statement and Framework for Action on Special Needs Education*. Salamanca: UNESCO, 1994.

United Nations. *Convention on the Rights of Persons with Disabilities*. Geneva: United Nations, 2006.

Van Dongen, Carol J. "Quality of Life and Self-Esteem in Working and Nonworking Persons with Mental Illness." *Community Mental Health Journal* 32, no. 6 (1996): 535–48.

Vickerstaff, Sarah, Chris Phillipson, and Ross Wilkie. *Work, Health and Wellbeing – The Challenges of Managing Health at Work*. London: Policy Press, 2011.

Vygotskij, Lev S. *Mind in Society: Development of Higher Psychological Processes*. Cambridge, MA: Harvard University Press, 1978.

Weber, Max. *Wirtschaft Und Gesellschaft*. Tübingen: Mohr Siebeck, 1922.

Wilson, John. "Doing Justice to Inclusion." *European Journal of Special Needs Education* 15, no. 3 (2000): 297–304.

WHO, *The World Report on Disability*. Geneva: WHO, 2011.

Index

Index

Index

Index

Index

Index

obsession, 260
obstacles, 108, 176, 177, 240, 311, 312
Office of National Statistics, 168
Oliver, Michael, 100
one-thought-too-many argument, 29
ontology of disability, 117
opportunities, 130, 190, 213
oppression, 117, 118, 175, 189
Organization for Economic Cooperation and Development, (OECD) 168

pain, 53, 95, 96, 101, 143, 159, 235, 243, 252, 258, 260
pain management, 235
Panzarino, Connie, 149
paraplegia, 102, 106, 150, 155, 180, 182, 183, 233
Parfit, Derek, 2, 5, 78, 145
partial-verticality needs, 285
participation, 93, 96, 117, 125, 130, 175, 202, 300
participation restrictions, 119
paternalism, 1, 175, 177, 189, 190
pathological condition of an organism, 73
patient-clinician encounter, 248
patient-physician relationship, 250
perception, 247
perception model, 79
persecution, 162
personal assistance, 234
personal development, 210, 214
personal growth, 257. *See also* development
personal heterogeneity, 312
personal preferences, 209
personhood, 4, 24, 27, 34–36, 38, 44, 48
    Lockean concept of a person, 24
phenomenological approach, 244–64
phenomenological approach to illness, 244, 266
phenomenology. *See* phenomenological approach
physical and mental limitations, 258
physical frailty, 260
physical habits, 263
pity, 97, 137, 148, 228, 239, 251, 280
Plato, 146
pluralism, 292
Pogge, Thomas, 273, 282–86
policy maker, 162
political philosophy, 4, 313
politics of difference, 122, 123, 134
politics of equal dignity, 123
politics of equal recognition, 122
politics of universal dignity, 134, 136

positive life satisfaction. *See* happiness
posttraumatic growth, 257, 261
potential, 127
potentialities, 213
potentiality, 125
poverty, 105, 189
preconception care, 107
predicament of impairment, 94
prejudice, 6, 64, 65, 95, 98, 126, 127, 228, 230
prenatal diagnosis, 3
prevention, 3, 142, 153
prevention campaigns, 107
prevention of impairments, 6
primary social goods, 5, 82
process between the individual and their environment, 304
protention, 246
psyche/ soma distinction, 249
psychiatric classifications, 143
psycho-emotional disablism, 124
psychological compensation, 159
public policy, 183

QuadPara Association of South Africa, 107
quadriplegia, 139
Quality Adjusted Life Years (QALY), 181
quality assurance systems, 199
quality of the present moment, 260

race, 42, 152
racism, 154
Rajapatirana, Chammi, 238
ramps, 314
Rawls, John, 5
Reader, Soran, 59
reciprocation, 43
recognition, 121, 132, 136, 301, 304, 305–10
    psychological model, 309
    status model, 309
redistribution, 282
reduced lifespan, 160
Reeve, Christopher, 258
reflective cognitive evaluations, 174
re-focus on the present, 258
rehabilitation, 6, 94, 96, 102, 120, 128, 233
Reinders, Hans, 62
relationship between happiness and income, 172
relationships, 29, 59, 67, 97, 145, 175, 178, 185, 227, 231, 234, 258, 262, 264, 302, 304, 306, 307–8, 314, 317
Rentenbach, Barb, 238

Index

Index

Printed in Great Britain
by Amazon